# WAGING PEACE

## ITAMAR RABINOVICH

Israel and the Arabs, 1948–2003

UPDATED AND REVISED

Library of Congress Cataloging-in-Publication Data

Rabinovich, Itamar, 1942–
Waging peace : Israel and the Arabs,
1948–2003 / Itamar Rabinovich.
—Updated and rev. ed.
p.  cm.
Includes bibliographical references.
ISBN 0-691-11982-1 (pbk. : alk. paper)
1. Arab-Israeli conflict—1993—Peace. I. Title.
DS119.76.R33   2004
956.04—dc22      2003069151

British Library Cataloging-in-Publication Data is available.

IN MEMORY OF MY MOTHER,
TOVA BUCHSBAUM RABINOVICH

# CONTENTS

# PREFACE

During the years 1992–96 I was privileged to serve as Israel's ambassador in Washington (February 1993–September 1996) and also as its peace negotiator with Syria (July 1992–November 1995). In this dual capacity, I was especially active on the Syrian track of the Israeli-Arab peace process and also took part in most of its other aspects. This unique opportunity to acquire a much deeper understanding of both the Arab-Israeli conflict and the peace process was grafted onto more than two decades of academic study of and writing on Israel's relationship with the Arab world. So when I returned to Tel Aviv University in September 1996, I decided to write two books: a specific account of Israel's relationship with Syria (this was published in 1998); and an overview of Israel's relationship with the Arab world, which was published originally by Farrar, Straus and Giroux in 1999.

The original manuscript was completed in March 1999; much happened in the next four years—Barak's brief tenure as Israel's prime minister, the collapse of the peace process in both the Syrian and Palestinian tracks, the outbreak and unfolding of the Palestinian-Israeli war of attrition, the formation of George W. Bush's administration and Ariel Sharon's two governments, the terrorist attacks of September 11, and the war in Iraq. It was time to write an essentially new book.

Two new chapters were added, bringing the narrative to the fall of 2003, and the original chapter 4 ("The Web of Relationships"), now chapter 6, was substantially revised. The conclusion was rewritten.

It is a pleasant duty to thank the institutions and individuals that helped me in writing this book: Tel Aviv University, my academic home; the Dayan Center and my friends and colleagues on its faculty and staff; The Yona and Dina Ettinger Chair; and Keren Braverman, Lydia Gareh, Efrat Harel, Dorit Moshkovits, and Marlene Sacho, who helped with research and typing. I am grateful to the staff of Farrar, Straus and Giroux and particularly to Elizabeth Sifton for their help with the original volume. I am indebted to Princeton University Press and especially to its director Walter Lippincott and to Hanne Winarsky for their advice and help with the present book.

I want particularly to thank my immediate family: Efrat, Iris, Orna, Itai, the two Uris, and Ayelet. This year we mark the seventeenth anniversary of the passing away of my mother, to whose memory this book is dedicated. For us the pain of her absence is as acute today as it was in 1986.

Tel Aviv
October 2003

# 1

# THE BACKGROUND

The Arab-Israeli conflict has crossed the half-century mark. A conflict between the small Jewish and the much larger Arab community in Palestine had first erupted in the late Ottoman period. It became fiercer and more significant after the First World War, the publication in 1917 of the Balfour Declaration, in which the British government supported the "establishment in Palestine of a national home for the Jewish people," and the establishment in 1920 of a British Mandate over Palestine on both sides of the Jordan River. During the next three decades, Arabs and Jews fought over rights and control, their conflict culminating in a war that broke out after the United Nations' decision in 1947 to partition the country between a Jewish state and a Palestinian-Arab one.[1]

Throughout the decades of conflict, the indigenous Palestinian Arabs were supported and helped by a large part of the Arab world, but it was the establishment of the state of Israel in 1948 and the invasion by five Arab armies that gave birth to the full-fledged Arab-Israeli conflict. Israel's victory, the consolidation of its existence and expansion of its original territory, the Arabs' military defeat, the failure to establish the Palestinian Arab state envisaged by the UN resolution, and the consequent problem of Palestinian refugees were the fundamental facts in the process that transformed the Arab-Jewish conflict in Mandate Palestine into the Arab-Israeli conflict we still know today.

The conflict's fifty-year history is evenly divided by the October War of 1973. For twenty-five years, the old wounds festered as efforts to heal them or at least address some of their causes failed for reasons that I shall analyze. But after the Israeli victory in October 1973, diplomatic procedures were inaugurated that four years later developed into an Israeli-Egyptian peace process, which in March 1979 produced Israel's first peace treaty with an Arab state, though this subsequently came to a grinding halt; the stasis lasted through the 1980s. Then a new phase of peace negotiations was inaugurated in October 1991 at the Madrid Conference. The ensuing set of negotiations gave birth to a second Arab-Israeli peace treaty in 1994, with Jordan, to a Palestinian-Israeli breakthrough, and to a significant degree of Arab-Israeli normalization; but even in its heyday in 1993–95 the "Madrid process" failed to bring about a comprehensive settlement of the Arab-Israeli conflict or to end the political disputes and the bloodshed between Israel and parts of the Arab world. New developments in 1996 slowed it down and in 1998 brought it near collapse.

The Madrid process represents the first sustained international effort to resolve the Arab-Israeli conflict.[2] It is significant that no comparable effort—as distinct from short-lived attempts, various mediation efforts, and partial settlements—had been undertaken before, and that twenty-five years of an uneven peace process have still failed to produce a comprehensive settlement. The Arab-Israeli conflict has indeed been one of the more complex and difficult international problems of the second half of the twentieth century. The first step to understanding its complexity is a recognition that there is no single Arab-Israeli dispute but a cluster of distinct, interrelated conflicts:

1. The core conflict between Israel and the Palestinians. This is a classic conflict between two national movements claiming title to and vying for possession of the same land. This original strand in the Arab-Israeli dispute was overshadowed for some fifteen years (1949–64) by the pulverization of the Palestinian community that had been dispersed during Israel's war of independence, and by the preeminence then of pan-Arab ideologies and Arab state interests. The resurgence of Palestinian nationalism in the mid-1960s and, ironically, the establishment in 1967 of Israeli control over the whole of Palestine west of the Jordan River restored a major role to the Palestinians in the Arab world. Their new importance was reinforced by the PLO's offensive against Israel, conducted with the defeat of the established Arab armies in the background.

2. A broader dispute between Israel and Arab nationalism. This is a national, political, cultural, and increasingly also religious conflict. Both sides came into this conflict carrying their historical and cultural legacies. The Jewish people's national revival in their historic homeland in the immediate aftermath of the Second World War and the

Holocaust, and after millennia of exile and persecution, unfolded during a head-on collision with an Arab national movement seeking revival, renewal, and power after a century of soul-searching and humiliation at the hands of Western powers. Unfortunately, most Arabs have perceived Zionism and Israel as either part of the West or, worse, a Western bridgehead established in their midst.

3. A series of bilateral disputes between Israel and neighboring Arab states created by geopolitical rivalries combined with other factors. Thus Egypt was drawn into war with Israel in 1948 by the Palestinian problem, but its decision to join the Arab war coalition and its subsequent conflict with Israel were also affected by the ambitions of Arab and regional leaders, by its sense of competition with Israel as the other powerful and ambitious state in the region, and by a desire to obtain a land bridge to the eastern Arab world through the southern Negev Desert. Similarly, Syria's bitter relationship to Israel has expressed both its genuine attachment to Arab nationalism and to the Palestinian cause, and its acute sense of rivalry with Israel for hegemony in the Levant.

4. The larger international conflict. The "Palestine question" has always been an important and a salient international issue. The interest and passion aroused by the "Holy Land" (*Falastin* to Arabs and Muslims), the saliency of what used to be called the "Jewish question," the rivalries of colonial powers and later the superpowers in the Middle East, and the overall geopolitical importance of the Arab world were some of the considerations and forces that have accounted for the significance in international affairs of the evolving Arab-Israeli conflict. It was not originally and was never allowed to be a local squab-

ble. Arabs and Israelis from the outset sought international support for their respective causes, while foreign governments and other actors—out of genuine commitment to one of the parties, in search of gain, or for the sake of peace and stability—have always intervened.

These international factors were magnified and exacerbated by the Cold War. The Middle East, because of its intrinsic importance, its geographical closeness to the Soviet Union, and its openness to change, became an important arena of Soviet-American competition. In the early 1950s, the Soviet Union shifted from initial support for Israel to sweeping support for the Arab states, and it exploited the Arab-Israeli conflict in order to weaken the Western position in the Middle East and enhance its own. After about a decade of fluctuation, the United States decided on a policy of open cooperation with Israel and other Middle Eastern allies against the region's radical and pro-Soviet regimes. So, in the Arab-Israeli wars in 1967 and 1973 and in other Middle Eastern crises, the two superpowers contended by proxy. Israel's power was increased dramatically by American aid and support, but the Soviet Union's military assistance to its allies and clients, the prospect of Soviet military intervention, and Soviet help in rebuilding the defeated Egyptian and Syrian armies were important in denying Israel the political fruits of its military power and achievements.[3]

Whereas in the 1950s and early 1960s it was the Soviet Union that tended to take advantage of the Arab-Israeli conflict, the equation was altered by Israel's victory in the 1967 war. Within a few years, the Arab world grasped that the key to regaining the territories Israel had gained in that war was to be sought in Washington. American endorsement of the principle of exchanging "land for peace," and a willingness and ability to act on it, were at least some of the time the basis on which the United States was able to orchestrate the Arab-Israeli peace negotiations and register several impressive achievements. For example, the Egyptian-Israeli peace process initiated after the 1973 war, the first major breakthrough in the Arab-Israeli conflict, was intimately linked to one of Washington's greatest Cold War accomplishments: Egypt's transition from a Soviet ally to a nation in the American orbit.[4]

## 1948–67

This was the formative period of the Arab-Israeli conflict. The 1948 war that gave birth to both the state of Israel and the Arab-Israeli conflict ended with a series of armistice agreements, not with a peace settlement. This fact has in recent years been the focus of a fierce debate in Israel among three schools of opinion: an orthodox, establishment-oriented, sometimes almost official historiography that blames this failure on the Arab world and its refusal to accept Israel's existence; a revisionist school that considers these critical years through a contemporary ideological prism, relying on several newly opened archives, primarily Israel's state archives, and that lays much of the blame on Israel and its leader, David Ben-Gurion, for refusing any sensible compromise or concession; and a further school of postrevisionists, also using newly available archival and other sources, that shuns both the apologetic tendency of the first historiography and the blunt revisionism of the second.[5]

This third group is interested less in allocating blame and discovering "missed opportunities" than in trying to understand the stalemate produced by the Arab-Israeli clash of interests and outlooks and in their asymmetries. Israel sustained heavy casualties in the 1948 war, believed that in the aftermath of the Holocaust the Jewish people was entitled to a secure homeland, and maintained that a belligerent force defeated in a war that it had itself initiated could not reasonably demand a reversal of its outcome.

Israel was also guided by a genuine, albeit sometimes exaggerated, existential insecurity and a fear that a "second round" might be initiated by its Arab adversaries, who had refused to accept the war's outcome and Israel's entrenchment in their midst. Under Ben-Gurion's leadership, Israel sought to stabilize the status quo, on the assumption that, once it had consolidated its existence and absorbed the postwar wave of Jewish refugees and immigrants, peace could be made on better terms a few years later. In a series of exploratory and then real peace negotiations conducted after the 1948 war, Israel offered some concessions, though not the ones demanded by its Arab interlocutors.[6]

From the Arab nationalist perspective, Israel was an illegitimate state that threatened the Arab world culturally and geopolitically. The few Arab leaders who agreed to negotiate with Israel insisted on far-reaching concessions (giving up the southern part of the Negev Desert, allowing a corridor to link Gaza to the West Bank, permitting the return of Palestinian refugees, jurisdiction over part of Lake Tiberias), both in order to legitimize any prospective agreement in Arab eyes, and because they

believed that only significant and painful Israeli concessions could redress some of the injustices done them by
Israel's very establishment and the expansion of its original territory, the defeat of the Arab armies, and the disintegration of the Palestinian community.[7]

A close look at the various attempts to arrive at peace
settlements between Israel and its Arab neighbors after
the 1948 war will point to many reasons and forces responsible for their failure, but at the root of the difficulty
lay the truth that the Arab and Israeli perspectives were
irreconcilable. In the circumstances obtaining at the war's
end, any concession that could possibly satisfy at least
some of the Arabs was perceived by Israel's leaders as an
existential threat. This state of affairs continued until
June 1967, when Israel's victory in the Six-Day War gave
it territorial assets that it could use as bargaining chips in
peace negotiations. Until then, the conflict had lingered
and festered. The limitations and shortcomings of the armistice agreements, friction over unresolved issues, the
impact of radical ideologies espoused by certain Arab
army officers on Arab politics, Israel's response to these
developments, and the Soviet Union's influence in the region combined to shape a full-blown Arab-Israeli conflict
by the mid-1950s. This meant a virtual absence of normal
contacts between Israel and the Arab world; a complete
Arab boycott; border clashes; individual and organized
group Arab violence against Israel and an Israeli policy to
retaliate against both; a second Israeli-Arab war in 1956
shaped by Israel's cooperation with Great Britain and
France, two declining colonial powers, versus revolutionary pan-Arab nationalists; an arms race; and perennial fear
of still more war.[8]

Soon events and developments occurred that led to the crisis of May 1967 and the Six-Day War in June. One was the completion of Israel's overland water carrier, bringing water from Lake Tiberias in the north to the more spacious but arid lands in the south, and the Arab decision to thwart a project designed to enhance Israel's absorptive capacity and thus consolidate its existence. A second was the return of the Palestinians and the Palestinian national movement to a directly active role in Middle Eastern politics with the emergence of various groups and organizations that subsequently assembled under the umbrella of the Palestine Liberation Organization. Third was the radicalization of Syrian politics under the Ba'ath Party's regime and the exacerbation of rivalries among various Arab states, particularly with regard to issues relating to Israel. Fourth was the intensification of Soviet-American rivalry in the region. And lastly there was a leadership crisis in Israel after David Ben-Gurion's second and final abdication in 1963.[9]

## 1967–73

Though the June 1967 war created a potential for a political settlement by gaining Israel new territorial assets, it also escalated the Arab-Israeli conflict to hitherto unfamiliar levels. Right after the war, Israel indeed considered the Sinai Peninsula and the Golan Heights as, essentially, temporary holdings to be used in order to obtain a genuine peace, but as time went by and peace failed to come, the situation progressively acquired the trappings of permanency, and the temporary holdings were tied to Israel by a variety of bonds and vested interests.

The West Bank and the Gaza Strip, which Jews considered parts of the historical Land of Israel and which had been parts of Mandate Palestine, were treated from the outset on an entirely different basis. Sovereignty over the West Bank and Gaza was, unlike that over the Sinai and the Golan, according to the Israeli interpretation at least, an open issue. Control over and title to these territories raised fundamental issues of security and identity—these were the lands of the Bible (much more so, in fact, than the coastal plains where most of Israel's population actually lived). In them lay the key to a historic compromise with Palestinian nationalism or, alternatively, to yet another effort to make an agreement with Hashemite Jordan; but neither the shape of such a settlement nor an available partner was readily apparent. Moreover, Israel's politics were altered by the powerful wave of messianic-mystical nationalism generated by Israel's acquisition of Judea and Samaria. (In the coded language of Israeli politics, the term "West Bank" is neutral but the biblical term "Judea and Samaria" expresses a claim to the heartlands of Jewish history.) This wave was reinforced by the Israelis' unprecedented sense of power after their great and swift military victory, and their determination never to return to the vulnerable borders of the prewar period or to a trauma like the one they had endured in May 1967.[10]

The military might that Israel displayed in June 1967 convinced the Arabs that they could not reasonably hope to end the conflict through a military victory. The effect of the 1967 defeat was qualitatively different from that of the defeats in 1948 and 1956—Israel's swift and stunning victory could not be explained away by the Western powers' direct participation or by the decay of the old order in the Arab world, for though King Hussein was a traditional Arab monarch, the Nasserite regime in Egypt and the Ba'ath regime in Syria were paragons of revolutionary Arab nationalism. In the Arabs' ensuing soul-searching, several alternatives were fiercely debated—return to the Islamic fold, further radicalization, staying with the familiar status quo. But a recommendation to draw yet another conclusion from the repeated failure to defeat Israel—to seek a political settlement based on a historic compromise—was not made.[11]

These Israeli and Arab frames of mind were chiefly responsible for the diplomatic stalemate over the next six years. Meanwhile, the Soviet Union hastened to rebuild and resupply the Egyptian and Syrian armies, while the United States supported Israel's insistence that its victory should lead to nothing less than a genuine settlement of the Arab-Israeli conflict. The UN's lengthy deliberations in the summer and fall of 1967 ended with the adoption of Security Council Resolution 242, an epitome of "constructive ambiguity": it has served ever since as the basis for the several efforts to resolve the Arab-Israeli dispute precisely because its careful formulation (along with the differences between the English, French, and Russian versions of it) has enabled all parties to claim the validity of their own interpretations.

The initial efforts at international mediation having failed, Egypt, with its armed forces rehabilitated with Soviet aid, resumed hostilities in late 1968. Limited fighting with Israel spread along the Jordanian and Syrian fronts; this "war of attrition" lasted until the summer of 1970. The Arab states' eagerness to regain the territories they had lost in June 1967 was supplemented and en-

hanced by Palestinian nationalism's quest for self-determination. Thus the Six-Day War gave new scale and impetus to a process that had already begun: the Arab states'
formation of the original PLO, the challenge presented
to the PLO by authentic Palestinian groups, the formulation of the Palestinian National Charter—in short, the
return of the Palestinian issue to the forefront of the
Arab-Israeli conflict.

After the June war, the relationship and balance between the Palestinian national movement and the Arab
states changed, the latter losing power and prestige while
the former seemed to offer new hope—of defeating Israel
through a popular war of liberation, and inflicting unfamiliar blows on it through a series of spectacular
terrorist acts. In addition, the Palestinians built virtually
independent territorial bases in Jordan and Lebanon, at
the expense of these states' sovereignty. Authentic Palestinian organizations led by Yasser Arafat and the Fath
took control of the PLO, ending the duality of the previous four years. Arafat became an important Arab leader,
wielding influence in summit conferences and at other
Arab meetings.[12]

In theory, some of these developments might have
been the basis for an Israeli-Palestinian accommodation.
Israel was in control of all of Mandate Palestine, but it
was not eager to add the Palestinian population of the
Gaza Strip and the West Bank to its body politic. Palestinian leaders had the authority and credibility to make a
compromise agreement that their predecessors had refused to consider. But accommodation and compromise
remained only theoretical options. Israeli attachment to
the West Bank intensified, while the PLO was carried

away by its initial successes to an inflated view of its power and prospects.[13]

By the summer of 1970, it had become clear that the PLO's efforts to organize a popular uprising in the West Bank and the Gaza Strip were unsuccessful. Still more significant, the Arab states' war of attrition against Israel had run its course, and Egypt's president, Gamal Abdel Nasser, responded positively to Secretary of State William Rogers's "initiative" for a cease-fire. The PLO's radical wing fought a rearguard action against what it viewed as capitulation. Western airliners were hijacked to Cairo and Jordan. In Jordan this defiance triggered a final showdown between the Palestinians and the Hashemite regime. For three years, King Hussein had tolerated the gradual erosion of his authority and sovereignty in Jordan by a movement that enjoyed the support of both the Palestinian majority among his own subjects and the larger Arab world. In September 1970, the Palestinians overplayed their hand, humiliating him and his loyalists, but the Jordanian army crushed the Palestinian opposition and expelled the PLO's fighting units from Jordanian territory without incurring significant criticism from Nasser, who had just made his own truce with Israel. A half-hearted Syrian intervention ended ignominiously: Hafez al-Assad, commander of the Syrian air force, refused to commit his planes to what he regarded as a senseless adventure, and without air cover the Syrian armored column invading Jordan fell easy prey to Jordan's small air force and was forced to turn around.

There was more to this episode than a minor military clash between Jordan and Syria. It was also a Soviet-American conflict by proxy. In the Cold War context, a

Soviet client had invaded the territory of an American
client, and had apparently been defeated by the latter's
armed forces, though it was also deterred by the deployment of Israeli land and air forces. Israel's moves were
closely coordinated with the United States, which viewed
this coordination as a successful implementation of
the Nixon doctrine—resolving a regional crisis with local
allies and without American troops. This was the first
in a series of exploits by Henry Kissinger that defined
his spectacular Middle Eastern diplomacy during the next
years.

In Israel a retrospective policy debate followed this episode. Henry Kissinger's chief partner on the Israeli side
had been Yitzhak Rabin, who was serving as ambassador
to Washington—a preparatory phase in his transition
from a military career to a political one. He and the government of Prime Minister Golda Meir as a whole took
pride in what they considered a clear demonstration of
Israel's strategic value to the United States, its contribu-
tion to pragmatism and stability in the region, and the
reinforcement of Israel's community of interests with the
Hashemite regime in Jordan. Curiously, the government's right-wing critics took exception to this latter
point; in their view, Israel should have remained neutral
in the Jordanian dispute and allowed the Palestinians to
defeat the Hashemite regime and take over the Jordanian
government, for they believed that, once the Palestinians
had their own state in Jordan, Israel could press its claim
to the West Bank. Thus the maxim "Jordan is Palestine."[14]

But this Israeli debate seemed almost academic. The
successful conclusion of the Jordanian crisis, the end of
the war of attrition, Nasser's subsequent death, and the

partnership and intimacy with the United States combined to generate a feeling that the status quo could be
indefinitely perpetuated. This, however, came from a
false sense of complacency.[15]

The war launched in October 1973 by Egypt and Syria
against Israel differed from those of 1948 and 1967. They
did not go to war in support of the Palestinians or drift
into it in an uncontrolled process of escalation. But the
Sinai Peninsula for Egypt and the Golan Heights for
Syria were parts of their national territories, and Israel's
control of them seemed unbearable. The real driving
force that planned and executed the war was Nasser's un-
derestimated successor, Anwar al-Sadat.

Sadat's new policy toward Israel was predicated on his
underlying decision to liberalize Egypt's politics and
economy and to reorient that nation from a Soviet to an
American focus. In order to implement these changes, he
had to disengage from the conflict with Israel. His concepts for a diplomatic settlement with Israel were very
modest (and very distant from the peace treaty he ended
up signing nine years later), but they were unacceptable
to Golda Meir in 1971, and he decided to launch a limited
war in order to break the deadlock.

Sadat relied on two partners. One was Syria's new
ruler, Hafez al-Assad, who seized full power in his country
in November 1970 after an internecine debate over Syria's debacle in Jordan two months earlier. Assad, a senior
member of the Ba'ath regime since its inception in March
1963, headed its more pragmatic wing. He did not believe
in the ill-defined notion of a "popular war of liberation"
but advocated cooperation with other Arab states against
Israel. When Sadat approached him in 1972, he agreed

to join Egypt in a war coalition, though he did not share
Sadat's concept of the war as a prelude to negotiations or
relish Syria's junior-partner position. Sadat's other partner was the group of conservatively governed, oil-producing Arab states. By the early 1970s, the first signs of the
"energy crisis" were visible, and the balance among the
oil-producing nations, the international oil companies,
and the Western powers was shifting. Sadat knew that in
launching war he could rely on the increasing political
and economic power of the Gulf Arabs.[16]

The PLO was not part of or privy to these preparations. Having been evicted from Jordan, it was busy building a new territorial base in Lebanon. The weakness of
the Lebanese state, the sympathy and support of several
factions within Lebanon, and the backing of other Arab
governments enabled it to build a "state within a state"
there—with virtual control over Palestinian refugee
camps in Beirut and in the south, autonomous political
and operational headquarters in Beirut, and an extensive
infrastructure in southern Lebanon, which it could use as
a base of operations against Israel.

## 1973–77

The October War of 1973 did indeed break the deadlock
and opened the way to a lengthy, intermittent effort to
convert the potential created by the 1967 Six-Day War
into peace negotiations that would settle the Arab-Israeli
conflict. The transition from violence to diplomacy was
facilitated by the absence of a clear outcome to the war,
which ended with Israeli troops on the Egyptian side of
the Suez Canal, a hundred kilometers from Cairo, and

also in Syrian territory, within artillery range of Damascus to the north. Only forceful intervention by the United States saved Egypt from a total military defeat. But Egypt did effect a successful crossing of the Suez Canal and managed to keep some troops inside the Sinai Peninsula. And Syria, before its troops were pushed back toward Damascus, had overrun the Golan Heights. Owing to an intelligence setback caused by political shortsightedness and a bureaucratic mind-set, Israel had been caught by surprise, and at first its armed forces performed poorly. Its recovery and subsequent performance were most impressive, but the meaning of the war's early phases could not be forgotten: the large number of casualties, the need for American resupplies, and therefore the collapse of an important element in strategic U.S.-Israeli cooperation—the belief that Israel could hold its own against any Arab coalition so long as the United States deterred the Soviet Union.

Given the war's ambiguous outcome and the danger of resumed hostilities, the chief protagonists sought an accommodation, and their early agreements became the starting points for a new Arab-Israeli diplomacy led and driven by President Richard Nixon and Secretary of State Kissinger, whose sense of urgency derived from several sources: the energy crisis, the quadrupling of oil prices by Iran and the principal Arab oil-producing states (which clearly took advantage of the war to effect a change they had been planning for some time), and the danger of a confrontation with the Soviet Union if war broke out again.

Beyond these immediate considerations, additional forces were at work. The debacle and shock of the early days in the October War disabused many Israelis of the sense of power they had enjoyed ever since their victory in 1967 and paved the way for significant changes in domestic politics and national-security policies. The full extent of this domestic change was manifested only in 1977, when the Labor movement, after fifty years of hegemony in prestate and independent Israel, lost power to the right-wing Likud alignment. But meanwhile a yearning for peace and a weariness with bloodshed provided public support for the concessions made in foreign policy by Prime Minister Meir and her successor, Yitzhak Rabin, in 1974 and 1975.

The Arab states were buffeted by contradictory forces. The Egyptian and Syrian armies' initial success, and the swelling of Arab economic power and political influence, tilted many Arabs against the notion of a compromise with Israel. These were the years (1973–82) of the "Arab Decade," when the rest of the world sought Arab oil and money and Arabs could reasonably hope that as a result Israel's base of international support might be undermined. Other Arabs were more cautious. If Israel could not be defeated even when caught by surprise, as it had been in 1973, with its military machine out of gear, what was the point of waiting for some prospective opportunity to fight it in the future? From that perspective, there was no value in a long-drawn-out effort to erode Israel's position when significant concessions might be obtained through diplomacy.[17]

After the October War, Sadat completed the move he had begun in 1972, when he expelled the Soviet Union's military advisers from Egypt, and placed his country squarely within the American orbit. Indeed, for Henry

Kissinger, his partner in this transition, the Israeli-Arab peace process was not only a mechanism for preventing another war, for directing Arab-Israeli relations on the path of resolution, and for calming the Arab oil-producers, but also part of a strategy designed to facilitate precisely this shift of allegiance. And the success of that strategy was one of the United States' greatest achievements during the Cold War. But Kissinger's effort to apply the same rule to Syria met with only limited success. Assad concluded one agreement with Israel and began negotiating with Washington, but he refused to abandon his pro-Soviet orientation.

Alongside the American mediation, a direct channel of communication between Egypt and Israel was opened after the October War: talks between Generals Abd-ul-Ghani al-Gamasi and Aharon Yariv at Kilometer 101, a site named for its sign marking the distance from Cairo. The talks revealed the potential for reconciliation inherent in the relationship between the two countries, but at the end of the day both preferred to have Washington's mediation. With American help, Egypt and Israel signed a number of agreements that led to a further agreement in January 1974. This stabilized the situation and indicated the direction further peace negotiations could take: it stipulated Israel's withdrawal from the Egyptian mainland and from the banks of the Suez Canal. Egypt thus emerged from the war with its first concrete achievement, while Israel could relish the opportunity to regroup and contemplate its next moves, taking comfort in the notion that a withdrawal from the Suez Canal was a sine qua non for starting a peace process with Egypt. (Israel could also ask itself whether it had been necessary to go through the October War to come to that conclusion.)

Kissinger's mediation efforts and the three accords they yielded—disengagement agreements between Israel and Egypt and then Syria in January and May 1974, and the Israeli-Egyptian interim agreement of September 1975—were referred to at the time as "step-by-step" diplomacy. As this implied, U.S. policy was to aim not for a comprehensive settlement of the Arab-Israeli conflict but for a series of partial, interim agreements. The pessimistic presumption was that a comprehensive, final settlement that met Arab demands and expectations and also addressed Israel's needs and concerns was not feasible under prevailing circumstances. Though almost everyone paid lip service to the idea of a comprehensive settlement by coming to a brief Arab-Israeli peace conference held in Geneva under UN auspices in December 1973, this was an essentially ritualistic affair designed to placate the Soviet Union and Arab nationalist opinion, both of which resented Washington's control of the negotiations and its preference for partial bilateral agreements.[18]

Syria boycotted this conference but was eager nonetheless to collaborate with the United States in negotiating a disengagement agreement with Israel. It was a protracted and arduous negotiation. Though Syria had fewer bargaining chips than Egypt, it was determined to obtain an equivalent agreement, and Assad bargained hard, reinforcing his diplomacy with a minor war of attrition. The agreement finally reached in May 1974 provided for Israel's withdrawal from the territory it had captured beyond the Golan Heights in October 1973 and from Quneitra, the provincial capital there. Like Sadat, Assad thus managed to win back a slice of the territory his country had lost in 1967. But whereas in the Egyptian case the postwar disengagement agreement was only a first step in a phased process, the Israeli-Syrian agreement of May 1974 had no sequel.

In the early summer of 1974, it was clear that Israel and Egypt were ready for the next stage of their negotiations, but the substantive issues were compounded by a procedural problem. Sadat was willing to defy the Arab nationalist demand for a comprehensive agreement with Israel, but he was not willing to go it alone. Syria had been Egypt's partner until now, but the idea of pairing the two again did not appeal to anyone; Assad had acquired the reputation of being a tough, meticulous negotiator, and the Golan Heights' limited terrain offered limited choices. A short-lived effort was made to bring in Jordan: Kissinger's idea was to offer Jordan a bridgehead in the area of Jericho as a prelude to its getting back the West Bank. To Israel's new prime minister and to the Labor Party as a whole, Jordan was a preferable partner to the PLO in resolving the Palestinian problem, but Rabin was not ready to make a bold move that would address this underlying issue in Israeli politics and public life, for though it might possibly provide a satisfactory solution it would certainly generate bitter controversies. This was not Rabin the mature statesman of the 1990s, but a political novice still, entrusted with ultimate responsibility at a very difficult time. So Rabin rejected Kissinger's initiative. Shortly thereafter, the Arab states, in a consensus formulated in a summit conference at Rabat, formally denied Jordan's claim to the West Bank and recognized the PLO as "the sole legitimate representative of

the Palestinian People" and as the rightful claimant to
those parts of historic Palestine that Israel might give up
in future negotiations.[19]

Given this sequence of events, Egypt decided to go it
alone in negotiations with Israel. After nearly a year of
arduous work, an interim agreement over the Sinai Peninsula was signed: Egypt regained its oil fields there and
the strategic Mitla and Gidi passes; a collateral U.S.-Is-
raeli memorandum of understanding was also signed that
advanced the two nations' strategic and diplomatic cooperation still further.

The interim agreement represented the high point of
Kissinger's "step-by-step" diplomacy, but it may also have
marked its end. At least one additional phase might have
been planned in the Sinai, but it was not at all clear that
Sadat was able or willing to face an angry Arab chorus led
by Syria. Kissinger showed his own ambivalence when he
allowed a senior State Department official, Harold Saunders, to state in a congressional hearing in October 1975
that the Palestinian issue was "the core of the problem."
If this was indeed the case, there was only a limited value
to negotiations that avoided it. In any event, the outbreak
of civil war in Lebanon in 1975–76 and the Ford administration's preoccupation with the presidential election in
November 1976 resulted in a virtual suspension of Middle Eastern diplomacy.[20]

## 1977–82

Jimmy Carter's election and the inauguration of his administration in January 1977 began a new phase in Israeli-
Arab relations. President Carter and his team—Secretary

of State Cyrus Vance, National Security Adviser Zbigniew Brzezinski, and Harold Saunders and William Quandt as the bureaucratic experts on the Middle East— were motivated by a host of new considerations: an open desire to distance themselves from their predecessors' policies, a genuine belief that a final and comprehensive settlement of the Arab-Israeli conflict could be made, diminished interest in East-West Cold War rivalries and a concurrent preoccupation with tensions between North and South, concern about the supply and price of oil, and a religiously inspired sense of mission. Carter's new Middle Eastern policy not only reversed Kissinger's but turned a comprehensive settlement of the Arab-Israeli conflict into a major goal. His administration's concept of comprehensiveness meant an international conference, cooperation with the Soviet Union, and the allocation of significant roles to Syria and the PLO. Carter made no secret of the fact that, in line with a Brookings Institution report which inspired his policies, he believed that Israel should withdraw practically all the way back to its pre-1967 borders and should allow for the establishment of a Palestinian state, in return for diplomatic recognition and peace that Israel would obtain from the Arab states.

These views and policies pitted Carter against Prime Minister Rabin and, after May 1977, his successor, Menachem Begin. But they also confounded President Sadat, who could not understand why the United States would want to bring the Soviet Union back to center stage in the Middle East and relegate Egypt, its newfound ally, to a role secondary to that of uncooperative Syria. Egypt's and Israel's concern with these developments led to their forming a direct channel of communication between them. By means of it, the groundwork was laid for Sadat's historic journey to Jerusalem and for the negotiations that led to the Camp David Accords of September 1978 and to the Egyptian-Israeli peace treaty of March 1979.[21]

Shared exasperation with the policies of the Carter administration certainly helped to start this direct Egyptian-Israeli dialogue, but both parties were also moved by more significant considerations. Sadat wanted, of course, to regain the whole of the Sinai Peninsula. In 1977, he understood that this was a realistic possibility but full peace had to be offered in return. Early in his presidency, Sadat had decided that disengagement from the conflict with Israel was integral to a realignment of Egypt's policies and politics, but he had not thought through a plan and had only a sense of direction, some rudimentary notions, and an understanding of the Egyptians' weariness. By 1977, he had several years' experience, self-confidence gained in the October War and its sequel, and a clearer idea of what had to be done.

In Menachem Begin, Sadat found a surprising, not to say unlikely, yet effective partner. On May 17, 1977, after defeats in previous elections, Begin finally won and became Israel's prime minister, a victory that ended Labor Zionism's hegemony and represented the first genuine transfer of power in Israeli politics. The accession to power of a nationalist right-wing politician was unanimously expected to exacerbate Arab-Israeli relations. But this expectation failed to take account of two significant changes in Israeli politics: as a newcomer, Begin was less constrained by convention than his predecessors had been; and as a nationalist ideologue, he was totally committed to the idea of the Land of Israel (Eretz Yisrael) yet not to the Sinai Peninsula—from which, it turned out, he was willing to offer full withdrawal in order to achieve peace.

A separate peace was not what Sadat had in mind. The discrepancy between his and Begin's ideas of what peace meant produced an early crisis in their direct negotiations that was resolved by the United States. Washington's initial response to direct Egyptian-Israeli dialogue had been quite cold, but the president and his team soon understood that, whatever their own hopes, once Egypt and Israel were in direct negotiation, both opportunities and dangers presented themselves that U.S. policy had to address. The unusual gathering at Camp David was the culmination of a process that made the United States a third, often dominant partner in the negotiations and introduced a kind of mediation-cum-arbitration into what had originally been direct give-and-take.

The Camp David Accords turned Arab-Israeli diplomacy into a full-blown effort to achieve peace. By extending diplomatic recognition to Israel, signing a peace treaty with it, and establishing normal relations with it, Sadat and Egypt violated a taboo that an Arab consensus had strictly enforced for more than three decades. There were two parts to the Camp David Accords—an Israeli-Egyptian agreement terminating the bilateral dispute between them, and a framework laying down the principles for resolving Israel's conflict over the Palestinians and its disputes with other Arab neighbors. But the two parts were not of equal importance. Begin and Sadat were primarily interested in their bilateral agreement, and both leaders saw to its strict implementation. Indeed, this was how the Arab world perceived the agreements: as Sadat's having broken ranks and made a separate peace with Israel. He was denounced and vilified, Egypt was ousted from the Arab League, and most Arab states severed diplomatic relations with Cairo.[22]

Sadat reacted angrily to this criticism. He viewed himself not as a traitor to the Arab cause but as a pathfinder showing the Arab world the only course open to it for regaining territories lost in 1967. When Assad and other critics accused him of being a careless and ineffective negotiator, he retorted that they were small-minded men who focused on minor details and failed to see the overall picture. He kept saying that his loudest critics would end up following in his footsteps—a judgment that was vindicated posthumously.

As for Begin, he exploited part of the potential created in June 1967 to resolve the "conflict of 1948" on the Egyptian front. His far-reaching achievement—Israel's peace agreement with Egypt—was the most significant breakthrough in Arab-Israeli relations to date, but the price was commensurate. Sadat was willing to offer Israel full peace and generous security arrangements in the Sinai, but he insisted on regaining the whole territory, every last square inch. By agreeing to this, Begin not only conceded the whole of the Sinai but established a precedent (in fact explicitly): full withdrawal for full peace.

Furthermore, if Begin expected Sadat to treat the Palestinian dimension of the agreement as a mere formality and allow Israel a free hand in the West Bank, he misunderstood. In the Israeli-Egyptian negotiation of 1977–78 Sadat had pressed for recognition of the Palestinians' "national rights." Begin, worried by the potential ramifications of this abstract principle, had put forth his autonomy plan, to which Sadat had reacted coldly. But once it was agreed on, Egypt pressed hard for a liberal interpretation of "full autonomy" for the Palestinians. A deadlock was reached on this issue, and relations between Israel and Egypt soured.

The failure to implement the Palestinian component of the Egyptian-Israeli peace treaty allowed Sadat and his successors a convenient justification for keeping bilateral relations between the two countries at a low level, or, as it came to be known, for "the cold peace." Egypt has kept its principal commitments to Israel (full diplomatic relations, a security regime in the Sinai, free access to Egypt for all Israeli tourists) but has imposed severe restrictions on the development of normal relations in the economic and cultural spheres and has continued its political and diplomatic rivalry. Thus the collapse of the "autonomy negotiations" in 1980, which seemed at the time only a temporary setback, was perpetuated over the next decade, and several events and developments helped: Jimmy Carter's loss in his reelection campaign, Sadat's assassination, the Lebanon war, the Iran-Iraq war, the changes in the PLO's standing and position, and new trends in Israeli politics.

## 1982–91

There were two aims to the war Israel launched in Lebanon in June 1982. One was to resolve once and for all the host of problems presented by the collapse of the Lebanese state in the civil war of 1975–76. But on another level, the war's plan reflected a much more ambitious effort to bring about a sweeping change in the whole region. As Ariel Sharon, architect of the war, saw it, Israel could transform its regional position by inflicting serious blows on Syria and the PLO and by installing a friendly regime in Lebanon. This flawed plan failed on both levels. Israel's regional position was not transformed, and the general challenge of the Lebanese problems has only continued. The confrontation with the PLO has been replaced by a confrontation with the Shi'ite community and two Shi'ite militias—Amal and, subsequently, Hizballah. The latter is a political movement and also a militia and terrorist organization operated directly from Teheran. During and after the conflict with Israel and the United States in 1982–84, Syria consolidated and further institutionalized its hegemony in Lebanon; as part of its strategic alliance with Iran, Syria affords it access to the Shi'ite community in Lebanon and acquiesces in its control of Hizballah, though it imposes limits on its activities.[23]

The Islamic revolution in Iran in 1979 that brought the Ayatollah Khomeini and his fundamentalist regime to power was a cardinal event in the modern history of the Middle East. For Israel, it put an end to a vital relationship the nation had established in prior years with the Shah of Iran, and placed Iran's considerable potential at the service of the Arab world's radical wing. Ever since, the Islamic Republic of Iran has agitated against Israel and against the notion of Arab-Israeli reconciliation, has used its extensive networks in the Middle East and other parts of the world for anti-Israeli terrorist activities, and has introduced new elements, like suicide bombings, into the Shi'ite-Lebanese and Palestinian conflicts with Israel. But at first these negative effects were mitigated by other developments. The fall of the Shah and the rise of the

Ayatollahs also upset a delicate balance of power in the Persian Gulf region. It had always been difficult to maintain stability when several rich but weak states, and two wealthy powerful states—one a conservative monarchy and the other a radical republic—were all in the act. When the conservative monarchy in Iran was taken over by revolutionary clerics, the balance became impossible, and indeed Iraq launched a war against Iran that lasted nearly eight years. The war gave the weaker Arab states in the Gulf region a breathing spell, but inevitably the end of the Iran-Iraq war in 1988 shifted the tension elsewhere; this happened in 1990.

While all this was going on, a substantial change occurred in the agenda and priorities of the conservative oil-producing states of the Arabian Peninsula. In the 1960s and 1970s, they had been genuinely concerned about the Arab-Israeli conflict and its radicalizing effect on their own polities; in the 1980s, different dangers were emanating from Iran and Iraq, which meant a change of attitude toward the conflict with Israel, as well as the peace process. The former was dwarfed by existential threats posed by Iran and Iraq; and peace between Egypt and Israel—the object of sharp criticism in 1978–79—now seemed more positive, stabilizing the western part of the region and freeing Egypt's armed forces to defend the Arabian Peninsula against the two radical republics. This change of perspective facilitated a reconciliation between Egypt and the other nations of the Arab world and enabled Sadat's successor to join them without having to give up the new relationship with Israel.[24]

At the same time, American leadership during Ronald Reagan's eight years in the White House lacked the drive, conviction, and determination that his two predecessors (and successor) displayed vis-à-vis the Middle East. Reagan seemed warmly disposed toward Israel, but he lacked any emotional commitment to the Camp David Accords, his rival's great achievement, and also lacked the messianic zeal that drove the Carter administration's quest to bring peace to the Middle East. Reagan's administration was damaged badly by a series of negative experiences in the Middle East—the crisis in Lebanon, the virtual rejection of his September 1982 "Reagan Plan," the Iran-Contra affair—and turned its foreign-policy efforts elsewhere, mostly to the great struggle against the Soviet Union. Secretary of State George Shultz did invest time and ingenuity in his efforts to revive the Arab-Israeli peace process, notably in 1987 and 1988, but drive and muscle were lacking. The effort to make an Israeli-Jordanian agreement (the London Agreement of 1987) and to turn the PLO into an acceptable partner (in 1988) failed.

The debacle in Lebanon was the beginning of the end of the Begin era in Israeli politics, but the Likud alignment's decline was not matched by a return to Labor ascendancy. The elections of 1984 and 1988 produced six years of power sharing under two versions of national-unity governments: the first gave a domestic political base for an (almost complete) Israeli withdrawal from Lebanon, but the Labor leader Shimon Peres's effort to revive the peace process, whether as prime minister (1984–86) or as foreign minister (1986–88), were to no avail; then Labor brought down the second national-unity government in 1990, when it believed that Likud was not responding to Secretary of State James Baker's efforts to restart the peace process.

At the core of the Likud-Labor disagreement were two conflicting approaches to an Israeli-Arab, or Israeli-Palestinian, settlement. Tactically, these differences were translated into a debate over the acceptability of various Palestinian negotiators and their affiliations to the PLO. Likud's opposition to the PLO was absolute. The Labor Party's leaders also refused to accept the organization as a legitimate negotiating partner but were willing to accept certain Palestinian negotiators whose relationship with the PLO was not direct or explicit. Still, at the end, it was Likud and its right-wing allies that were able to form a new government, and the Labor Party went back to the opposition.

Not every twist and turn in Israeli politics during the 1980s derived from the Likud-Labor rivalry and their respective ideologies, but a significant pattern could be identified: between 1977 and 1992 Israel was governed for thirteen years by a Likud prime minister and for only two years by a Labor prime minister. This shows the preeminence, however slight, of conservative nationalist forces in the Israeli body politic. Thus it was a right-wing Israeli government that confronted the massive changes of the early 1990s.[25]

On the other side, three forces had contended since 1967 to be the effective and legitimate representation of the Palestinian cause: the PLO, Jordan, and ill-defined local forces in the West Bank and the Gaza Strip. The PLO was dealt a severe blow in the Lebanon war of 1982; the subsequent removal of its headquarters and fighting forces to Tunis and to the Yemen was a severe handicap. But there was no one else to take advantage of its predicament. The failed London Agreement of 1987 was the last time an effort was made to have Jordan be Israel's principal partner in resolving the Palestinian issue, but it failed before its feasibility could be tested.

When the Palestinian uprising, the *intifada*, broke out spontaneously in 1987, it was sustained by individuals and groups that were not part of the PLO's hierarchy, yet the political capital it generated was ultimately captured by the PLO, though the road it traveled was far from straight: first acceptance of a formula for a two-state solution in 1988, then the establishment of a dialogue with the United States, the breakdown of that dialogue after the PLO's fresh drift into sponsorship of terrorism, and misguided support of Saddam Hussein's Iraq after his invasion of Kuwait.

## THE TURNING POINT OF THE
## MADRID CONFERENCE

The Madrid Conference of October 1991 finally placed the Arab-Israeli peace process on a qualitatively different footing. This first sustained effort by the international community to resolve the old conflict[26] was the product of three principal developments.

First, the decline and dissolution of the Soviet Union put an end to the Cold War's deleterious effects on Arab-Israeli issues. It left the United States as the sole power capable of exercising influence for settlement, while the Soviet Union's Arab clients lost their chief source of aid for their subsidized weapon systems. Rulers like Syria's Hafez al-Assad found themselves looking for substitutes, seeking out the United States, and dealing with the repercussions of the fall of Eastern European dictators. Israel, on the other hand, was a clear beneficiary. Soviet and Eastern-bloc hostility was replaced by normal (in several cases friendly) relations.

Also, the arrival in Israel of nearly a million immigrants from the former Soviet Union had a very significant substantive and psychological effect on the Arab-Israeli balance. In absolute terms the addition of a million Jews to the Arab-Israeli demographic equation may not seem very impressive. Israel now has 5 million Jewish and 1 million Arab (or Palestinian) citizens; also, more than 2 million Palestinians live in the West Bank and the Gaza Strip. The overall number of Palestinians is estimated at about 7 million (and the total population of the Arab world at more than 200 million). Still, the disappearance of the radical Arabs' principal mainstay and the influx of 1 million Jews to Israel sufficed to persuade many Arabs that time was not necessarily on their side.

Second, the United States, having already benefited from the Soviet Union's decline, saw its position and standing in the Middle East rise to a new level after the world witnessed its willingness and ability to field half a million soldiers and build an international coalition for the liberation of Kuwait and the defense of Saudi Arabia. The war weakened Arab radicals and the PLO. (The PLO leaders, aware of their diminished position, consented to being demoted, as it were, to only indirect representation at the Madrid Conference.) The United States also emerged from the war determined to take advantage of its enhanced influence and prestige in order to seek a comprehensive solution to the Arab-Israeli conflict. The Bush administration saw this as a prerequisite for stability and for a reorganized Middle East. It also believed, given

Iraq's launching of Scud missiles against Israel in the Gulf War, that the danger that weapons of mass destruction would be used in future wars was more acute. A political settlement was vital.

Third, the Palestinians' uprising in the West Bank and in Gaza beginning in late 1987, the *intifada*, had a long and profound effect on the Israeli public. Ever since the 1967 war twenty years before, Palestinians had failed to devise an effective strategy for their struggle against Israel, and whenever Israeli society weighed the costs of keeping the status quo or working out a new compromise, the balance had tilted toward maintaining the status quo. But in 1988, a significant body of opinion in Israel was no longer willing to pay the costs of a perpetuated status quo. It is impossible to understand Yitzhak Shamir's acceptance of the "Madrid framework" or the Labor Party's victory in the 1992 elections without understanding the effect of this change.

It took several months of hard work by Secretary of State James Baker, including nine trips to the Middle East, to build upon these developments and put together the formula for convening an international conference. A compromise had to be worked out between Arab and Israeli points of departure. As I have already noted, a weakened PLO had to give up hopes for direct participation in the conference and in ensuing negotiations; Syria, which had hoped for years for significant roles for the Soviet Union and the UN, one single Arab delegation, and continuous negotiation thereafter, finally agreed to a process cosponsored by the Soviet Union but dominated by the United States, and on comparatively loose coordination among four Arab-Israeli negotiating tracks. Israel

accepted the notion of an international conference and
was willing to turn a blind eye to the Palestinian delegation's real source of authority.

The final texts of the letter of invitation to the Madrid
Conference and of the different letters of assurance given
by the United States to the different participants clearly
expressed the bitter arguments over these principles and
terms, and the nature of the compromise solutions finally
worked out by Secretary Baker and his team. Thus the
phrase "territories for peace" was not included in the text
of the letter of initiation to the Madrid Conference or in
the specific letter of assurances sent to Israel, but it was
mentioned in the letters of assurance addressed to the
Arab invitees. For Shamir's government, the fact that the
Palestinians formally had no separate representation but
were present only as part of a Jordanian-Palestinian delegation was an achievement.

Another Baker achievement (and Syrian concession)
was the formation of a second, multilateral negotiation to
supplement the bilateral one. Working groups were established to focus on five regional issues: water, refugees,
arms control and regional security, environment, and economic cooperation. The original idea was to generate discussion of how to achieve regional cooperation on these
matters and paint visions of a better future, which would
facilitate the concessions that all the parties on the bilateral track would have to make. This plan proved to be
particularly fruitful, even though Syria and Lebanon refused to join these multilateral talks. It enabled a group
of states from outside the region to take an active part in
the peace process, bringing in Arab states from the Gulf,

the Arabian Peninsula, and North Africa, and accelerating Arab-Israeli normalization.

At the Madrid Conference, where for the first time the international community, led by the United States, committed itself to a sustained effort to resolve the Arab-Israeli conflict, a framework and a set of rules were accepted by all parties. As we have seen, a measure of ambiguity was maintained, but the Madrid formula was more explicit than, say, Security Council Resolution 242 had been. Diplomatic ambiguity and various protestations notwithstanding, it was clear that Israel wanted full peace with the Arabs, and the Arabs wanted massive territorial concessions. "Territories for peace" of course did not mean "all of Israel's occupied territories for peace," but the phrase was nonetheless unacceptable even to Shamir's government, although its leaders had come to understand that their advocacy of "peace for peace" was unrealistic.

The Madrid formula also showed that a new balance had been struck between the Palestinian and larger Arab components of the conflict. Earlier, choices had to be made in practice between Palestinians and the Arab states. The Geneva Conference and Kissinger's "step-by-step" diplomacy were both predicated on a conscious policy to bypass the Palestinians and the Palestinian issue. President Carter's attempt to put the PLO and the Palestinian issue at the center of a comprehensive settlement was an important reason for its failure. True, the Camp David Accords and the Egyptian-Israeli peace treaty incorporated the notion of interim or transitional Palestinian self-government, but this remained a dead letter. The Bush administration had, prior to the Gulf crisis, focused exclusively on the issue of Palestinian autonomy. But in 1991, the idea of dealing simultaneously with the Palestinians *and* with the Arab states was one of the keys to Jim Baker's success.

Yet the forces that produced the Madrid successes could not take them beyond a certain point. The opening conference was impressive, but during the next nine months and five rounds of negotiations in Washington, no progress was made. It was clear from the outset that a breakthrough could happen only on the Syrian or the Palestinian track, that progress with Jordan and Lebanon would have to come later. However, the Syrian and Palestinian protagonists were unwilling to make the concessions needed for progress, let alone for a breakthrough. The Bush administration, having invested a great deal of effort and political capital in Madrid, was not ready for the cost and pain entailed in goading the parties on; it was openly critical of Shamir and his government and was willing to wait for the Israeli elections of June 1992, hoping that a Labor victory would lead to change.

# 2

# MADRID AND OSLO: YEARS OF HOPE

As the century drew to a close, the four-year period from June 1992 to May 1996, shrouded as it was by both nostalgia and controversy, loomed ever more distinctly as a notably significant chapter in the evolution of Arab-Israeli relations. A hospitable regional and international environment, the newly formed Madrid framework, American leadership and support, and, above all, the determination of two Israeli prime ministers to move toward peace and several Arab partners' positive response to this, produced the most ambitious and sustained effort yet to settle the Arab-Israeli conflict.[1] These ambitions endowed the period with significance, and a number of important breakthroughs changed the contours of Arab-Israeli relations; these produced negative reactions, though, and underlined the limits to achieving a notion of peace that would be acceptable to both Arabs and Israelis.

The term "peace process" is often used rather loosely, but in those years it had a very concrete meaning: four formal tracks of bilateral negotiations supplemented by discreet informal ones, five working multilateral groups, a concerted international effort to give financial and economic support to Arab peacemakers, and two economic conferences (in Casablanca and Amman). These led to the Oslo Agreement between Israel and the PLO, a peace treaty between Israel and Jordan, semidiplomatic relations established between Israel and four other Arab states, a significant degree of less formal Israeli-Arab normalization, and a widespread sense that the Arab-Israeli conflict was finally on the way to reconciliation and resolution.

Yet the negative reaction to the same set of developments was hardly less significant.[2] Palestinian opponents of the peace process, some of them encouraged and supported by Iran, conducted a terrorist campaign designed to undermine it. Radical Israeli opponents of their government's peace policies perpetrated and condoned a massacre of Palestinian worshipers at the Tomb of the Patriarchs in Hebron in February 1994 and, separately, the assassination of Prime Minister Rabin in November 1995. Violent conflict continued along the Israeli-Lebanese border between Israel and Hizballah, exacting a high toll of casualties on both sides and culminating in Katyusha rocket attacks on northern Israel and two large-scale Israeli military operations in Lebanon. This conflict in Lebanon had local causes, but it should be seen in the context of Iran's effort to undermine the peace process, and of the failure to reach an agreement between Israel and Syria. The peace process was not well received by large segments of public opinion in the Arab world and was bitterly criticized and rejected by the Arab intelligentsia. In Israel it was pursued by a government that relied on a very slim majority, and opposition rose to the agreement made with the PLO and to the agreement contemplated with Syria. This culminated in the assassination of Rabin and the subsequent election of Benjamin (Binyamin, in Hebrew) Netanyahu, who promised to respect the agreements made by his predecessors but also to shift the peace process to an entirely different premise.

The progress made during 1992–96 had one additional and unanticipated effect. Israelis and Arabs had been familiar for some fifteen years with the benefits and limitations of the separate peace between Egypt and Israel, but notions of a comprehensive Arab-Israeli peace remained remote and abstract. The peace process of 1992–96 brought it close and made it more palpable; it showed both sides how limited the concept of peace was that would be acceptable to their societies and political systems.

It may seem odd that the period should be defined by two Israeli elections. But the fact of the matter is that, in the configuration that determined the ebb and flow of the peace process, Yitzhak Rabin's electoral victory in June 1992 marked the beginning of a new chapter, and Benjamin Netanyahu's triumph in 1996 brought it to an end. The 1992–96 peace process unfolded through four distinct phases: from the Israeli elections of June 1992 to the signing of the Oslo Accords in September 1993; from then to the signing of the Israeli-Jordanian peace treaty in October 1994; from then to Rabin's assassination in November 1995; and from then to the Israeli elections of May 1996.

## THE ROAD TO OSLO

Yitzhak Rabin's electoral victory in June 1992 was universally interpreted as the first step in a revived peace process, and Rabin himself stated clearly that he could produce an agreement on Palestinian self-rule within nine months. But neither Rabin nor his eventual partner, Yasser Arafat, envisaged himself signing an agreement like the Oslo Accords in a festive ceremony in Washington fourteen months later. And yet both leaders, in their different styles and within their different environments, adjusted and made new choices.

Rabin arrived in the prime minister's office in Jerusalem in July 1992 as a mature, experienced, and authoritative political leader. Fifteen years after his earlier resignation, he had eradicated the memories of that episode and, more broadly, of his rocky first tenure (1974–77), and now he projected the image of a confident senior leader, Israel's ultimate authority on matters of national security, a direct and trustworthy man, a political leader who was a reluctant politician.[3]

Rabin won twice in 1992. In February, having failed in earlier challenges, he defeated Shimon Peres in the Labor Party's primaries and became the party's leader and its candidate for the premiership. He had finally succeeded in persuading not only the rank and file but part of the party apparatus that he alone could defeat Shamir and the Likud and could return Labor to power. The conventional wisdom in Israeli politics was that Israeli voters had shifted to the right, that they thought Peres was too dovish. Only Rabin, it was felt, identified as he was

with national security and more centrist policies, could
attract swing votes in the center of the Israeli political
spectrum. So Labor's campaign in the subsequent general
elections presumed that, though a significant number
of voters might be ready to switch their votes away from
the Likud, they remained reluctant to cast them for
Labor. Accordingly, it focused on the candidate and not
on the party. Rabin hammered away on two principal
issues: Shamir's inability to move the Madrid peace
process forward, and his mismanagement of Israel's relationship with the United States, as evidenced by the
manifest tension between his government and the Bush
administration. Rabin promised that if elected he would
galvanize the peace process and argued that an agreement to give the Palestinians some kind of autonomy
could be reached within nine months. (A settlement with
Syria did not seem realistic to Rabin at the time and was
not a real issue.)

Rabin won, but only barely so. An analysis of the voting
figures in June 1992 shows that the Israeli body politic
remained evenly divided between right and left, and that
in fact the right received several thousand more votes
than the rival bloc but ended up with a slightly smaller
representation in the Knesset. Rabin formed a coalition
with the left-wing Meretz and with Shas, the latter
being an unusual combination of an ultra-Orthodox party
and a grassroots movement of Israelis of North African
extraction.

The key term in the new government's agenda was "a
change of national priorities." Rabin, who did not believe
that a comprehensive Arab-Israeli peace was likely in the
near future, was ready to offer concessions in order to

reach an accommodation with the Arabs, but not to return to the 1967 borders. Nor did he believe in simultaneous negotiation with Israel's four Arab protagonists, in which the Arab position would be dictated by the most radical Arab party while Israel would have to make simultaneous concessions on several fronts. Rabin preferred a gradual approach, and in the meantime Israel's domestic, regional, and international positions could be improved.

As minister of defense only a few years before, Rabin had conducted Israel's campaign against the *intifada* sternly and severely, but its lessons were not lost on him. He knew that the cost of holding on indefinitely to the West Bank and Gaza had become prohibitive. An ultimately futile effort was diverting too many resources to the West Bank from Israel proper and exacerbating Israel's relationship with the rest of the world, most significantly with the United States. For Israel's new prime minister it was essential that peace negotiations begin again, that good relations be restored with the United States, that Israel obtain the $10 billion in loan guarantees which the Americans were willing to underwrite and invest them in expanding the economy and strengthening the infrastructure. Israel needed not only to absorb its new immigrants from the former Soviet Union but to prepare for the future.

Yet Rabin was not enamored of the format established in Madrid. Simultaneous formal negotiations with four Arab delegations were not likely to lead to the kind of breakthrough with the Palestinians or Syrians that he wanted. (Lebanon and Jordan could not be counted on to act first, since Lebanon was subordinate to Syria, and Jordan would need the legitimacy of a prior Syrian or

Palestinian agreement.) But for the time being, he saw no reason to insist on a different format. His initial preference was to move first on the Palestinian track. In 1989–90, he had cooperated with Secretary Baker in trying to start an Israeli-Palestinian negotiation; given what he knew from that experience, his own readiness, and Arafat's diminished stature, he thought an agreement on self-rule could be reached within nine months: the Palestinian negotiators would be ones who were acceptable to the PLO but not representing it directly. Such an agreement would not, of course, solve the Palestinian problem, but it would take the edge off the confrontations, move people on to a course of accommodation, open up the larger peace process, and improve Israel's international standing.

Yet there were significant advantages to predicating the peace process on an early agreement with Syria, a powerful state ruled by an authoritative government, in contrast to the fragmented Palestinians. Hafez al-Assad was difficult to negotiate with, but Israel's experience showed that once he made an agreement he kept it. An agreement with Syria would also resolve Israel's problems in Lebanon, encourage Jordan to seek agreement, and thus strengthen Israel's hand with the Palestinians. Still, Syria was likely to insist on discussing only a final settlement, to settle on nothing short of Israel's full withdrawal from Syrian territory, and to offer less than what Israel had in mind.

Rabin's original preferences were modified during Secretary Baker's final trip to the Middle East in July 1992. Baker went first to Damascus and then, in Jerusalem, impressed Rabin both with his account of Assad's willingness to come to a genuine peace agreement and with the

Bush administration's willingness to help in reaching it. From that point on, Prime Minister Rabin realized that the only practical course open was to forget about the comparative advantages of this or that possible breakthrough and explore instead the possibilities afforded by the new circumstances.[4]

To begin with, the new government decided to cease building new settlements for Jews on the West Bank. To Syria it offered an implicit acceptance of the principle of withdrawal as a component in a prospective settlement. The effect of these small but significant gestures was felt during the sixth session of talks held in Washington from August 24 to September 2. The format did not change, but those sessions were marked by a new atmosphere, and substantive progress was made.

Syria responded to Israel's opening gambit by presenting, on September 1, 1992, a draft of a proposed Declaration of Principles about a Syrian-Israeli peace agreement. The concepts underlying this draft and the positions presented in it were all totally unacceptable to Israel, but, in contrast to Israeli-Syrian relations during the previous four rounds of Washington talks—an acrimonious dialogue of the deaf—its very presentation and its mention of a Syrian-Israeli peace agreement were emblematic of significant changes.

By the end of 1992, this good momentum had been all but dissipated. The Palestinian delegation to the talks in Washington, operating under instructions from the PLO leaders in Tunis, and the Israeli delegation were at cross-purposes. (The Palestinian delegation, composed of residents of the West Bank and the Gaza Strip, was headed by a distinguished Palestinian nationalist, Dr.

Haidar Abdul Shafi from Gaza, but it was common knowledge that for all intents and purposes the group was controlled and monitored by the PLO leaders in Tunis.) And the Israelis and Syrians were bogged down by Syria's insistence on Israel's commitment to a full withdrawal from the Golan Heights as a precondition to any further give-and-take. In December, Israel cracked down on the radical Islamic opposition in territory under its direct control by deporting some four hundred members of Hamas, the Islamic Resistance movement, to Lebanon. The Arab parties at the Washington talks knew very well that Hamas was challenging them, too, but they responded to Israel's move by suspending their participation in the negotiations.

What were the principal forces that were slowing down or stalling the hoped-for peace?

One was the continued discrepancy between Israeli and Arab outlooks. Syria tried hard to rally the four Arab negotiating parties, and indeed the larger Arab world, behind its own concept of a prospective settlement with Israel and of the procedural aspects in the negotiations. Assad was determined to maximize Arab coordination and to seek a comprehensive settlement or an approximation of one. When, in late July 1992, the Arab foreign ministers were invited to Damascus to formulate their strategy in the aftermath of the Israeli elections and in anticipation of the sixth round of the Washington talks, their joint statement of July 25 alluded to some flexibility (the term "peace agreement" was used for the first time), but it also foreshadowed Syria's and the PLO's opposition to the main thrust of Israel's peace policies. The statement noted approvingly the new Israeli government's "relative change in tone and approach" but criticized its failure to declare "its commitment to the basic principles of comprehensive, just and lasting peace in the region through full implementation of Security Council Resolutions 242 and 338 and the principle of the return of all occupied Arab land, including Jerusalem, in return for peace." The foreign ministers "emphasized anew the . . . principles and elements on which the peace process is based." This meant, overall, a "commitment to the objective of comprehensive peace in the region." But the foreign ministers also pledged to "respect and ensure the Palestinian people's right to self-determination and set up their independent state on their national soil"; they stressed "the linkage between the transitional and final stages in the Palestinian track," and pledged to work to eliminate not only "the obstacles that block completing the Palestinian representation to include the inhabitants of Jerusalem and the diaspora," but also the obstacles to "PLO participation in an official manner in the peace process." They also insisted on "the illegitimacy of all forms of Israeli settlement" and called for a "comprehensive solution in all fronts and in all tracks . . . rejecting any attempt to fragment and deal with each party individually."[5]

During the next few months, Syria and the PLO were in fact successful in upholding these principles. The PLO was, indeed, concerned to obtain formal legitimacy for itself in the peace process and to block any interim agreement that was not linked to a final arrangement that met Palestinian nationalism's basic expectations. It made sure that no progress was made in Washington so long as these two principal goals were not met. And a genuine progress between Syria and Israel was totally overshadowed by Assad's insistence on Israeli commitment to a full withdrawal from the Golan Heights. Outside the conference room, Assad objected to any informal, discreet contacts with Israeli diplomats, refused to engage in public diplomacy, and declined to exercise a restraining influence on Hizballah's activities in and from Lebanon.

A second difficulty concerned political developments within the United States. The revival of the "Madrid process" in the summer of 1992 coincided with the diminishing diplomatic effectiveness of the Bush administration. Shortly after Secretary Baker's trip to the Middle East in July, President Bush asked him to leave the Department of State and move to the White House as his chief of staff. It was a desperate effort to salvage Bush's ailing campaign for reelection. Dennis Ross, Baker's chief aide in Israeli-Arab matters, went along with him. Deputy Secretary Lawrence Eagleburger was appointed acting secretary of state. Eagleburger was an authoritative diplomat and policy-maker and he had at his disposal an experienced "peace team," but the reality and perception of a waning presidency undermined his effectiveness. Hafez al-Assad, for one, went on participating in the talks as much to build a new relationship with the Americans as to arrive at a settlement with Israel and regain the Golan Heights. But from his perspective there was no sense in offering concessions to a president whose future prospects appeared increasingly uncertain or, later, after Clinton had defeated Bush, in making concessions in anticipation of working with a new president about whom Assad knew practically nothing. This transitional phase ended only in February 1993, when Bill Clinton's new administration signaled its assignment of high priority to the Arab-Israeli peace process.

A third difficulty was the direct challenge presented by the radical Islamic opponents of peace with Israel. Hamas and the smaller Islamic Jihad were inspired by several sources: opposition to the very notion of a peaceful settlement with Israel, a more specific opposition to the "Madrid process," opposition to and criticism of Yasser Arafat and his team, and Iranian encouragement. The actions of Hamas, the more active and effective of the two, were shaped by a terribly effective logic—violence and terrorism against Israeli targets would undermine the Israeli people's support for peace and would force Israeli counteractions that would disrupt it.[6] And, indeed, by stepping up its deadly activity—Hamas killed three Israeli soldiers in the Gaza Strip on December 7, and an Israeli border-police officer was abducted and murdered on December 13—Hamas provoked Rabin to his radical effort to emasculate, if not destroy, the Hamas infrastructure in the West Bank and the Gaza Strip: the deportation of some four hundred Hamas activists to Lebanon.

When Warren Christopher, the new secretary of state, went to the Middle East in February 1993, this marked the revival of the peace process, which by April was fully back on track. Rabin had his first working visit to the Clinton administration in March, and the Washington talks were resumed in April. Rabin's visit to Washington was especially important, for it laid the foundation for a warm personal relationship between Clinton and Rabin and for a close working relationship between their governments. But progress was clearly neither smooth nor linear. Rabin completed his work in Washington but had to cut short his visit to the United States because of a wave of terrorist knifing attacks in Tel Aviv.

Coherence and clarity marked the architecture of the new American administration's Middle Eastern policies: a "dual containment" of Iraq and Iran in the east and pursuit of Arab-Israeli peace in the west, two mutually reinforcing policy prongs. By cultivating an Arab-Israeli peace, Washington hoped it would be easy for its conservative Arab allies to support "dual containment," and fostering Israeli-Syrian and Israeli-Palestinian reconciliation should diminish the ability of Iran and other fundamentalist Muslim states to agitate and subvert.[7]

The administration also believed that this Middle Eastern policy had an unusual asset: an authoritative Israeli prime minister who was determined by his own choice to move toward peace and who was ready to offer indispensable concessions. During the previous twenty years, the United States and Israel had cooperated for much of the time, but as a rule American presidents and secretaries of state had to extract concessions from reluctant Israeli prime ministers (including Rabin himself during his first tenure). Here was a unique opportunity.

In their discussions with Rabin in March, Clinton and his team were quite explicit about their preference for effecting the first breakthrough on the Israeli-Syrian track, which seemed eminently feasible given Rabin's willingness to offer significant (though still not specific) territorial concession and assuming Assad's willingness to make peace. They believed Assad could deliver an agreement he would sign, and considered that an Israeli-Syrian peace could be a prelude to an American-Syrian rapprochement; this would detach Syria from Iran's sphere of influence, as it were, and be the key to a desirable realignment in the Middle East. Rabin was responsive to this view, but he reminded the Americans that from Israel's point of view a breakthrough would be welcome on either track.

In April, the State Department official in charge of the peace process, Edward Djerijian, was dispatched on a secret mission to President Assad. He bore a letter from President Clinton that was intended to persuade him to open additional discreet channels to Israel and to adopt a bolder, more forthcoming approach in the negotiations. Djerijian's mission, then a second letter from Clinton, a meeting in Vienna between Secretary Christopher and Foreign Minister Shara, and further work between the Israeli and Syrian delegations in Washington all failed to produce results. Nor did U.S. diplomacy succeed in helping the Israeli and Palestinian delegations. Israeli diplomacy, resorting to unorthodox methods, produced a final breakthrough on this track only by means of secret bilateral negotiations that went on in Oslo for several months.

The Oslo talks began, like several similar informal and unauthorized Israeli and Palestinian dialogues, in January 1993. On the Israeli side it had the sponsorship of Deputy Foreign Minister Yossi Beilin, who operated through two of his academic protégés. Beilin took his time before briefing his superior, Foreign Minister Shimon Peres, about these talks, and Peres took his time in reporting to the prime minister.[8]

Rabin's response was complex. He himself was not enamored of the Madrid format and had lost faith in the formal negotiations in Washington. He had authorized some of his own confidants to deal indirectly with the

PLO and in March 1993, during his visit to Washington, had agreed to have Faysal Husseini, the most prominent Palestinian leader in East Jerusalem, join the Palestinian delegation to the Washington talks. Husseini was known to have close ties with the PLO, and his participation in the talks could conceivably be construed as a crack in Israel's adamant claim that Jerusalem's status as an Israeli city was not negotiable. This latter point was finessed by the admittedly weak argument, familiar since 1989, that since Husseini had a West Bank address he could be regarded as a West Banker and not necessarily a Jerusalemite. And as for the PLO connection, Rabin felt that the pretense of dealing with presumably independent local leaders was wearing thin. Husseini was an authentic local leader, whatever his affiliation with the PLO, and his participation in the Washington talks was a last-ditch effort to see whether there was any value to dealing with local leaders by bypassing the PLO. In retrospect, it is clear that Rabin was not really surprised to discover that Husseini, too, received his marching orders from Tunis. For him, the whole episode was a transition to the ensuing negotiation with the PLO.

So, in May 1993, Rabin agreed to formalize and elevate the status of the Oslo talks and dispatched the director general of the Foreign Ministry, Uri Savir, to head the Israeli team there. Rabin's concession was dual: he agreed in fact to negotiate with the PLO, an organization he had until recently demonized, and he assigned the principal work in this negotiation to Shimon Peres and his team. The original division of labor in Rabin's government had reflected the lingering rivalry between the prime minister and the man he had defeated in the party primaries just five months earlier: Rabin had taken charge of the four tracks of bilateral negotiations with the Arabs, while Peres was left with the five working groups in the multilateral talks. Now Rabin was altering the internal balance in his government, but he regarded this as a secondary issue compared with the prospect of a breakthrough with the Palestinian nationalists.[9]

The Oslo negotiations continued into early August. The Palestinian delegation, composed of Abu Alaa (or Ahmad Quray), a senior member of the PLO hierarchy, and two associates, at Israel's insistence provided ample proof that they were valid and effective PLO representatives. On the Israeli side Savir was reinforced by Joel Singer, a retired international lawyer with the Israeli Defense Force. Rabin kept his own close aides and the defense establishment in the dark, and Singer's participation in addition to his own overseeing of the negotiations was intended to ensure that security issues would be covered. By early August, the broad lines of an agreement had indeed been put together.

The core of the agreement was predicated on the model established by the Camp David Accords in 1978. Palestinian self-rule was to be established in the West Bank and the Gaza Strip for a transitional period of five years. At the end of the second year, negotiations would begin over final-status issues. Israeli military forces would be redeployed in several stages—from Gaza, then from Palestinian cities in the West Bank, and then in a series of "further redeployments" during the final-status negotiations. Israeli settlements on the West Bank would not be affected, and their future, as well as the issues of Jerusalem, of water rights, and of refugees, would be addressed in the final-status negotiations.

But the agreement taking shape in Oslo was different from the autonomy plan of 1978–79 in several significant respects. For one thing, the PLO had earlier refused to endorse the autonomy agreement, and Israel was led by a government resigned to the need to prevent Palestinian statehood. But the Oslo Accords were signed by the PLO and by Israeli leaders determined to effect a historic compromise with Palestinian nationalism and aware that an agreement on self-rule would likely lead to Palestinian statehood.

It was precisely his realization of the magnitude of the issues involved in the Oslo Accords that led Rabin to resort to an unusual measure: before an agreement was concluded in Oslo, he wanted to establish whether Israel had any option vis-à-vis Syria. On August 3, during a meeting in his office in Jerusalem with Warren Christopher, he asked the secretary of state to use the "hypothetical-question" technique when he went next to Damascus. As we have seen, the effort during the previous few months to develop an effective Israeli-Syrian communication had been made to no avail. Rabin now asked Secretary Christopher to inquire of Assad whether, "on the assumption that his own demand would be met," he would be willing to make peace with Israel on the basis of terms acceptable to Israel.

Rabin modeled the terms on the Israeli-Egyptian peace treaty of 1979—contractual peace, full diplomatic relations, normalization, security arrangements, implementation in phases over a five-year period, and "interface"—a heavy dose of normalization at the outset in return for a very small withdrawal on Israel's part, to enable Israel to "test" the new relationship before withdrawing from the rest of the territory it had seized in the war. Rabin emphasized to Christopher that this must remain secret, that it was a hypothetical question, and that, since he had not presented it as part of his platform in the 1992 elections, he would have to submit such an agreement to a referendum before it had legitimacy.

Secretary Christopher and Dennis Ross presented Rabin's hypothetical gambit to Assad on August 4 and returned to Rabin's office on August 5 with a response that they regarded as positive and he viewed as disappointing. Assad envisaged an implementation period of six months rather than five years; he took exception to the term "normalization"; security arrangements were welcome as long as they were for both parties and "on equal footing"; and the notion of "interface" was unacceptable. Assad clearly thought he was beginning a protracted bargaining process, but this was totally unacceptable to Rabin. Not only did he not want a lengthy and arduous tug-of-war over every issue, big or small, but he felt it was an inherently flawed process. Since Syria regarded full Israeli withdrawal from the Golan Heights as a given, the bargaining process would be restricted solely to Israel's terms, which were bound to be whittled down. Christopher and Ross went back home and left on their summer vacations—only to find out later in August that Israel had gone ahead and concluded the Oslo Accords.[10]

Still, the Clinton administration had been briefed in general terms about the secret negotiations between Israel and the PLO. In fact, Rabin and Christopher had discussed them on August 3, but the briefings were vague enough so that the Oslo breakthrough was a surprise. But the administration wasted no time in being surprised, disappointed, or angry: most of its decision-makers and policy-makers had thought a Syrian-Israeli agreement was the best starting point, but they recognized the historic significance and policy implications of Israel's agreement with the PLO. After the Israeli and Norwegian ministers of foreign affairs briefed Christopher and Ross in California, the administration decided not only to endorse the Oslo Accords but to endow them with the added value of an impressive signing ceremony on the White House lawn on September 13.

From that point on, the Israeli-Arab peace process was predicated on the Israeli-Palestinian agreement, and prospects for an Israeli-Syrian agreement diminished. Hafez al-Assad's positions and attitudes, as revealed by the hypothetical exercise in August, had had a chilling effect on Rabin, who also felt that he could not "overload the circuits" in Israel itself, that the Palestinian settlement had to be digested before a second painful concession could be accepted in Israel.

But Assad and the Clinton administration had a different idea. Assad chose to ignore the distinction between a hypothetical deposition with an honest broker and an actual commitment made in the course of a negotiation. His position was reinforced by Christopher's view—a promising start unnecessarily nipped in the bud—and his determination to go ahead with Israeli-Syrian talks once the Oslo Accords were signed. The Americans invested considerable efforts in placating Assad, persuading him not to agitate against Oslo and in fact to send his ambassador in Washington to the signing ceremony. They also promised Assad to resume the work begun in August, and indeed they obtained Rabin's commitment to cooperate in new talks in four months. This is how the term "commitment" was introduced into the vocabulary of the Israeli-Syrian negotiation.

Fourteen months after taking office, Rabin thus effected the first breakthrough toward peace. The Oslo Accords and the Washington signing ceremony were momentous: the ground had been laid for a historic compromise between Israeli and Palestinian nationalism; by addressing this core issue and by going through the rites of mutual recognition with the PLO, Israel also laid the groundwork for normalizing its relations with other Arab states and its own international position, while Palestinians for the first time since 1947 had a real chance for statehood.

The prospects were exhilarating, but the euphoria of the moment could not conceal the gravity of the remaining problems or the difficulties inherent in the very wording of the Oslo Accords. Compromises and concessions generated criticism on both sides; criticism and opposition were bound to increase after the initial shock wore off and problems of implementation came to the fore. There was an ironic symmetry to the criticism leveled at Rabin by his Israeli critics and at Arafat by his Arab ones: Rabin was accused of making an agreement with the leader and organization he himself had demonized, endowing them with legitimacy, giving away parts of the Jews' historic homeland, and undermining the security of Israel and Israelis. Arafat was charged with having sold out, offering Israel legitimacy and recognition in return for self-rule under Israeli tutelage, abandoning the Palestinian diaspora, and relegating Palestine's crucial final status to an ill-defined future moment.

Now the principles in the Oslo Accords would have to be converted into detailed, agreed-on implementations. This required a sense of partnership and genuine cooperation. In the absence of clarity about the future, both leaders would have to win each other's confidence while keeping the support of their own constituencies. Yet, throughout the West Bank and the Gaza Strip, Israeli settlers and Palestinian Arabs would pursue different, often contradictory agendas. The PLO's former foot soldiers were to become a gendarmerie entrusted with keeping law and order but also with foiling attacks against Israel and Israelis. Important questions would have to be answered by both parties. Would Arafat actually move to Gaza and turn the Palestinian Authority there into the center of Palestinian life, or would he keep the PLO headquarters in Tunis and its "embassies" and offices around the world as the real locus of Palestinian nationalism? Would the Israeli public reelect the government that had signed the Oslo Accords, or would the critics come to power to stop the process before the final-status negotiations?

## THE CRUCIAL YEAR OF 1994

Some of these questions were answered during the following year, which Israel and the PLO spent negotiating the implementation agreement for a Gaza and Jericho plan (it was signed on May 4, 1994, in Cairo), and the Paris Agreement, which regulated economic relations between Israel and the Palestinian Authority. This was arduous work, and yet the first phase was concluded successfully: by the summer of 1994, there was a functioning Palestinian administration in Gaza and a less significant extension in Jericho. Arafat had moved to Gaza and was spending most of his time there.

But some of the anticipated difficulties arose as well. Chief among them were violent efforts made to derail the peace process. On February 25, a Jewish settler killed twenty-nine Muslim worshipers at the Tomb of the Patriarchs in Hebron; a few weeks later, on April 6 and 13, Hamas killed twelve Israelis in suicide bombings in two Israeli towns.

Israel's next major initiative was to seek a full-fledged peace settlement with Jordan, a popular, noncontroversial move that would require only moderate concessions in return for which Israel would have peace along its longest border, the prospect of warm relations and actual cooperation with King Hussein's friendly regime, and increased leverage with both Syria and the Palestinians.[11] But several significant obstacles had to be overcome first. One was the Clinton administration's reservations. It felt beholden to Syria: it wanted to hold Rabin to his commitment first to resume serious give-and-take with Assad once the agreement with the PLO was in place. It also doubted that Jordan would make a full peace; after all, the Hashemite kings had not yet done so despite decades of secret diplomacy. Also, there were disputes over land and water that had to be resolved, and to help in this Jordan would have to defy Syria and move on its own.

But Rabin persisted. He saw the advantage in several developments. King Hussein was not pleased with the Oslo Accords and the prospect it gave of a Palestinian state on Jordan's border claiming the allegiance of most of his subjects. But once his government overcame its initial anger, the members understood the advantages of having a close working relationship with Rabin during this crucial period, and the Americans, despite their reservations and different priorities, were finally persuaded to offer support: Jordan was offered debt relief, the possibility of strengthening and modernizing its armed forces, and, not least, an opportunity to erase the negative legacy of its role in the Gulf crisis and during the Gulf War period. Israel had experienced a long tradition of secret personal diplomacy with Jordan. So the talks in Washington were sidestepped during 1994 by personal diplomacy at the highest level, which achieved the breakthrough; the official delegations resumed work in earnest only at the final phases, and not in Washington. And the warm personal relationship between King Hussein and Prime Minister Rabin was indispensable in the two countries' completion of a peace treaty in one year; it was signed in October 1994.

The character and pace of Israel's negotiations with Syria were very different. In late April, when the Cairo Agreement with the Palestinians was about to be signed, Rabin was stunned to hear from Secretary Christopher that Assad had a new precondition for resumed negotiations: the full withdrawal, conditionally and hypothetically suggested by Israel via the United States in August 1993, must mean withdrawal to the lines of June 4, 1967, that is, *before* the 1967 war. The difficult truth was that between Israel and Syria there was no established border. A line separating Mandate Syria from Mandate Palestine had been drawn in 1923; the 1948 war had ended with an armistice agreement, in 1949, that in certain respects was ambiguous: it referred specifically to an "armistice line," leaving the border issue for future settlements. Then, between 1949 and 1967, Syria took advantage of superior topographical conditions to establish itself in the al-Hamma enclave in the southern foothills of the Golan Heights and on the eastern shore of Lake Tiberias, Israel's most important water reservoir. The term "lines of June 4, 1967," which presumed this territory was Syrian, had appeared before in the Israel-Syria negotiations, but the cutting edge of Syria's demand had all along been "full withdrawal." Syria's insistence now on the June 4 lines could be explained as tactical (a desire to do better than Egypt, which had made its peace according to the international border) or principled (in line with Assad's traditional railing against the region's partition by the colonial powers). But in any event Rabin viewed it as unjustified and illegitimate; to him it cast doubts on Assad's intention actually to conclude an agreement, let alone swiftly, and it reinforced his sense that an Israel-Syria agreement was not likely during his first term.

Still, Rabin was not interested in pushing Assad into a corner or in straining his relationship with the Clinton administration, which, from its remote and lofty vantage point, saw little difference between the acknowledged international border and the June 4 lines. By July 19, a formula had been found for grafting the lines of June 4 onto the original hypothetical, conditional suggestion made in August 1993. Assad now authorized his ambassador in Washington, Walid Muallem, to open an "ambassadors' channel" with his Israeli counterpart, the present author. We met regularly and frequently for several months, always in the presence of one or two American diplomats. This ambassadors' channel proved to be most effective: the two nations could with relative ease explore each other's real positions and establish the possibilities and limitations of any future relationship.

## CASABLANCA AND AFTER

On October 31, 1994, shortly after Jordan and Israel signed a peace agreement, the first Middle East Economic Conference opened in Casablanca. Several themes converged here: one was the notion of "Arab-Israeli normalization," which Israel's agreement with the PLO had made much easier to implement; another was the idea of having multilateral talks in which Israel, various Arab countries, and other nations discussed regional issues and means of cooperation that among other things would facilitate any concessions made in bilateral negotiations. A third idea, identified closely with Foreign Minister Peres, was that a durable Arab-Israeli peace should rest on a common effort to resolve regional socioeconomic problems and to elevate the general population's standard of living. A calmer and better integrated Middle East was a positive idea for everyone.

In many respects, the Jordan-Israel peace and the Casablanca Conference were the high-water marks of the 1992–96 period. Soon several negative trends became apparent, and two of them were devastating. But first there was the signing on September 28, 1995, of Oslo II—the agreement that extended Palestinian self-rule to the West Bank. The negotiations had been more difficult and more protracted than expected. The implementation of the

Cairo Agreement had been considered fairly successful, and a sense of partnership did develop at least among some of the Israeli and Palestinian decision-makers and negotiators, but several obstacles obstructed the next phase. To begin with, the implementation of Palestinian self-rule in the West Bank was a more complex and difficult matter than in Gaza, which is a more compact area where the number of Israeli settlements and settlers is smaller. The West Bank is close to Israel's main cities, contiguous to Jerusalem, and dotted with Israeli settlements large and small. The Palestinian negotiators were eager to control as much territory as possible before the final-status talks began and before the Israeli elections, both scheduled for 1996. Rabin and Peres were equally determined to keep as many bargaining assets as they could for as long as possible.

The core of the agreement finally reached stipulated a division of the West Bank into several categories: Area A would consist of the main cities, in which a full transfer of civil and security authority to the Palestinian Authority (PA) would take place gradually as Israel withdrew; Area B would include more than 450 villages under the PA's civil authority, but with Israel maintaining overall responsibility for security until mid-1997; Area C would include state lands, thinly populated areas, and the Jewish settlements, which would remain under full Israeli security jurisdiction, with a limited PA jurisdiction over the area's sparse Palestinian population. All told, less than 30 percent of the West Bank would be transferred to direct Palestinian control at that phase.

Later on, Israel was to continue its withdrawal in three further redeployments. Israeli negotiators agreed to this scheme, which the Palestinians argued was predicated on the autonomy plan in the 1978 Camp David Accords ("a withdrawal of Israeli armed forces will take place and there will be a redeployment of the remaining Israeli forces into specified security locations"), but only at a later date and in circumstances that have since become controversial in Israel. The logic underlying Israel's acceptance of the arrangement was intimately linked to its anticipation of the final-status negotiations: every Israeli withdrawal should facilitate a concession that Arafat would have to make if those negotiations were to succeed. Another important stipulation of the agreement concerned the election, under international supervision, of an eighty-two-member legislative council, to be held twenty-two days after Israeli soldiers had withdrawn from the main cities of the West Bank (except Hebron).

This Oslo II agreement was a particularly important milestone. The original Oslo Accords had had far-reaching *potential* consequences, but actually getting through the first phase of implementation to the second was not inevitable; the second agreement provided for that transition and brought the Palestinians to the verge of statehood. Israeli negotiators defined it as "a historical agreement that put an end to the Israeli domination of the Palestinians and to the concept of the 'Land of Israel' and which set in motion the beginning of cooperation between the two peoples who decided to divide the land between them for the sake of the mutual object of peace, security and economic development."[12]

The next phase of negotiations coincided with the temporary collapse of those between Israel and Syria. Between November 1994 and June 1995, significant efforts were made to develop a dialogue between the security establishments of the two countries: the relatively open discussion between the ambassadors in Washington had clearly demonstrated that this was indispensable to any real progress. So, in December 1994, a first meeting was held between the chiefs of staff of Israel and Syria. This important and "normal" act revealed the depth of the gap separating the two protagonists' view of the security issue. Syria insisted on full Israeli withdrawal from the Golan Heights, of course, but maintained that this did not require extensive security arrangements, which would be invasive and humiliating given that Israel enjoyed overall military superiority. For Israelis who viewed the Golan Heights primarily as a security necessity, withdrawal from most, let alone all, of it would obviously have to be offset by an impressive array of other security arrangements.

President Assad, unhappy with what he regarded as excessive Israeli expectations and demands, suspended further negotiations between the military officers and insisted that a set of underlying principles be agreed upon before they met again. Most of the principles important to Assad were quite acceptable to Israel, as it happened, but for more than four months Assad's insistence that Israel agree to so-called equality as an underlying principle proved to be an insurmountable obstacle: Rabin held that, though most security arrangements could be implemented on an equal basis, their *territorial* dimensions could not be equal, because of the two countries' differences in size and topography. In May 1995, a compromise formula was finally worked out, which led to the drafting of a "nonpaper" on "the aims and principles of the security arrangements."

After this, the Syrian and Israeli chiefs of staff met again—in Washington in June. A genuine give-and-take developed in the course of that meeting, but afterward misunderstanding and disagreement recurred. Assad now wanted Israel to give up its own demand for a manned early-warning station on the Golan Heights before any further discussions ensued. Rabin refused to comply with this negotiating style and insisted that the sequence agreed on in May be kept. On this sticking point the negotiation was stalled, and it was renewed only after Rabin's assassination.

By that time, several other negative developments had occurred. Foremost among them was a string of terrorist attacks launched by Hamas. In October 1994, twenty-two Israelis were killed by a suicide attack on a bus at the very center of Tel Aviv; in January 1995, twenty-one Israeli soldiers were killed when two explosive charges were detonated in a bus station; and in July, five Israelis were killed in another suicide bombing in a bus in the city of Ramat Gan, near Tel Aviv.

These terrorist attacks had a devastating effect on the Israeli public's attitude toward the unfolding possibility of peace with the Arabs. Not all of the attacks originated in areas under the Palestinian Authority's control, but the prevailing perception was that they did, that Arafat and his colleagues were not totally committed to preventing anti-Israeli terrorism by Muslim fundamentalist opponents of the peace process, that Arafat did not consider Hamas a dangerous challenge whose infrastructure and ideology had to be uprooted lest his own strategy be destroyed, but as a legitimate, significant political force he would rather co-opt than fight head-on, as a potential partner if his agreement with Israel collapsed.

Arafat's familiar proclivity to equivocate in difficult and complex situations was, indeed, compounded by issues that grew out of the Oslo Accords, though not exactly as the Israeli public perceived it. Oslo, being a phased conditional formula for resolving the Israeli-Palestinian conflict, required Arafat to deal simultaneously with two conflicting constituencies. He had to persuade Israel that he had buried the hatchet and was a partner solicitous of Israeli security, but he also felt that he had to keep the Palestinians mobilized and motivated for the tug-of-war with Israel that lay ahead. Whatever his sense of partnership with the Rabin-Peres government, Arafat knew well that profound disagreements could be expected over the final-status issues. Meanwhile, his promises and exhortations to his Palestinian constituency—the struggle continues, it's a *jihad* (holy war), we know from Islamic history that agreements made with infidels may not be binding, Jerusalem will be liberated—were noted and amplified by Israeli opponents of the very idea of making peace with Arabs.

This was embarrassing to the Israeli government, but not as devastating as was the reformulation of the security issue, which occurred as an unanticipated consequence of the Oslo Accords. Rabin, a leader preoccupied with national security, oversaw the government's effort to guarantee that reconciliation with Palestinians would have no adverse effects on Israel's national security. He also believed that peace with the Palestinians and Israel's other immediate neighbors would set the stage for dealing with the more serious, even existential threats presented by

Iraq and Iran. But he failed to foresee that a terrorist campaign in Israel proper might be launched by Arab and Muslim enemies of the peace process, and Israel had no answer to the suicide bombings. During the six years of the *intifada*, 172 Israelis were killed; in 1993–96, close to 300 Israelis were killed by terrorists. As a result, many Israelis began to equate the Oslo peace process with an actual loss of personal security. Whatever the immediate or more remote benefits accruing to Israel and to themselves from the Oslo Accords, they were less palpable and seemed less significant than this, not to mention the apparent new dependence on the Palestinian Authority's cooperation for security, not only in the West Bank but in general.

By the summer of 1995, public disenchantment with the implementation of the Oslo Accords and growing opposition to the idea of withdrawal from the Golan Heights began to erode the government's support base and legitimacy. The Oslo II agreement was only barely approved in the Knesset, and the government was only barely able to fend off an attempt by the "Golan Lobby" to entrench the 1981 Golan Law, which extended Israeli law to the Golan Heights. This would have been a mortal blow to the beleaguered Israeli-Syrian negotiation.

More ominously, opposition to the government's peace policies was becoming still uglier and more vehement. There were violent demonstrations, calls for civil disobedience (a concept imported from the United States), disruption of public order, and much incendiary rhetoric. As it turned out, in this context of violence, delegitimization, and demonization a small fanatical group was operating with the belief that the only way to stop the peace process was to assassinate Yitzhak Rabin. One of its members acted on November 4, and his action proved, indeed, to be terribly effective.

The declining fortunes of the peace process in Israel were matched by growing opposition and eroding support on the Arab side. Euphoria had not been part of the Arab response to the Oslo Accords from the outset, of course, and most of the Arab world wanted simply to get the conflict with Israel over with and turn its attention to other issues. It was grudgingly willing to endorse Oslo and to offer Israel a measure of acceptance and normalization, but even this grudging acceptance was never universal. Soon it was clouded still further by criticism of the Oslo Accords themselves, by Syria's unhappiness with the failure to achieve progress, by Islamic and other radical agitation, and by both popular and official fear that normalization might lead to Israel's domination of the Middle East. Israel's massive participation at the Casablanca Conference and some less-than-tactful rhetoric in Israel fanned these anxieties. The term "New Middle East," used by Shimon Peres as the title of a book outlining his vision of peace in the region, became the focus of this criticism of Israel's intentions.[13] Peres had wanted to propose a future in which Israelis and Arabs worked together to resolve the region's underlying problems, first and foremost poverty and scarcity of natural resources, but his book and the ideas it expounded were received by a suspicious Arab world as paternalistic at best or, more commonly and at worst, as demonstrating Israel's quest for hegemony. As Hafez al-Assad put it in an interview in *Al-Ahram*:

I believe that they want a dark future for us. . . . I believe that the long-term goal of the others is to cancel what is called the Arabs, what is called Arabism. . . . I mean canceling our feelings as a nation, canceling Arab feelings, canceling pan-Arab identity. . . .

We, as Arabs, certainly reject this because . . . Arabism is not a commodity to trade in even though this is what the others seek.[14]

Egypt played a significant part in the development of this attitude. During the previous fifteen years, Egypt had been embarrassed by its separate peace with Israel and criticized Israel for failing to implement the Palestinian part of it. Now, with a larger peace process unfolding, and when an Israeli-Palestinian agreement had been signed, with Egypt's help and support, the nation was visibly unhappy with the restructuring of regional politics, and Cairo, too, saw Israel as striving for regional hegemony at its expense. It did nothing to improve its own bilateral relationship with Israel, and waged a vociferous campaign against Israel's potential as a nuclear power, noting its policy of studied ambiguity about nuclear weapons and its refusal to sign the Treaty on Non-Proliferation of Nuclear Weapons. Egypt tried to obstruct Washington's policy of extending the terms of that treaty indefinitely upon the expiration in 1995 of its original time frame and, when this failed, suspended its participation in the multilateral working group on arms control and regional security. In the event, this Egyptian policy resulted in the suspension of all the multilateral tracks on which Israeli-Arab negotiations had been proceeding.[15]

Rabin's assassination thus happened when the peace process he had launched was already receding, and dealt it a near-fatal blow. Peres's attempt to revitalize and accelerate peace negotiations can be viewed in retrospect as its Indian summer.

## AFTER RABIN

Throughout all this period and for everyone involved, domestic politics and foreign policy were closely intertwined. This was especially true between Rabin's assassination and the Israeli elections. Shimon Peres, as Rabin's successor, had to make an early dual decision: when the next Israeli election should be held and on what platform he would run. If he called an early election, he would run as Rabin's avenger and the principal issues would be the government's support of the Oslo Accords and its efforts to assign responsibility for the assassination. Or he could keep the original date—late October 1996—by which time he would have to run on his own terms and on the strength of new policy decisions he would make during the intervening months.

Peres chose the latter option, which presented him with the next decision to be made: should he seek to finalize an agreement with Syria, or should he try to speed up final-status talks with the Palestinians (scheduled to begin in May) and seek to telescope them into the next few months?

One of Peres's closest associates, Yossi Beilin, had just concluded another secret, unauthorized negotiation with the Palestinians: he and Abu Mazen had drafted a final-status agreement, which offered the Palestinians statehood and sovereignty over most of the West Bank, though it kept most of the Jewish settlements and settlers under

Israeli rule. It also proposed an ingenious solution to the issue of Jerusalem: Abu Dis, a village (or suburb) bordering Jerusalem on the east would be named Al-Quds and become a capital for the Palestinian state, contiguous to Jerusalem proper. Beilin argued that, using this draft, final-status negotiations could be completed by May, and that such an agreement would win the support of a majority of Israelis, and would give the government a program both for winning the elections in October and for consolidating the peace process.

Peres was not convinced. He preferred a different plan favored by some of his other aides and by the Clinton administration: to get a swift deal with Syria and to predicate on it a comprehensive settlement of the Arab-Israeli conflict. Peres's idea of an Israeli-Syrian settlement was quite different from what Rabin's had been. He was interested not in a lengthy phased implementation but in rapid execution, he did not see security as the key issue, and he did not believe in assigning military officers an important role in the negotiations. In keeping with his larger view, the new prime minister believed that the way to build a durable peace was to create a web of common economic interests and to increase Syria's own prosperity. There was also a significant difference in his view of "normalization." Rabin had not believed that Syria would willingly offer more normalization than Egypt had, and he thought Israel could settle, for the time being, on a formal peace. Peres held that Israel should insist on early engagement and economic cooperation, that this was the only way to deal with the underlying issues and place an ensuing settlement on a solid foundation.

Peres's preferences and his sense of urgency ran against the grain of Assad's character and style: cautious, suspicious, deliberate. Assad was attracted by Peres's apparent willingness to de-emphasize the security dimension, but he was taken aback by Peres's insistence that "normalization" and direct economic cooperation with Israel were crucial.

Just as Rabin's gambit via Secretary Christopher in August 1993 had been a breakthrough, Peres's interest in making a swift deal with Assad provided the opportunity for a second breakthrough. But prospects for an agreement soon faded. Peres explained to Secretary Christopher and his team that his willingness to come to terms with Syria was conditional on Assad's agreement to an early meeting: he knew that Assad would make peace only on the basis of Israel's full withdrawal from the Golan Heights, and he was willing to bite this bullet, but only if his own terms were met, which could be established only through negotiations; Peres wanted an early indication of seriousness, and he knew he could hardly go into the election campaign as a prime minister who had given up the Golan and gotten nothing in return.

A public meeting between himself and Assad was the litmus test. But Assad rebuffed the idea. He, too, cared about swift negotiations and was agreeable to some relaxation in their format, but he would not upgrade the negotiations significantly, would not engage in serious public diplomacy, and certainly would not meet Peres before an agreement was reached.

Relations further deteriorated during negotiating rounds that took place at a conference center at the Wye Plantation, near Washington (later to become much better known), where Israel and Syria were represented by mixed civilian and military delegations. Together with a group of American diplomats, the two teams stayed for several days at a time under the same roof, shared meals, and talked more freely than they ever had before. Progress was made, but too slowly for the Israeli government's domestic political agenda and timetable. Peres, grappling with the question of whether to move up the elections to late May, needed to know in January whether an agreement might be reached by the spring, so as to fit into a political schedule leading to October elections, and the reports he received from the Wye Plantation were not clear. Progress continued, but not much on security issues, and Syria resisted Israel's new insistence on genuine economic cooperation.

Peres therefore decided to move up the election to May 29. This displeased Assad. (Eventually, his spokesmen would argue that an agreement had been well on its way and that Peres's decision destroyed that prospect.) But he agreed to continue negotiating at Wye in anticipation of the vote; negotiations continued. Israel suspended them in early March, after the suicide bombings staged by Hamas and Islamic Jihad in three Israeli cities in late February and early March and the Syrian delegation's refusal to condemn them.

This terrorist wave in February and March exacted a large number of victims, and it inflicted a deadly blow on the peace process. Benjamin Netanyahu's victory over Shimon Peres in the May elections was the result of several forces at work, but there can be little doubt that the suicide bombings were the single most important one. Before them, Peres enjoyed a comfortable lead (some twenty percentage points) in the polls, but by early March that had gone, and he never fully recovered. Netanyahu's campaign, on the other hand, used the terrorist attacks to assail the credibility of Peres and his policies and to offer the Israeli voter a magic formula of "peace with security." Netanyahu pledged to respect the Oslo Accords but to replace Peres's policy with a more aggressive insistence on Israeli security and Palestinian compliance and a more deliberate pace in the peace negotiations. If the suicide bombings were designed by Iran and its Palestinian clients to stop the 1992–96 peace process, they proved to be morbidly effective.

Iran's offensive against an Arab-Israeli peace was mostly focused on Lebanon, where Hizballah had long been Teheran's principal instrument both for expanding its influence in and through the Shi'ite community there, and for launching attacks against Israel's "security zone" in the south and against Israel itself. Together with the cycles of terrorist attacks within Israel, the continuing violence along the Israeli-Lebanese border cast an ominous shadow on all the diplomatic maneuvers aimed at peace. And Israelis were hard put to accept Syria's complex conduct in this matter. As the dominant power in Lebanon, Syria could have put an end to Hizballah's attacks, but Assad had no intention of doing so, believing as he did in negotiating from a position of strength and in applying pressure tactics. If Israel was vulnerable to a steady stream of losses in southern Lebanon, that was all the more reason to keep the pressure on until a satisfactory agreement was reached. All the arguments made by U.S. and Israeli diplomats that this policy was undermining Assad's credibility in Israeli eyes and Israeli public support for a settlement with Syria were to no avail. Nor was Assad interested in prematurely jeopardizing his strategic alliance with Iran. If an agreement with Israel came and if a diplomatic dialogue with Washington began, a change might ensue vis-à-vis Teheran, but the prospect seemed remote.

At various points over the years, this complex Syrian policy in Lebanon became untenable. When, in late July 1993, Israel had launched a large-scale operation in southern Lebanon—Operation Accountability—Syria responded to Secretary Christopher's urging that he get Hizballah to accept "understandings" on the basis of which a cease-fire could be worked out. And from December 1995 to January 1996, at the height of its negotiation with Peres, Syria did put serious pressure and limitations on Hizballah's activities—to the point of having Iran look for alternative supply routes to its Lebanese clients, and not have things always sent by air via Damascus.

But in early 1996, yet more events—those that brought an end to the Wye Plantation negotiations—led to a further Israeli-Syrian deterioration. After the terrorist attacks in February and March, and in order to stabilize the situation and to shore up the Peres government, the Clinton administration launched a global campaign against terrorism, inaugurated in an impressive international summit meeting at Sharm al-Sheikh, at the tip of the Sinai Peninsula, and continued in Washington. This pushed Syria into a dangerous corner: the campaign had a clear anti-Iran purpose, but Assad regarded it as a hostile American-Israeli action also aimed at isolating Syria. An emerging strategic understanding between Israel and Turkey further exacerbated his paranoia. He responded by giving Hizballah the green light to accelerate activity in southern Lebanon and to launch Katyusha rockets against northern Israel, in disregard of the "understandings" of July 1993. In so doing, he did much to draw Prime Minister Peres to decide on yet another large-scale operation in Lebanon—Operation Grapes of Wrath.

Operation Grapes of Wrath is remembered primarily for one of its tragic unintended consequences—the death of more than a hundred Lebanese civilians by misguided Israeli artillery shells. But it had several other significant consequences: the alienation of Israel's Arab voters, many of whom decided not to vote in May, and the humiliation of Secretary Christopher by Hafez al-Assad, when the former was laboring to arrange a cease-fire and a new set of understandings. Ironically, an improved set of understandings and a monitoring mechanism were eventually worked out.

The monitoring agreement was drafted by diplomats representing five countries: the United States, France, Israel, Syria, and Lebanon. It was the second text agreed upon by Israel and Syria in a four-year negotiation that failed to produce the agreement both countries were after. The draft was actually completed during the final days of the Peres government but was signed by Benjamin Netanyahu's government in early July. By then the Arab-Israeli peace process had shifted to a new phase.

# 3

# YEARS OF STAGNATION

On October 24, 1998, a memorandum was signed in the East Wing of the White House after nine days of tripartite American-Israeli-Palestinian negotiations at the Wye Plantation conference center. At the core of it was an Israeli agreement to transfer control within three months of 13 percent of the West Bank to the Palestinian Authority. In return, the latter agreed to wage a genuine campaign against the fundamentalist Islamic and terrorist opponents of the peace process, once again to make a ceremonious revocation of the offensive paragraphs of the Palestinian National Charter that called for the elimination of the Israeli state, and, apparently, also to abstain from proclaiming statehood on May 4, 1999, which was the end of the five-year transitional period stipulated at Oslo. This agreement ended nearly two years of stalemate during which the very future of the Oslo Accords and of peace in the Middle East was in question. It brought Israeli-Palestinian relations back to the track charted by the

Oslo Accords and, in so doing, set the stage for final-status negotiations; it postponed, though it did not eliminate, the dangers of a crisis over the unknown circumstances of May 1999.[1]

It was significant that it was a right-wing Israeli prime minister who grudgingly handed over the city of Hebron to the Palestinian Authority, committed his country in January 1997 to further implementation of the Oslo Accords, and then in October 1998 signed a broader agreement in which he once again committed himself to the "Oslo process," now modified to meet his demands and requirements. Yet Benjamin Netanyahu's words and actions after signing the Wye Agreement did not reflect a conversion to a belief in a genuine political settlement with the Palestinians or a sense that Yasser Arafat was and should be his partner in this process. It was difficult to know whether his rhetoric after signing the memorandum was triggering a lingering resistance in an ideological leader who had journeyed from the right wing to the pragmatic center, or was a political tactic designed to keep his reluctant cabinet and uneasy coalition together.

By the same token, it was difficult to know how authentic was Yasser Arafat's commitment to dealing with the Palestinian foes of the peace process and to ending the ambiguity and ambivalence that he himself had exuded about reconciliation with Israel. It was important for Arafat to rally his own constituents and not to appear as an Israeli accomplice and collaborator. But did he decide to establish a single line of authority, to confront the fundamentalist opposition, and to reach out to the Israeli public, or was he merely offering temporary concessions to a right-wing Israeli leader in order to get an additional 13 percent of the West Bank on the road to statehood and independence?

It is easier to understand and explain Arafat's acceptance of the terms of the Wye Agreement than to trace the path that led his Israeli counterpart to it, after total opposition to the Oslo Accords and to any territorial concessions in the West Bank. Three years after coming to power, Benjamin Netanyahu remains an enigmatic figure, the object of bitter controversies, a prime minister who leads his country through a complex and crucial period without a clear and credible articulation of his goal.

A great deal happened in the Middle East, and in Arab-Israeli relations, in the years after May 1996—with the electoral defeat of Shimon Peres and the peace policies he represented, the Arab world's complex reaction to Netanyahu's victory, and the transition from the first to the second Clinton administration and to a different U.S. policy about the peace process. But the dominant developments are two interrelated ones: the deliberate slowdown of the peace process, which brought it to the verge of collapse; and the effective, albeit reluctant, endorsement of the "Oslo process" by part of the Israeli right wing. Netanyahu is central to both developments.[2]

Netanyahu came to power at the age of forty-six, Israel's youngest prime minister. His victory in the elections of May 29, 1996, was the culmination of a stunning thirteen-year drive for political power. In 1983, Netanyahu was drafted by Moshe Arens, then Israel's ambassador to the United States and a future defense and foreign minister in Likud governments. Arens was making a systematic effort to bring back to the fold the offspring of former Revisionist Movement or Herut Party leaders who had

distanced themselves from Likud over the years. Netanyahu was the son of Professor Ben Zion Netanyahu, an
eminent historian of medieval Spanish Jewry and a prominent disciple of Ze'ev Jabotinsky, the founder of Revisionist Zionism. The elder Netanyahu, when he pro-
nounces on Israeli politics, reveals a classic formulation
of right-wing Zionism, hardly affected by the passage of
time and articulated with great authority and conviction.[3]
Arens brought Benjamin Netanyahu, who had lived much
of his life in the United States, to the Israeli Embassy in
Washington as deputy chief of mission. He subsequently
served as Israel's ambassador to the United Nations, entered full-fledged politics through the Likud primaries,
served as deputy foreign minister, and, in 1992, right after
Likud's electoral defeat and Rabin's election, he made a
successful bid for the party leadership.

In 1992–93, Netanyahu, then still leader of the opposition, wrote a book published as *A Place among the Nations:
Israel and the World*, in which he elaborated his view of
Jewish history, Zionism, and the Arab-Israeli conflict and
peace process. For the most part the text consists of familiar Israeli right-wing views and arguments rehearsing the
case against Israel's making territorial concessions,
against the notion of a Palestinian state, and for the
"peace-for-peace" formula. Netanyahu was clearly as-
sisted by researchers and professional writers, but the
book reflects his personal style and formative experiences—as a politically oriented diplomat in Ronald
Reagan's Washington and as an exponent of Likud views
in the United Nations and at the Madrid Conference.

Genuine peace, Netanyahu argues, can be made and
maintained only between democratic governments. In the

absence of democracy in the Arab world, Israel cannot hope for a Western European or North American type of peace. Peace in the more modest sense of the term—absence of war—can be made and kept in the Middle East only from a position of strength and must be predicated on a bedrock of security and deterrence. The problem in the Middle East is not an Arab-Israeli territorial dispute but the Arabs' refusal to accept the reality of Israel's existence and its right to exist. But if Israel stands firm and receives full support from the West, the Arabs will come around to accept both Israel's reality and its right to exist. The West Bank and the Golan Heights are a defensive wall crucial for Israel's survival and must not be surrendered. A Palestinian state in the West Bank would present a mortal danger to Israel, and in any event there is already a Palestinian state—Jordan. The "demographic argument" made against this—that if Israel holds on to the West Bank and the Gaza Strip it will cease to be either Jewish or democratic—is a "demographic demon; a false argument."[4]

In 1993, the time of the Madrid Conference, Netanyahu's book laid out a particular strategy for Israel. The emphasis was on the Palestinian issue. The Gaza Strip was seen as the easier part: "Since administration of Gaza by its Arab residents does not pose an extraordinary security risk for Israel, it makes sense for most of the territory (with minor modifications for Jewish settlements) to be granted the fullest possible autonomy. I envision an arrangement whereby Israel would be in charge of security and foreign policy while all other areas of authority would be transferred to the self-administering authority under the rubric of Israeli sovereignty." Netanyahu further en-

visaged an international effort to invest in Gaza's economy, thus sparing both Gazans and Israelis the need to
have Gazan workers making their daily trips to and from
Israel's cities. After an interim trial period of at least ten
years, "Israel could consider offering the Arabs of Gaza
an even greater degree of self-rule."[5]

With regard to the far more complex problem of "the
Arab residents of Judea and Samaria," Netanyahu offers
a particular interpretation of the Camp David Accords.
Limited autonomy for the Palestinians would give them
"the ability to conduct their lives with a minimum of in-
terference from the central government." But Israel's
needs and expectations in the West Bank were far greater
than in the Gaza Strip; there were security needs and the
imperatives of Jewish settlement. The powers of Palestinian self-rule had to be curtailed, and freedom of movement for Israel's security forces had to be guaranteed.
There could not be a contiguous area of Palestinian self-
rule but "a system of four self-managing Arab counties:
Jenin, Nablus, Ramallah, Hebron. . . . Together these
counties encompass the great majority of the West Bank's
Arab population and they take up no more than one-fifth
of the land. . . . Control over vital matters would have to
remain in the central Israeli government's hands."[6]

This would be an interim arrangement. Later, following twenty years of cooling off, when the final settlement
is discussed, the question should be considered whether
West Bank residents should be offered Israeli citizenship.
Israel would justifiably insist on an oath of allegiance and
on military service and full payment of taxes, and most
residents of the West Bank would probably opt to retain
their Jordanian citizenship.

Shortly after the publication of his book, Netanyahu was asked his response to the Oslo Accords. For several months he was hard put to cope with a dual challenge: not only had the Rabin government signed an agreement that ran against the grain of everything Netanyahu stood for and argued for, but it appeared to be riding on the crest of a major historical wave. Later, when a backlash developed in Israel and terrorist acts undermined the Israeli public's support for the Oslo Accords, Netanyahu led the opposition to the government's policies. Public-opinion polls in 1994 and 1995 showed him running neck and neck with Rabin.

Rabin's assassination in late 1995 had a devastating immediate effect on Netanyahu's standing. The Israeli public's revulsion with his political and personal affiliation with the political campaign against Rabin and with the radical right wing gave Rabin's successor an advantage, but after Peres's decision in January to advance the elections to May, a wave of terrorist attacks in three Israeli cities in late February and early March completely erased Peres's lead and placed him and Netanyahu in more or less the same position some ten weeks before the elections.

With that campaign a new electoral system was also introduced in Israel—a direct election of the prime minister. Netanyahu's victory by a very slim edge can partly be explained by the effect of the new system, by the superiority of his campaign, and by other personal, political, and social forces at work. But the May 29 elections were also a referendum on the peace process, and in that referendum the line expounded by Netanyahu won—by only six-

teen thousand votes in the total electorate, but by a significant margin of some 10 percent of Jewish voters.

Netanyahu's campaign relied on mutually reinforcing
positive and negative messages formulated on the basis of
a shrewd reading of the average Israeli voter's frame of
mind. Netanyahu continued with criticism of the Oslo
Accords, yet he undertook to accept them and continue
the peace process with modifications that would make it
more deliberate and "secure." The Oslo Accords were
binding international agreements that had been under-
signed by the United States, and Netanyahu well understood that, as a serious contender for power, and certainly
if elected prime minister, he could not renounce his predecessors' contractual obligations. And he also understood that, without committing himself to respect the
Oslo Accords and proceed with the peace process, he
could not expect to attract the floating votes at the center
of the Israeli political spectrum. The slogan "secure
peace" proved to be extremely effective for this crucial
bloc of Israeli voters.[7]

The negative part of Netanyahu's and Likud's platform
included harsh criticism not only of the Oslo Accords and
the subsequent diplomatic work, but of Arafat's failure to
comply with his commitments and of Peres's willingness
to ignore this, of the Accords' shift of some of the responsibility for security to the Palestinian Authority, of the
Israelis' ensuing loss of any sense of personal security, and
of his opponents' alleged intention to "divide Jerusalem"
and acquiesce in the formation of a Palestinian state. This
vilification of Netanyahu's rivals and their policies proved
to be very effective, as did his promise to deliver a "secure
peace." But many Israelis and many of Israel's diplomatic

partners wanted to know more about the candidate's specific ideas with regard to the future of the unfolding of Arab-Israeli relations. As election day drew closer, Netanyahu—in a series of interviews, in a television debate with Shimon Peres, and through the Likud Party's written platform—outlined the following strategy.

In order to resuscitate the stalled peace process, he would try, if elected prime minister, to reconvene the Madrid Conference, at which he would "suggest emphasizing several new channels through which to reduce the level of tension in the region, minimize the arms race and find ways to supervise the introduction of certain weapons. . . . This, in any event, is the right approach to dealing with Syria. An agreement based on withdrawal from the Golan in return for a peace treaty and normalization has no value. Furthermore, Syria is in fact not interested in such an arrangement. For Assad regaining the Golan is a fourth priority."[8] A normal peaceful relationship with Israel would open Syria up and endanger Assad's rule, and a peace agreement signed by a country like Syria would be no more than a piece of paper. Under these circumstances, a "nonterritorial" negotiation on issues such as security and water would suit both sides.

In a different vein, Netanyahu sought to use Washington's aversion to Syria's association with terrorist groups as both a stick and a carrot: "Just as there are no American technology transfers, oil sales or trade with Iran and Iraq, Syria should be warned that it would be subject to the same sanction." But if Syria expelled Palestinian terrorist groups from its territory and dismantled Hizballah in southern Lebanon, "there should be no reason why, after a period of time, Syria should not be removed from the State Department's terror list."

As for the Palestinians, "the Oslo Accords established facts on the ground. I am forced to accept them as starting points. A government I will lead will hold negotiations with the Palestinian Authority on a fair concept of peace. As for Arafat, it is not my heart's desire to meet him. I will meet him only if he meets all his commitments to us and if Israel's interests require that I do so."[9]

The Likud Party's issues platform expanded further on this issue: "The Government of Israel will carry out negotiations with the PA to achieve a permanent peace arrangement on condition that the Palestinians fully honor all their obligations. Most important among these are the clauses in the Palestinian Charter which call for the destruction of Israel and that they prevent terror and incitement against Israel." Israel's commitment to the Oslo Accords under a Netanyahu government was thus made contingent on the PA's compliance with its own commitments. The notion of an Israeli-Palestinian settlement was given a very narrow interpretation:

> The Government of Israel will enable the Palestinians to manage their lives freely within the framework of self-government. However, foreign affairs and defense and matters which require coordination will remain the responsibility of the State of Israel. The government will oppose the establishment of an independent Palestinian state. . . . Israel will keep its vital water resources in Judea and Samaria. . . . The IDF and other Israeli security forces will enjoy complete freedom of action . . . in all places in their struggle against terror. . . . Security areas vital for the defense of Israel and

Jewish settlements will remain under full Israeli sovereignty. . . . The Jordan River will be the eastern border between the State of Israel and the Hashemite Kingdom of
Jordan. The Kingdom of Jordan may become a partner in
the final arrangement between Israel and the Palestinians in
areas agreed upon in the negotiations. . . .

. . . United and undivided Jerusalem is the capital of the
State of Israel. Activities which undermine the status of Jerusalem will be banned and therefore PLO and PA institutions
in the city, including the Orient House, will be closed.[10]

With regard to the policy of allowing Jews to establish
settlements in the West Bank, Netanyahu was careful and
evasive: "I certainly don't rule out new settlements, that's
obvious. But my view about settlement activity has always
been . . . that it has to be built on economic infrastructure
which means larger urban centers." This settlement activity need not be a burden on the Israeli taxpayer: "One of
the things I intend to do is to allow [settlement activity]
through market forces. . . . I will not subordinate the government budget to it . . . but allow it simply through the
release of public lands and transportation lines and allow
natural growth."[11]

The positions Netanyahu presented stood in stark contrast to the policies Rabin and Peres had pursued and
were clearly unacceptable to Israel's negotiating partners
in the three unfinished "tracks" of the peace process—the
Palestinians, Syria, and Lebanon. In the case of Syria, the
substantial negotiations conducted by the Rabin and
Peres governments had not produced a written agreement, and the issue was strictly one of policy: since, contrary to what Netanyahu had said, Assad was interested
only in a territorial negotiation, what would both nations

choose to do if Netanyahu won? Would a formula be
found for resuming negotiations, would the conflict by
proxy in Lebanon deteriorate into a full-blown conflict,
or would the familiar mixed pattern of muted conflict and
quest for negotiation continue?

The issue with the Palestinians was far more complex.
Netanyahu's public positions were inconsistent with the
Oslo Accords and with his promise to respect them. His
commitment was couched in terms sufficiently broad to
attract many Israeli voters worried that the pace of the
peace process was too rapid and worried by the loss of
personal security; they were willing to settle for a vague
promise to negotiate for peace in a deliberate, secure way
that would be acceptable to the Palestinian leadership.
(Alongside his public position, Netanyahu gave private
assurances to the Habad movement that he would not
cede any territory in the West Bank to the Palestinians.
The Habad movement was particularly active in the final
phase of his campaign.) Insistence on the PA's full compliance with its contractual commitment could not be
faulted—after all, agreements are signed in order to be
respected—but it also provided an escape mechanism,
should a new prime minister decide to suspend implementation of the Oslo Accords.

Victory only slightly moderated Netanyahu's stated
positions. He realized that at least some of his convictions
would have to be modified. Necessities of statecraft required him to polish some of the rough edges in the original draft of the new government's platform. But it still
stated that the government would "insist on preserving
[the Golan Heights] under Israeli sovereignty," though it
stipulated elsewhere that "the Israeli Government will

hold negotiations with Syria without any preconditions."
The assertion that "the Jordan River will be Israel's eastern border" was omitted, but opposition to Palestinian
statehood was retained, as was a fairly narrow concept of
Palestinian self-government.[12]

But when his government's platform was published, Israel's new prime minister had in fact headed in a direction
bound to lead him away from the principles and policies
he had advocated prior to his election. We do not know
what Netanyahu had in mind when he announced, on the
eve of the elections, that despite his own opposition to
the Oslo Accords he would respect them if elected. It was
first and foremost a (successful) bid for centrist voters, but
did Netanyahu also feel that he would in fact be fortunate
to inherit a compromise with Palestinian nationalism
rather than to have to make it himself, that while continuing to criticize the Oslo Accords and seeking to modify
them he might actually proceed on the road to peace? Or
did he perhaps toy with the idea that one could profess to
accept the Oslo Accords but in effect emasculate, perhaps
even destroy, the process they had set in motion?

Netanyahu's assumption of ultimate responsibility for
Israel's policies in June 1996 was not a simple unilinear
process. If he had not known it before, Israel's prime minister soon discovered that it was extremely difficult to get
off the Oslo track. The reality of Israeli-Palestinian relations had been altered permanently—once by the *intifada*
and then by the initial implementation of the Oslo Accords. To suspend further implementation was likely to
lead to conflict. Israel was infinitely stronger than the Palestinian Authority, but could it afford the price of victory

over the Palestinians? The direct cost—the effect on Israel's relations with Jordan, Egypt, and the other Arab powers and on Israel's international relations, particularly vis-
à-vis Washington—was prohibitively high. But there
were numerous countervailing forces—Netanyahu's personal and party legacy, the opposition of right-wing members of his cabinet and coalition, mistakes made by the
Arab participants in the peace process.

Netanyahu took a step forward and soon thereafter
seemed to backtrack. He signed an agreement to withdraw Israeli soldiers from Hebron, and then immediately
authorized construction of a new Jewish neighborhood in
the Har Homa section of Jerusalem that was intended to
drive a wedge between the city and Arab Bethlehem. He
sent messages to Syria expressing interest in renewing negotiations, and then endorsed legislation sponsored by
the Golan Lobby intended to entrench Israel's presence
on the Golan Heights. To some extent this was political
maneuvering by a prime minister trying to preserve a precarious coalition, but there seemed also to be personal
vacillation. As late as August 1997, Netanyahu delivered
a speech to the graduating class of Israel's National Security College in which he fell back on his 1993 book and
argued that peace agreements and normalization made no
sense in the Arab-Israeli context: "As long as the regimes
around us are not democratic and inherently peace-seek-
ing we will not be able to afford any arrangements in
which the security dimension is not dominant. No arrangement will survive if we fail to keep security and defense zones." And yet, fourteen months later, the very
same leader signed the Wye River Memorandum and ini-

tially carried his cabinet and coalition with him. The path that took them all from the formation of Netanyahu's government to that historic point unfolded in three phases.

## EARLY TRANSITION AND ADJUSTMENT

Benjamin Netanyahu's adjustment to the reality and responsibility of power was matched by the Arab world's complex reaction to Israel's new government, then gradual adjustment to it. At first, this reaction consisted of shock and concern. Public-opinion polls had indicated since early March that Peres and Netanyahu were running neck and neck, and yet the Peres defeat came as a surprise. Arabs thought of Netanyahu as a foe of the peace process and assumed that a radical change in Israeli policies would ensue. An Arab summit conference on June 21–23 issued an explicit warning to the new Israeli government:

> The Arab leaders affirm that any violation [*ikhlal*] by Israel of these principles and bases on which the peace process is founded, any retraction on the commitments, pledges, and agreements reached within the framework of this process, or any vacillation in implementing them will set back the peace process and will entail dangers and consequences that will plunge the region back into a spiral of tension and will compel all the Arab countries to reconsider the steps they have taken toward Israel within the framework of the peace process. The Israeli Government alone will be fully responsible for these consequences.[13]

But there were nuances in the various Arab reactions. Yasser Arafat was the most anxious. He depended on Is rael for implementation of the next phases of the Oslo process, and he had come to trust Shimon Peres and his team, with whom he presumed a final-status agreement could be negotiated. What was he to make of Netanyahu's criticism of the Oslo process, his opposition to Palestinian statehood, his narrow concept of Palestinian autonomy, and the assignments in his government given to people and parties widely perceived as implacable opponents of the PLO—Ariel Sharon, Rafael Eytan, and the National Religious Party?

Egypt was more ambivalent. On the one hand, as patron of the Palestinians and needing to defend its own peace with Israel, it feared the prospect of a deep crisis, but there was also an element of relief. Egypt had been visibly uncomfortable with the sweeping scope and rapid pace of the peace process over the previous eighteen months, and especially wary, as we have seen, of Peres's vision of "a new Middle East." President Hosni Mubarak and his government had genuinely hoped for a Peres victory, but they could see a silver lining in his defeat: a more modest scope and a more deliberate pace to the unfolding developments, with Israel clearly responsible for both.

Syria was particularly strident in its criticism of the new Israeli government. Syria had been unhappy with the two Labor prime ministers, though both had seriously negotiated with its representatives. Having refused to listen to friendly advice about the wisdom of concluding a deal with either of them before the elections, it now confronted an Israeli prime minister who was openly hostile and who seemed to rule out the possibility of an Israeli-Syrian settlement. Angry commentaries expressed Syria's frustration, but in private its diplomats were willing to meet with representatives of the new government in order to divine its real intentions.

Jordan stood in a category by itself. King Hussein and his government were the only Arab party to have supported Netanyahu during his election campaign, being concerned that a victorious Peres would proceed swiftly to a sweeping agreement with Syria and to the establishment of a Palestinian state. Netanyahu managed to persuade him that he would keep the peace process going at a level and pace suitable to Jordan's political needs.

According to the Oslo process's agenda and schedule, final-status talks, launched formally in May 1996, were actually scheduled to begin in September. The interim arrangements were supposed to end five years after the Cairo signing of the implementation agreement, which meant that May 4, 1999, became the target date. A major item on the agenda was Israel's withdrawal (or redeployment, to use the vocabulary of the peace process) from most of Hebron. Unlike the other cities of the West Bank, Hebron, a city with about 120,000 Palestinian inhabitants, had a Jewish settlement in its midst. The presence of this group of radical Orthodox settlers, the city's general historic and religious significance, and the memory of the massacre perpetrated against the city's Jewish population in 1929 only worsened the complex issue of the Israeli Defense Force's redeployment. Peres had not been keen on going through with the redeployment after the election, and he passed this issue on to Netanyahu.

Upon completing the "redeployments" from the six main cities of the West Bank, the second Oslo agreement committed Israel to proceeding with three "further redeployments" prior to final-status negotiations. The origin of that idea lies in the Camp David Accords, which stipulated that during final-status negotiations Israel would withdraw its troops to "security locations"; in the summer of 1995, at a late phase of the negotiations leading to the second Oslo accord, Israel agreed to three "further redeployments," a concession that made sense only in the context of a genuine final-status negotiation: if Israel were to hand over most of the West Bank to Palestinian Authority control, it might as well do it in phases, and use the phasing as a way of facilitating the concessions Arafat would have to make, too. But for a government formally opposed to Palestinian statehood and committed to a narrow view of Palestinian self-government, this notion made little or no sense.

Netanyahu was, indeed, determined to change both the agenda and the pace of Israeli-Palestinian diplomacy. He refused to meet with Arafat and wanted the latter to settle for lesser officials—first his own policy adviser (June 28), then the foreign and defense ministers (July 23 and September 18, respectively). He indicated several times that he was in no hurry about redeployment in Hebron, a complex issue. Most significantly, he insisted on "reciprocity" and "compliance," themes that had figured prominently in his election campaign, when he had accused Peres of being too lenient and of being willing to overlook Arafat's and the PA's failure to discipline or control terrorist organizations that struck at Israel, failure to complete the revision of the Palestinian National Charter, and failure to cease its hostile propaganda against Israel. He now demanded that the Palestinians comply "fully" with these commitments before Israel took another step.

A demand for full compliance with an agreement is, of course, perfectly valid. But, given the context in which the demand was made, Palestinians, Arabs in general, and the world at large saw this as an attempt to change the rules of the Israeli-Palestinian game. Rabin and Peres had argued that Israel, as the senior and more powerful party to the agreement, did not have to insist on a literal interpretation and implementation. The shift from that approach to a strict insistence on "full compliance" was widely perceived as a manifestation of the new government's negative attitude and of its proclivity to use Israel's preponderance vis-à-vis the Palestinians to impose rather than negotiate a settlement.

The awkwardness of Israel's relationship with the Palestinians was matched by dim prospects with Syria. The new prime minister was now fully briefed on the course of the 1993–96 negotiation. He knew that Hafez al-Assad was willing to make peace with Israel but only on the basis of the latter's complete withdrawal from the Golan Heights. Assad now demanded also that the new government endorse the whole legacy of the negotiation conducted by its predecessor and commit itself to that full withdrawal. Netanyahu knew very well that the positions he himself had advocated with regard to Syria and the Golan Heights were not realistic, but he was not willing to accept this demand. Assad, grasping the full significance of the change in Israel, rather than modify his position chose to dig in more firmly.[14]

In late July, Netanyahu tried a different approach. An agreement would be worked out that would have Israel withdraw its soldiers from the "security zone" in southern Lebanon: this would be conceived and perceived as a first, "confidence-building" phase in a broader Israeli-Syrian settlement (hence the name "Lebanon First" given to this initiative). The idea was stillborn. In fact, it was not a new idea, and Syria had systematically obstructed earlier attempts to break the logjam in this fashion. As Syria saw it, Israel's predicament in Lebanon was Syria's most effective instrument for pressuring Israel to move in the Golan Heights, and it was not about to give this up. Furthermore, it suspected that a separate Israeli-Lebanese negotiation would be used to lure Lebanon away from Syria. It lost no time in foiling the new Israeli initiative.

Nor was Netanyahu successful in building his relations with Jordan's King Hussein and Egypt's President Mubarak. With the passage of time, and as Netanyahu's Palestinian policy became more evident, Cairo and Amman expressed disappointment and criticism; both could live with a virtual suspension of Israeli-Syrian negotiations, but neither could accept Israel's new policy toward the Palestinians. Egypt's anger was contained— Cairo had a stake in Arafat's success but was content to take advantage of the new turn of events in order to slow down "normalization" of Israel's position in the region. For Jordan, the political challenge was much more acute. Given that the majority of Jordan's citizenry was Palestinian and given the criticism the king had endured for making a peace with Israel, he believed that a suspension or collapse of Israeli-Palestinian efforts could undermine his own position. He expected subtlety from Netanyahu; he had wanted more deliberation and modesty in Israeli diplomacy, and he had not expected such a dramatic reversal of policy.[15]

This transitional phase was terminated in September by two unrelated developments, the first between Israel and Syria, which brought the two countries to the verge of military confrontation.

This was a classic case of an unintended escalation nourished by misperceptions and mutual suspicions—all this exacerbated by the new Israeli leaders' inexperience and the Syrian leaders' unfamiliarity with their counterparts. A redeployment of Syrian troops from Beirut to the Beqaa Valley in eastern Lebanon, close to the Syrian border, had been planned for some time as a demonstration of the incremental normalization of life in Lebanon. But on the other side of the border, it was seen as a potential buildup for a surprise attack against Israel. In turn, Syrians, knowing there were no offensive intentions on Syria's part, saw Israel's deployment for such an eventuality as preparation for a potential attack. This spiral of mutual suspicion threatened to escalate into real hostilities. The tension eventually eased, but the episode demonstrated the dangerous potential in the Israeli-Syrian relationship, particularly when there was no ongoing direct dialogue between the two.

The other development was much graver. On September 24, the Israeli authorities opened for public viewing and in the service of tourism the Hasmonean Tunnel, which runs from the Western Wall along the base of Temple Mount. The tunnel, of immense archaeological interest, had been readied for opening during Rabin's tenure, but government policy then had been not to open the tunnel except in coordination with the Palestinian Authority. Given Arab, Muslim, and international sensibilities regarding anything that had to do with the holy places in Jerusalem, it was decided to wait for the right moment; the tunnel and its opening would not in any case interfere with the status quo in Jerusalem. The Netanyahu government's decision to disregard these considerations to open the tunnel on September 24 as an assertion of Israel's sovereignty in Jerusalem was yet another symptom of its inexperience, and it played directly into Arafat's hands. Arafat saw a golden opportunity to reverse the rules of the game that Netanyahu had played since June. He called for protest marches denouncing the tunnel opening as a "big crime against our religion and our holy places." In the following five days of violence, fifteen Israeli soldiers and sixty Palestinians were killed. Some of the violence was spontaneous, but there is little doubt that the Palestinian security officers who took an active part in the fighting were in most cases authorized if not encouraged to do so by Arafat.

By reacting in this fashion, Arafat may well have damaged his cause in the long run. For many Israelis it was proof that the Palestinian Authority could not be trusted to be a genuine partner in protecting Israeli security, that Arafat gave his cooperation only so long as his expectations were met, that if final-status negotiations were deadlocked violence could be expected. But in the short run his action was most effective. Netanyahu was now anxious to talk to him. President Clinton invited both men, as well as King Hussein and President Mubarak, to Washington for a meeting on October 1 and 2. The Jordanian monarch accepted the invitation; Egypt's president chose not to.

## THE ROAD TO THE HEBRON AGREEMENT

The Washington summit conference quickly accomplished two important goals: it defused the crisis that had erupted after the tunnel opening, and it resuscitated Israeli-Palestinian negotiations. But these were arduous, and it took three months more to reach further agreements about Israel's redeployment in Hebron and future relationship with the Palestinian Authority. Also, the Washington conference expressed important changes in Washington's outlook on and role in the Israeli-Arab peace process.

Ever since the formation of the first Clinton administration in January 1993, the Israeli-Arab peace process was high on Washington's foreign-policy agenda. The president, the secretary of state, and their assistants invested a significant portion of their time in it, and its achievements were among their most notable foreign-policy successes. Indeed, the Clinton administration's cooperation with the Rabin and Peres governments was a unique phase in American-Israeli history. In earlier stages, it invariably took American pressure on reluctant Israeli prime ministers to make territorial and other concessions in order to effect progress (even Begin's negotiation with Sadat, which had originated as an Israeli-Egyptian initiative, could not be concluded without American participation), but under Rabin and Peres the moving force was an Israeli leadership determined to move toward peace, and reconciled to the notion that both sides had to make concessions in order to reach and implement an agreement. During the Rabin years, this was buttressed by a quite warm and intimate relationship between the president and the prime minister, and the Clinton administration openly supported Peres in the 1996 election campaign.

After Netanyahu's victory, the administration felt that it had lost this secure Israeli footing. Its nervousness was exacerbated by Secretary of State Warren Christopher's disenchantment with Syria, and by changes in the Middle East (the formation of an Islamist government in Turkey, unrest in Saudi Arabia) that made it less hospitable to a major investment of U.S. efforts. As the presidential elections of November 1996 drew closer, the prospect of open disagreement with an Israeli prime minister openly allied with conservative Republicans grew more alarming. It remained important to preserve the American achievements in the Arab-Israeli peace process and to avoid its breaking down, but American willingness and ability to invest significant resources were limited.

This calculus was altered by the outburst of violence in September. Just a few weeks before the election, President Clinton took the political risk of convening a summit that could end in failure. In the event the meeting was successful, but Netanyahu's mobilization of the organized right-wing Jewish community in the United States and the Republican leadership in Congress to keep the administration at bay was a harbinger of future developments.

The Washington summit was followed by a round of intensive negotiations held at the Erez checkpoint between Israel and Gaza. Secretary of State Christopher presided at the outset, but as the negotiations lingered on, leadership passed to the principal American negotiator, Dennis Ross. In the absence of mutual trust and effective communication between the Israeli and Palestinian lead-

ers, the United States had to go from being a facilitator
to being a combined mediator, partner, and guarantor.

One level of the negotiation dealt with the redeployment in Hebron. On another level, Arafat and the Palestinian Authority were eager to obtain control over Hebron, but they wanted also to ascertain that this would
not be a final act of a moribund process, but would be
fitted into a broader agreement on the implementation of
Oslo II. More specifically, they demanded that a date be
set for resumption of final-status negotiations, that a
timetable be set for the implementation of Israel's three
further redeployments, and that agreement be reached on
other issues pending since 1995—the opening of air- and
seaports in Gaza, the establishment of a "safe passage"
between the West Bank and the Gaza Strip, and the release of Palestinian prisoners from Israeli jails.

Benjamin Netanyahu, in turn, had many dilemmas and
problems. Israeli withdrawal from Hebron would be seen
by many Israelis as an act of withdrawal from part of the
historical, biblical Land of Israel. In agreeing to go
through with the agreement to do this, he would be the
first Likud leader to offer and implement such a concession. And even if he were to do so by arguing that he had
no choice but to fulfill the contractual obligation undertaken by his predecessors, what was he to do about the
sweeping commitment to three further redeployments?

The problem was not limited to Netanyahu's personal
soul-searching. He was the first Israeli prime minister to
have been elected by a direct popular vote, but as he and
the Israeli political system soon discovered, the new election law did not mean that the prime minister was immune to pressure from his own cabinet and coalition;

though the law made it more difficult to unseat him than before, he still had to form and maintain a parliamentary coalition. Netanyahu's not very large coalition (it originally consisted of sixty-six members) had a rightist complexion; within it, several of his Likud colleagues and members of the National Religious Party formed a hard core of opposition to making any territorial concessions in the West Bank. The argument that governments are constrained by domestic political opposition has been used all too often in Arab-Israeli negotiations, but Netanyahu did face a genuine, significant opposition within his own party and coalition.

Netanyahu understood that he had no choice—he had to redeploy in Hebron, and he had to reiterate the basic Israeli commitments at Oslo II—but he fought to recast these commitments in terms that would be or at least appear to be new and more congruent with his own outlook. By mid-January 1997, an agreement had been reached that was embodied in three documents: a protocol to implement the redeployment in Hebron; a "note for the record" prepared by Dennis Ross as a summary of a meeting between Netanyahu and Arafat; and a letter from Secretary Christopher to Netanyahu. These three documents were supplemented by two additional instruments: a letter from Dennis Ross to the secretary of the Israeli cabinet that formalized the original compromise worked out by King Hussein, suggesting that the term "mid-1998" be left vague.

The security arrangements detailed in the protocol were different enough from past ones to enable Netanyahu to argue that he had obtained a better, indeed satisfactory, security regime in Hebron. In the note for the record, Israel reaffirmed its promise to proceed with implementation of Oslo II, which meant first and foremost the three further redeployments. It undertook to carry out the first redeployment during the first week of March, to negotiate the other pending issues, and to resume the permanent-status negotiations within two months of the implementation of the Hebron protocol. Arafat, for his part, reaffirmed the following principal promises: to complete the revision of the Palestinian National Charter, to fight terror and prevent violence, to strengthen security cooperation, to prevent incitement and hostile propaganda, to combat systematically and effectively terrorist organizations and infrastructure. The note also stipulated that "the exercise of Palestinian governmental activity and location of Palestinian governmental offices will be as specified in the Interim Agreement" (in the coded language of Israeli-Palestinian relations, this meant the Palestinian Authority's undertaking not to engage in "governmental" activity in Jerusalem) and that Oslo II should be implemented on the basis of "reciprocity."

That last point was repeated and reinforced in Secretary Christopher's letter to Netanyahu. The letter was essentially intended to assuage Israelis, but it addressed a major Palestinian concern by stating the American administration's "belief that the first phase of further redeployments should take place as soon as possible and that all three phases of further redeployment should be completed within twelve months of the implementation of the first phase of further redeployments but no later than mid-1998." Israel, it was implied, would determine the scope of the redeployments.

The Palestinian Authority and the United States could note with satisfaction that a Likud prime minister was about to withdraw Israeli soldiers from most of Hebron and that he formally reaffirmed the principal commitments of Oslo II. Netanyahu, in turn, could claim that he had committed Arafat to respond to his criticisms of the Oslo Accords and that he had formalized the principle of reciprocity and established a formal link between Arafat's compliance with these commitments and Israel's own further undertakings. In fact, though Israel's redeployment in Hebron was carried out in accordance with the protocol, the larger agenda addressed in the note for the record and the secretary's letter was not implemented. Further progress in Israeli-Palestinian relations was delayed for nearly two years.

In other words, the Hebron Agreement ended up being only and precisely that—an agreement on Israel's redeployment in Hebron. To address and implement the larger agenda—reaffirming and implementing the unfinished components of Oslo II—the three partners to the Hebron Agreement had yet to make some fundamental decisions.

Israel's prime minister felt ill at ease with the agenda itself, requiring those three further redeployments by mid-1998, leaving less than a year before the end of the five-year transitional period. Israel could not realistically expect to complete the process without ceding a significant portion of the West Bank. For the first redeployment, scheduled for March 1997, Netanyahu offered 2 percent, and Arafat scornfully rebuffed this. So Netanyahu and Arafat were miles apart, and bridging the gap was likely to take a long time, and from the Israeli vantage point, giving up land in three predetermined moves made little if any sense.

Thus, in March 1997, Netanyahu proposed that Israel and the PA telescope the whole process and, instead of proceeding with the implementation of Oslo II, meet for a Camp David–style conference, allocating three to six months for completing the final-status negotiations. The underlying argument was quite persuasive. The Oslo process, it was said, had been intended to go in phases so as to build confidence between the parties; whatever its initial achievements, it was clearly not building confidence, and it ought to be replaced by something else. This valid argument was briefly endorsed by the new secretary of state, Madeleine Albright, but it was rendered useless by one problem—mistrust. Arafat and many other Arabs had no trust in Netanyahu and his government, and they saw his offer as a transparent maneuver to extricate himself from the Oslo commitments.

This policy problem was exacerbated by a political one. Even if Netanyahu wanted to go through with genuine implementation of the Hebron accords, he might not have had a working majority in his cabinet and coalition. One right-wing member of his party and cabinet, Benny (Binyamin) Begin, resigned after the agreement was signed. Menachem Begin's son refused to remain a member of a government that had voted to hand over part of the Land of Israel to foreign control. Nor did Begin conceal the contempt he had for Netanyahu. Other right-wing Likud coalition members and members of the National Religious Party threatened to topple the government if it decided on further withdrawals in the West Bank. Their threat was aggravated by the dissension of

other cabinet and coalition members—Finance Minister
Dan Meridor resigned in June 1997 and Foreign Minister
David Levy in January 1998—and others distanced themselves owing to personal differences with Netanyahu or
unhappiness with his style and performance. As time
passed, pressure built among more moderate or pragmatic members of the government, who began to suspect
that Netanyahu had no intention of implementing the
agreement. Netanyahu himself was increasingly preoccupied with his government's survival, and his perpetual
maneuvering created a zigzag effect: if Netanyahu signed
the Hebron Agreement in January, he tried to balance it
in February by placating his right-wing critics with the
Har Homa construction in Jerusalem. The Palestinians
considered this a provocative act, and Arafat responded
by suspending the negotiations.

As might have been anticipated, the principle of reciprocity also obstructed rather than facilitated progress.
Arafat had been reluctant to take on the Islamic fundamentalist opposition to his negotiations with Israel, to
complete the revision of the Palestinian Charter, to stifle
anti-Israeli rhetoric, or to engage overtly in security cooperation with Israel. Even when things had been at their
best, he was determined to keep the option of joining
forces with the fundamentalists if things turned sour, to
keep his people mobilized, and to refrain from appearing
as an Israeli accomplice. By 1997, he must have realized
this conduct had alienated part of the Israeli public and
had helped to undermine Peres and bring Netanyahu to
power, but if he considered a policy change he was discouraged by his—and many others'—suspicion that
Netanyahu was actually seeking to emasculate the Oslo

process, in which case he was not about to alter his own conduct. And thus, throughout this period, Arafat persisted both in presuming that the Oslo process offered the best way to achieve the historic goal of Palestinian statehood, and in refusing to make any additional investment of acting on the Hebron Agreement commitments. Netanyahu argued, in turn, that, given this failure to offer "reciprocity" and "compliance," he wasn't about to have Israel make additional withdrawals.

At the core of the original Oslo process had been the idea that it took time to make a transition from conflict and hostility to a settlement predicated on compromise and partnership. These last had not always been present during the brief golden period of Israeli-Palestinian relations, but they were glaringly absent after June 1996. Any concessions made and cooperation secured were offered grudgingly. Both parties presumed they were locked in conflict, and each acted to maximize its position in the West Bank and in East Jerusalem.

Under these circumstances, it was difficult to get them to cooperate in the crucial and sensitive area of security. Given the devastating effectiveness of the Islamic terrorist campaigns of 1994–96 and the significance attached to this theme by Netanyahu, terrorist attacks were now particularly agonizing. During the first thirty months of Netanyahu's government, suicide bombings occurred in Tel Aviv and Jerusalem, though they did not have the impact of the earlier ones—partly because of effective countermeasures taken by Israel and at least sometimes by the Palestinian Authority, and also through sheer luck and, perhaps most important and ironic, the slowdown in the peace process. Iran, Hamas, and Islamic Jihad did not have to invest an effort comparable to that of the years 1993–96 in order to obstruct a faltering peace process.

So the security cooperation between Israel and the Palestinian Authority was erratic. Conducted both bilaterally and trilaterally (with the CIA as the third party), it affected and expressed the fluctuations of the general Israeli-Palestinian relationship. Security, after all, was at the core of the "reciprocity" and "compliance" issues. Arafat, in offering some cooperation some of the time, withholding it at other times, and occasionally tolerating or encouraging anti-Israeli violence, was walking a very fine line. Throughout this period he continued to act on the assumption that the Oslo process still offered the best prospects, but favoring it was not a policy he pursued with enthusiasm or consistency. And as time went on, his motivation changed. His primary effort became to cultivate a new relationship with the United States and, specifically, with the Clinton administration. The primacy of obtaining control over additional land in the West Bank was clear, but as long as this was not feasible, Arafat was willing to settle, as an interim goal, on the dividends earned in a new relationship with the world's leading power.

President Clinton had made a personal political investment in Israeli-Palestinian relations and taken some political risks to defuse the crisis in September 1996. But if it took three months to negotiate the Hebron Agreement, only to encounter fresh difficulties and disappointments when it came to implementation, what were the prospects for the United States in the final-status negotiations?

Warren Christopher's successor, Madeleine Albright, had a different order of priorities, as was seen in her decision to delay her first trip to the Middle East (in sharp contrast to Christopher's trip to the region less than a month after the inauguration in 1993). During her first weeks in office, it became evident that only part of the Hebron Agreement would be implemented and that a fresh effort would have to be made to get the three further redeployments. This was not an attractive prospect, and it was made even less so by the Israeli government's demonstrable willingness and ability to mobilize conservative Republicans in Congress and a significant part of the organized American Jewish community against it. In theory, a president who had just been reelected should have been immune to such considerations, but political circumstances in early 1997—and a Republican majority in both houses that enhanced the influence and importance of every single member of Congress—dissuaded the administration from open confrontation with the Israeli government. President Clinton and several of his aides made no effort to hide their criticism of Israel's prime minister and his government, though they avoided a showdown. The United States lowered its profile in the peace process but, despite criticism and advice to the contrary, refused to walk away from it. Clinton believed that the United States must make real and visible efforts to prevent the collapse of a diplomacy closely identified with the American position, and that at the end of the day Netanyahu would go through with the second redeployment.

Four factors converged in the fall of 1998 in order to bring that about.

First, Washington made it abundantly clear that, even if Arafat and the Palestinian Authority did not fully comply with their own commitments, it expected Israel to provide the key to further progress and to implement the redeployments. The American peace team established a middle ground of 13 percent as the effective range of Israel's next withdrawal in the West Bank. It brought Arafat down from his initial demand for a withdrawal from some 40 percent, it subsequently obtained Netanyahu's personal agreement to this figure, and then it set to work on constructing an agreement into which this withdrawal could be fitted and on helping Netanyahu to bring the rest of his government and coalition along.[16]

In the course of this protracted process, President Clinton was going through the first stages of his worst personal-political crisis. The Lewinsky affair exploded during Netanyahu's visit to Washington in January 1998, when the question of U.S. pressure on Israel was at the fore, and began to simmer down in the early fall of 1998, at the time of the Wye River Conference. There the president was first and foremost trying to solve a difficult and dangerous problem in the Middle East, but he was also trying to conduct normal presidential business and demonstrate his own personal effectiveness. By making the conference possible, by sustaining Clinton's personal participation, and by making their own political contributions, the president and his administration exerted an unusually effective influence on Israeli-Palestinian relations.

A second important consideration was the imminence of May 4, 1999. This date had seemed quite remote when the Hebron Agreement was completed in January 1997, but now all parties were dangerously close to the end of the transitional period. Arafat began to threaten publicly that he would announce Palestinian independence and statehood unilaterally; Israel threatened to respond with its own unilateral actions. Israel is, indeed, not short of potential responses, but a major crisis over a unilateral Palestinian declaration of independence would be undesirable for any Israeli prime minister. Arafat's and his colleagues' consternation with Israel and their own rhetoric notwithstanding, they still preferred to reach their goals by an agreement with Israel and were worried about the repercussions of a unilateral declaration. The explosive potential in this situation was fully exploited by U.S. diplomacy in bringing the parties together at the Wye Plantation.

Third, a deal was gradually crystallizing. After all, the territorial aspect of the agreement had been put together by mid-1998; it then had to be matched by a political structure that would meet Netanyahu's requirements. On the face of it, Arafat had done this when he signed the Hebron Agreement. What was the value in yet another undertaking to revise the Palestinian Charter or the practical and political value of further reaffirmations of all the old points? Yet, in substantive and political terms, it was important for Netanyahu to be able to show that Israel's territorial concession would be matched by something; on a deeper level, he and his associates had to ask themselves about the rationale of giving up 13 percent of the West Bank at that particular juncture. Keeping a commitment, mending relations with the United States and other nations, keeping the peace process going—these were all weighty reasons, but they had been for years. A new prospect was now needed for Netanyahu's government to agree to a new situation in which the Palestinian Authority would control 40 percent of the West Bank and have an international airport in Gaza.

Lastly, the domestic political base in Israel for implementing the 13 percent withdrawal was put together. The link between Netanyahu's personal and domestic political calculus and the implementation was an especially intricate business. Netanyahu had concluded earlier that what had already been implemented as part of the Oslo process was irreversible, and that at least part of the remaining Israeli commitments had to be implemented as well. These conclusions were linked to a presumption that in a reelection bid Netanyahu would need centrist as well as right-wing votes, that he would run as a leader who had lived up to his promises. But when would the next election be held? Could Netanyahu keep his coalition together until 2000? Could he, more specifically, withdraw from 13 percent of the West Bank *and* keep the National Religious Party, the settlers' movement's closest ally, in his coalition? Or did he perhaps want an early election, right after an agreement, in which he might lose the votes from the radical right wing but steal the Labor Party's thunder?

For many months, Netanyahu seemed to think of and try every political option and maneuver—a "national-unity government" with the Labor Party, splitting the Labor Party and attracting part of its parliamentary caucus into his coalition under the banner of "saving the peace," buttressing the coalition by promising its right wing to avoid, delay, or fail to implement an agreement, and promising its more pragmatic members to make the deal and carry it out. Finally, in September 1998 he decided to make Ariel Sharon, minister of national infrastructures, his main ally, and to rely on this leader of the radical right in the final stage of negotiating the agreement.

On October 14, Netanyahu appointed Sharon foreign minister; Sharon immediately announced that he would not vote for any agreement stipulating a withdrawal of more than 9 percent, but he made it clear that he would be the prime minister's partner in negotiating such an agreement at the Wye Plantation.

Sharon's own journey from right-wing radicalism to this position paralleled and supplemented Netanyahu's shift from his preelection positions to his postelection policies. Sharon had grown up in the tradition of Labor Zionism's activist school. In 1973, having retired from the armed forces as a general, he joined Likud; he left his mark on Israel's relationship with the Arab world as the architect of the subsequent war in Lebanon and as the secular patron of the settler movement.[17]

At the age of seventy, Sharon was acting under the influence of multiple considerations. He clearly remained critical and dubious of the ongoing peace process and specifically of the two Oslo Accords. But he was also eager to rehabilitate his reputation and image that had tarnished during Israel's debacle in Lebanon in 1982–83. He also clearly relished his standing as the one substantial person in Netanyahu's government, though his relationship with Netanyahu was awkward. As a rule, he criticized him from the right, but when he had been in charge of resolving disputes between Israel and Jordan over water rights, he proved to be most accommodating.

Sharon's work in resolving the water issue and the Jordanians' exasperation with Netanyahu made Sharon a pivotal figure in Israeli-Jordanian relations. For years, this Likud leader most closely identified with the slogan "Jordan is Palestine" had been anathema to the Jordanians. But in the 1998 circumstances, they were willing to hold on to him as a pillar of effectiveness and pragmatism in the confusing landscape of Israel's new politics. As for Sharon himself, he regarded his new relationship with the Hashemites as a model for the kind of accomplishments he envisaged for himself in Israeli politics. Why couldn't he, drawing on his nationalist credentials and his gift for plain, tough talk, cast himself as the senior, mature figure of Israel's right wing who could offer the key to a reasonable compromise, a compromise for which he alone could mobilize sufficient support?

A glimpse into Sharon's recent thinking is afforded by the synopsis of a presentation distributed by his office in May 1998 under the title "Security and Coexistence: An Alternative Approach to Breaking the Deadlock between Israel and the Palestinians." The final two paragraphs— "a summary"—read as follows:

> The way I view the situation today, it is possible to reach an agreement with the Palestinians in the interim phase, which would be somewhat similar to the concept of nonbelligerency. This will give Palestinians the possibility of keeping and holding to the Oslo Accords, and Israel the necessary time to examine and see that conditions for a true and lasting peace have materialized.
>
> Finally, I wish to emphasize that this alternative approach of crisis avoidance, and the concept of "less than peace" agreement, which I have presented here, should be considered as a *fallback position*: if at a certain point it becomes clear to all parties that the current efforts to reach an agreement

fail, then I believe it would be in the interest of both Israel and the Palestinians to adopt this approach as a means of breaking the deadlock and reviving the peace process.[18]

It is apparently with this view in mind that Israel's new foreign minister went to the Wye Plantation. He is reported to have argued that any agreement reached there should be seen as an interim one for some twenty years. This is clearly not what the Palestinians, the rest of the Arab world, and the United States had in mind. Nor was it clear how Sharon and Netanyahu really viewed the agreement they concluded. Did they believe that they could freeze the status quo for so long, or did they realize that this was not the last stop in their journey toward the middle ground of pragmatism and compromise?

In stark contrast to the partial progress made in Israeli-Palestinian affairs, there was no movement whatsoever in Israel's relationship with Syria. The negotiations suspended in March 1996 were not renewed, despite several attempts by the American peace team, the European Union's special envoy, and a whole host of private intermediaries. Technically, the chief obstacle was Syria's insistence that "the negotiations be resumed at the point at which they had been interrupted" and Israel's rejection of this demand and of the interpretation on which it was based. For this terminology was coded language for a very sweeping demand: Syria's version of the 1993–96 negotiation had it that Prime Minister Rabin had committed Israel to withdraw from the Golan Heights, that Peres had reaffirmed this commitment, that these commitments were legally binding, and that fresh negotiations must proceed from this point of departure. The Israeli version was that there was no commitment, agreement, or promise to withdraw; that a hypothetical, conditional position had been deposited with the United States to be matched by Syrian acceptance of a settlement package, which never happened. Netanyahu had a letter from Secretary of State Christopher in September 1996 expressing the view that the only agreement reached during the negotiations, the "nonpaper" on the security arrangements, was not legally binding; oral exchanges were surely even less binding than this nonpaper.

The gap between these two positions could in fact have been bridged, but the real obstacle was not procedural but substantive. As the negotiations of 1993–96 clearly established, President Assad was willing to sign a peace treaty with Israel but insisted on a full Israeli withdrawal from the Golan Heights, and the peace package he has thus far offered does not meet Israel's criteria. The "hypothetical formula" facilitated negotiation, but suspension of the talks left Syria with nothing achieved. Since June 1996, Assad has faced an Israeli prime minister elected on a platform that explicitly precluded full withdrawal from the Golan Heights. Thus Assad now insists on an explicit (not hypothetical) American or Israeli commitment as a precondition for renewing the negotiations, but he is not anxious and certainly not desperate for this. And he is not interested in negotiations for their own sake. In his view, the very fact of holding a Syrian-Israeli negotiation would play into Netanyahu's hands, enabling him to argue that the peace process had been revived and, on that basis, to advance the cause of Arab-Israeli normalization. Assad therefore demands that a new phase of ne-

gotiations be predicated on Israel's explicit commitment
to withdraw from the Golan Heights.

This has not been acceptable to Netanyahu, for two
main reasons. Like his predecessors, on procedural and
practical grounds he has resented Assad's attempt to dic-
tate conditions and to open a negotiation with a guaranteed bottom line, which would leave the Israelis with very
little leverage. Then there is the substantive and ultimately most important obstacle: was Netanyahu interested in and could he deliver an agreement with Syria that
was predicated on Israel's withdrawal from the Golan
Heights? Netanyahu had shown that he could disengage
from his past record and election promises, but would he
be able to make this Syrian deal? On various occasions he
indicated that he was interested in a negotiation with
Syria and realized that it could not be conducted effectively if he continued to hew to his past positions. He was
also willing to offer various different formulations that
implied an unspecified withdrawal in the Golan Heights.
But he did not agree to Assad's demands.

Assad, needless to say, has been unhappy with an in-
definite stalemate in which there has been some progress
in Palestinian matters and none with Syria. His most effective means of putting pressure on Israel has been
through Lebanon. By allowing and sometimes encouraging Hizballah to operate against Israeli forces in southern
Lebanon, he has produced a steady stream of casualties,
and Israel's decision-makers have to take notice. But the
Israelis' sensitivity to these casualties, by now a familiar
aspect of the Arab-Israeli conflict, is only worsened by
the apparent senselessness of this policy. Israel's presence

in the security zone of southern Lebanon had been intended not to advance a policy agenda but to maintain a status quo until conditions were ripe for a political solution, whereupon Israel would depart. Sustaining casualties for such a point is particularly onerous. Yet Israel faces only a few options here. It is broadly agreed that the only fundamental solution can be political-diplomatic, and that Syria holds the key to it. For a government and a significant portion of the public that does not wish to withdraw from the Golan Heights, however, this is not a viable possibility.

Nor is the option of escalating Israel's military responses or activities attractive to most Israelis. After Operation Litani (1978), the Lebanon war and its sequel (1982–85), Operation Accountability (1993), and Operation Grapes of Wrath (1996), the prospect of getting back or deeper into the Lebanese morass is simply not considered by most participants in the policy and public debates. A third option—having the Israeli Defense Force leave Lebanon under the aegis of an explicit or implicit understanding with the government of Lebanon—was tried in the first moments of Netanyahu's government and was rebuffed by Syria. A second effort was made in March 1998, when Israel executed a diplomatic maneuver concerning Security Council Resolution 425, a document dating back to 1978. The resolution called for Israel's withdrawal from southern Lebanon, and Israel had always refused to accept it, arguing that it had no claims in southern Lebanon and would be happy to leave once the threat to its own security along that border were removed. By accepting the resolution, Israel created some pressure on the Lebanese government to respond in a way that might lead to Israel's withdrawal. But this pressure could never be as strong as Syria's pressure on Lebanon, and this initiative went nowhere. The net effect has been to reduce the policy debate to the pros and cons of unilateral Israeli withdrawal.

In December 1998 the situation changed again with the collapse of Netanyahu's coalition. It is moot whether the prime minister could (and should) have stayed the course or whether his government was doomed by the tension between policy (the need to come to an agreement after nearly two years of procrastination) and politics (the refusal of several right-wing coalition members to support the government through implementation of the Wye Agreement). Netanyahu got the cabinet and the Knesset to approve the Agreement, but his coalition ran out of steam soon thereafter. On December 21 the coalition and opposition joined forces in a vote that dissolved the Knesset and stipulated an early election, called for May 17, 1999, with June 1 as the date for a possible second round in the prime ministerial election.

During the next few weeks the stage was set for a lengthy, contentious election campaign. The formation of a new "center party" meant that for the first time in Israel's political history there would be a three-way race. Netanyahu and his election advisers chose to focus their campaign on the peace process and away from socioeconomic issues and from the prime minister's character. The strategy was to repeat the success of 1996 and to depict Netanyahu as a resilient, uncompromising leader who, despite the recent Wye Agreement and in contrast to his meek competitors, would not yield to Arab and, specifically, Palestinian pressures.

Aside from a minor Israeli redeployment and several meetings of joint committees established by the Wye Agreement, implementation was suspended in anticipation of the elections. Some protests notwithstanding, Arafat agreed to this and agreed, in fact, to delay the declaration of Palestine's independence and statehood to the fall. For one thing, he (and for that matter the Clinton administration) was reluctant to affect the Israeli election adversely. Whatever their sympathies, each had discovered in 1996 that an overt effort to help Netanyahu's rivals could backfire; passive communication of one's preferences seemed the safer option. Inasmuch as Arafat was concerned, this meant that he was not going to overtly support the Labor candidate, Ehud Barak, or the centrist Yitzhak Mordechai or be critical of Netanyahu, but likewise he was determined not to embarrass Israeli supporters of the peace process by staging a major crisis before the elections.

In Arafat's strategy, investment in Washington's goodwill remained cardinal and continued to yield handsome dividends, notably when in mid-December 1998 President Clinton visited Israel and the Gaza Strip—as agreed on and announced at the Wye River Conference. The visit was meant to reinforce the implementation of an agreement that was likely to encounter difficulties. Yasser Arafat and the Palestinians could easily note the political and diplomatic advantages of having the president of the United States visit Gaza, while Netanyahu was promised that Clinton's presence would be used to guarantee a definitive public abrogation of the offensive paragraphs of the Palestinian National Charter. Chairman Arafat registered yet another milestone on his way to Palestinian statehood, and the Israeli prime minister could claim he had obtained the final revision of the document over which he had chided Peres in 1996.

# 4

# EHUD BARAK AND THE COLLAPSE OF THE PEACE PROCESS

Ehud Barak was elected as Israel's prime minister on May 17, 1999; on July 6 he presented his coalition government to the Knesset. He had conducted his election campaign as Yitzhak Rabin's heir—a high-ranking military man and a former chief of staff of the IDF—who went into politics in order to provide Israel with peace embedded in a solid new security regime.[1] But as prime minister, Barak adopted a style radically different from Rabin's. Rabin moderated his bold decisions through his preference for gradualism; Barak sought to cut the Arab-Israeli Gordian knot with one bold stroke. He concluded that the phased approach to Israeli-Arab peacemaking had run its course, and acted out of a deeply held conviction that the failure to reach a swift comprehensive Arab-Israeli settlement would inevitably lead to a large-scale collision.

Barak set a formidable challenge for himself by formulating ambitious goals and a brief timetable in his public statements. During his first visit to the United States as prime minister, Barak's spokesmen told Israeli reporters that he had presented President Clinton with a program for a final peace agreement that would resolve all outstanding issues among Israel, the Palestinians, Syria, and Lebanon. These issues would include the most intractable problems, such as Jerusalem and the resettlement of the Palestinian refugees. The Israeli reporters were told that "Barak wants to remove the phased approach once and for all off the agenda and proposes that Arab leaders come to discuss the whole gamut of issues. . . . The Barak plan sets a timetable of fifteen months, until October 2000, to reach a breakthrough on all tracks: a final-status Israeli-Palestinian agreement, peace agreements with Syria and Lebanon, and regional arrangements for the refugee and water problems."[2]

On other occasions, Barak emphasized that he was setting a fifteen-month deadline in order to find out whether Israel had a "real partner" on the Arab side. Barak and his spokesmen did not elaborate in public on the essential components of his plan, but they let it be understood that he estimated an agreement could be reached on terms that were quite acceptable to both Palestinians and Israelis. This agreement would include an independent Palestinian state, contiguous in the West Bank and connected to the Gaza Strip through an elevated bridge; a unified Jerusalem under Israeli sovereignty; the Jordan River serving as a security border; and refugees rehabilitated in their countries of residence without "right of return" to Israel. Barak was said to be willing to predicate the peace settlement with Syria on Israel's withdrawal from the

Golan Heights, while insisting that the border be pushed back from the shoreline of Lake Tiberias.[3]

Barak's domestic political moves reflected his decision to devote his first two years in office to completing—or at least significantly advancing—the peace process. The elections of May 1999 were conducted by the "two ballots" method, which meant that the voter cast one ballot for the direct election of the prime minister and another for a party list. Barak won an impressive personal majority (56.08 percent) but emerged with a weak parliamentary basis. His own list won only 26 out of 120 seats, and the larger center-left bloc, the natural supporter of his peace policy, failed to obtain the requisite number of seats for building a coalition.

Against this backdrop the prime minister–elect had two choices. One option was to form a coalition government with the Likud, with a parliamentary caucus decimated to 19; to settle on modest progress in the peace process; and to seek to turn the Likud into a partner for an ambitious program of sociopolitical reform. The second option was to add the Orthodox Sephardi Shas (the third largest party, now holding 17 seats) to the coalition alongside the left-wing Meretz Party, in the hope that in return for the accommodation of its agenda on funding a separate school system and "church and state" issues, the Shas leadership would overcome the nationalistic proclivities of its voters and support Barak's bold vision for ending the Arab-Israeli conflict.

Barak chose the second option, working on the assumption that under the leadership of Rabbi Ovadya Yossef, Shas would become an effective partner to his peace policies. On July 4, 1999, he introduced a government resting on a coalition composed of 73 members of the Knesset. He also assumed that a government conducting an energetic peace policy could rely on the votes of the Arab Knesset members without adding them to the coalition.

This strategic choice was supplemented by a second major decision: to focus the initial and main effort of the government's peace policy on the Syrian, rather than Palestinian, track. Barak did not advertise this choice. According to his own statements, Barak remained committed to the idea of reaching final-status agreements with both Syria and the Palestinians within a reasonable time frame, but he clearly preferred a "Syria first" policy, seeking to obtain an early agreement with Syria and then proceed to negotiate with the Palestinians from a better bargaining position.

This premise—as well as the whole tenor of Barak's policy—was questioned by a significant portion of Israel's foreign policy and national security establishment. Questions were raised as to whether a government resting on a fragile coalition would be able to complete agreements entailing significant concessions on both the Syrian and Palestinian tracks. There were also more specific questions regarding Barak's ability to achieve an agreement with Syria, based on withdrawal from the Golan and approved by a referendum, with the Palestinian issue hovering in the background.

Barak's preference for the Syrian track was shaped by the same considerations that had guided his three predecessors—Rabin, Peres, and Netanyahu—to choose a "Syria first" policy. The Syrian-Israeli conflict was perceived as less complex than the Israeli-Palestinian dispute, as an essentially territorial conflict between two sovereign states rather than a nationalist and communal conflict over land and rights. Assad was also seen as a better partner than Arafat for a swift negotiation. Barak, in a typically determined fashion, pushed from this vantage point to an early resumption and conclusion of the Israeli-Syrian negotiations.

Given the comparatively cordial welcome offered to Israel's new leader by both the Syrian government and media, it began to seem that the prospects of an Israeli-Syrian agreement were better in the latter half of 1999 than they had been in the previous decade. And yet the efforts to resume the negotiations met with a series of unanticipated difficulties. It took a full six months—until December 1999—to restart the negotiation.[4]

Two of the difficulties were of an apparently technical nature. For one, Hafez al-Assad continued to insist (as he had done vis-à-vis Netanyahu) that the negotiations be resumed only "at the point at which they had been interrupted," and that that "point" included an Israeli agreement to withdraw to the lines of June 4, 1967. Barak was familiar with the history of the Israel-Syrian negotiations and well knew that Assad would not sign a peace treaty with Jerusalem without a full Israeli withdrawal from the Golan. Even if he accepted this as part of the negotiation's bottom line, Barak was not willing to accept it as the point of departure. By effectively surrendering his trump card before the start of the negotiations, he would be left without any leverage or bargaining chips once the negotiations began to unfold. Barak also wanted to establish the degree of flexibility in the Syrian insistence on Israel's withdrawal to "the lines of June 4, 1967." Such lines had never been drawn on a map. Barak wanted to ascertain Assad's willingness to settle on a formal Israeli acceptance of his demand, in return for Syrian flexibility regarding the actual location of the lines. When this issue was first put on the agenda in the mid-1990s, the Israeli negotiators and their colleagues on the U.S. "peace team" assumed that what mattered to Assad was the principle of obtaining an Israeli withdrawal beyond the (1923) international boundary, that he was primarily interested in the al-Himmeh salient (south of Lake Tiberias), and that he would be willing to accommodate Israel's needs regarding the shoreline of Lake Tiberias and northern Jordan. It was made amply clear to Assad that this was a "red line" for a country preoccupied with its water supply.[5]

A second difficulty arose from the loose ends left in the aftermath of the negotiation conducted with Assad in the fall of 1998 by the American business magnate Ronald Lauder on behalf of Benjamin Netanyahu. Lauder, a Republican who had served as ambassador in Vienna on behalf of the Reagan administration, was supposed to conduct the negotiation unbeknownst to the Clinton administration. Yet Lauder was accompanied on his trips to Damascus by a Lebanese-American middleman who was connected to several parties, including the Clinton administration. Later, Lauder gave the U.S. government a report, and a version was leaked to the Israeli media. According to Lauder's early report to the Clinton administration (subsequently modified), his negotiation with Assad was conducted on the basis of an Israeli agreement to withdraw to the *international* boundary (rather than the lines of June 4). This led Barak to believe that he could restart negotiations on terms that were more comfortable from an Israeli point of view. It took several weeks to discover that the report—and the set of assumptions it produced—were erroneous. (The Syrians continue to deny this version of events and have sought to belittle the significance of the whole Lauder episode.)

Beyond these particular issues lies the more fundamental question of Assad's intention ever to consummate negotiations with Israel. There was, in the 1990s, a school of thought that had argued all along that Assad never intended to reach an agreement with Israel, and that his participation in the peace process was motivated purely by the political dividends he expected to reap in Washington. But even those who did not share this view had to contend with the question of the extent to which—and the conditions under which—Assad was interested in resuming and completing negotiations with Israel in 1999–2000.

The principal change during this period was the decline of Assad's health, and the subsequent urgency that was now vested in the issue of succession. Assad died in June 2000. During the preceding months his physical and mental decline was all too evident. This decline was matched by a loss of authority and political power. The process of promoting his son, Bashar, and building him up as heir apparent, was accelerated. Some of Hafez al-Assad's closest friends and associates were removed by younger men who were closer to Bashar and viewed as better partners for the new ruler. Assad's gradual decline gave Syria's foreign minister, Faruq al-Shara, a degree of authority and freedom of action that he had not known in the past.

Hafez al-Assad's power remained unchallenged, but the removal of several former partners and associates, the widespread unhappiness with the adoption of the dynastic principle, and the discontent with Bashar's persona created significant pockets of criticism and opposition for the first time in many years. Part of the criticism was directed at the very idea of settlement with Israel and the compromises and concessions it entailed; these were easier targets than Assad's nepotism. Assad, aware of his decline, chose to focus on his chief priority: ensuring the succession to his son.

But this was not the only set of forces brought to bear on Syria's negotiations with Ehud Barak. Assad's desire to regain the Golan before stepping offstage, the need to secure Washington's goodwill and cooperation at this sensitive juncture, and the potential for conflict in Lebanon (given Barak's pledge to the Israeli public to get the IDF out of Lebanon within his first year in power) all modified and affected the Syrian-Israeli negotiations.

Barak first made that pledge during the election campaign, and it was, indeed, dismissed by many as a mere campaign promise. But he did repeat it after his election and thereby changed the dynamic shaping the Israeli-Lebanese-Syrian triangle throughout the 1990s. Israel's policy had been predicated on the assumption that its problems in South Lebanon could be resolved only through an agreement with Syria. The hegemonic power in Lebanon, Syria in fact encouraged Hizballah's attacks in order to extract greater concessions from Israel. Barak's promise (or threat) to take Israel out of South Lebanon by July 2000 altered this equation. How would Hizballah conduct itself if Israel were to withdraw unilaterally from South Lebanon? How should Syria act on its own and with regard to Hizballah and its Iranian sponsors? Could Damascus risk escalation along the Israeli-Lebanese border, given the complex state of affairs in Syria's domestic politics?

Against this backdrop, the quiet diplomacy of the summer and fall of 1999 yielded a positive outcome. In December 1999 the resumption of the Israeli-Syrian negotiations was announced. Moreover, Assad agreed to upgrade the negotiation from the bureaucratic to the political level and nominated Foreign Minister Faruq al-Shara as the Syrian negotiator. Barak, in turn, decided to overlook the difference in rank and status and put himself at the head of the Israeli delegation. Negotiations began in Washington on December 15. Barak was accompanied by his foreign minister, David Levy; the minister of tourism (and former chief of staff of the IDF), Amnon Shahak; and a team of negotiators headed by Reserve General Uri Sagi (who, like Barak and Shahak, had participated in earlier phases of the Israeli-Syrian peace process).

In December 1999 and January 2000 two rounds of negotiations were held under President Clinton's aegis, in Washington and in Shepherdstown, West Virginia. The Washington talks were overshadowed by Faruq al-Shara's sulking conduct, notably his refusal to shake Barak's hand and his strident speech.[6] Such details may seem trifling within the larger context of two enemies making an effort to move from a state of hostility and belligerency to a state of peace, but symbols and rituals are significant both in conflict and during a transition to peace. This was particularly true for the Israeli-Syrian relationship. It was widely assumed that in the event of an agreement with

Syria, Barak would have to hold a referendum. It was also
assumed that in order to win this referendum, he would
have to persuade Assad to engage in "public diplomacy"—
a series of gestures designed to persuade the Israeli public
that Syria had had a change of heart and was now ready
for genuine peace with yesterday's enemy. But during the
Washington talks and throughout this period, Syria held
on to its familiar position: refusal to engage in any public
diplomacy, and continued pressure exerted on Israel in
the Lebanese and Palestinian arenas as long as an
agreement had not been reached.

However, in the closed sessions held in Washington,
Shara was more forthcoming than his public conduct suggested. Furthermore, strident tone notwithstanding, he
incorporated two intriguing phrases in his public statement: that the conflict with Israel was no longer existential but territorial, and that peacemaking with Israel constituted a transition from struggle to competition.[7] This
motif was essential to Syria's concept of a prospective settlement with Israel—Israel would no longer be an enemy
but would remain an adversary and a competitor. By signing a peace treaty with Israel, Syria could end active conflict with the Jewish state but not reconcile itself to its
legitimacy. The struggle would therefore continue in
other (that is, nonmilitary) ways. This concept of peacemaking with Israel is, in fact, not so different from the
policies pursued by Egypt, although the latter's leaders
stopped short of an explicit adoption of the notion of "an
ongoing struggle," preferring to use sifted terms such as
"cold peace" and opposition to "normalization."

The Shepherdstown talks took longer than the brief
meeting in Washington but ended in failure. The chief

obstacle was familiar: Syria's insistence on an explicit Israeli commitment to withdraw to the lines of June 4, 1967, as a precondition to any progress. Barak alluded to his willingness to withdraw, and to start preparing Israeli public opinion for withdrawal to the lines of June 4, 1967, as an abstract concept, but he refused to make an explicit commitment prior to assessing Assad's flexibility regarding the actual demarcation of the June 4 lines and in particular the shoreline of Lake Tiberias. According to American diplomats who participated in the talks, Syria's Foreign Minister Shara indicated that Syria could be flexible in this matter. But he refused to elaborate, and, as it turned out during the Clinton-Assad meeting in Geneva in March 2000, his statement had no real value.

The failure of the Shepherdstown talks subsequently became a bone of contention between Barak and his critics. Participants such as Ambassador Martin Indyk and Barak's own chief negotiator, Uri Sagi, have argued that Barak developed "cold feet." They felt that his failure to make an explicit commitment prevented a breakthrough with a Syrian partner otherwise ready to make a deal. Raviv Druker's critical book on Barak's tenure claims that pollsters warned Barak that Israeli public opinion was opposed to the concessions demanded by Syria.[8] Rob Malley, a former official of the National Security Council, argued that Clinton was resentful of Barak's conduct at Shepherdstown—so much so that, angered by a change in Barak's position during the Camp David Summit in July 2000, he told him: "I can't go to Arafat with a retrenchment! You can sell it. . . . This is not real. This is not serious. I went to Shepherdstown . . . and was told nothing by you for four days. I went to Geneva and felt like an Indian doll doing your bidding. . . ."[9]

Barak still insists that it would have been a grave mistake to offer Assad an explicit commitment to withdraw, and that it was Assad's insistence on this precondition that obstructed the talks. Barak also attributes great importance to the fact that an American draft of a proposed text for an Israeli-Syrian peace treaty was leaked to the Israeli press. The U.S. peace team prepared the draft in an effort to demonstrate how close the parties were to agreement. The Syrians leaked a doctored version of the text, to show that it was in fact closer to a "nonbelligerency" agreement than to a peace treaty. Later, (in order to counter this attempt or perhaps owing to another consideration by an American or Israeli participant) a different, more attractive version of the text was leaked to an Israeli journalist. Indeed, in the postmortem of the Shepherdstown talks, the Syrians complained that the leak embarrassed Assad and made it difficult for Syria to resume the negotiations.[10]

As had been the case in earlier instances, the very fact that a high-level Israeli-Syrian meeting took place agitated the Israeli political system. The prospect of an agreement with Syria predicated on a full Israeli withdrawal from the Golan seemed close and realistic. The Golan Lobby had become powerful during the past decade, and its campaign against Barak's Syrian gambit was facilitated by two crucial forces: Hafez al-Assad's refusal to invest any effort to win over Israeli public opinion, and the inherent difficulty of persuading the public to endorse an agreement that had yet to be made.

In hopeful anticipation, Barak's government began a campaign to build support in the United States for a massive aid package, to be received when an agreement with Syria was signed. It suggested that the Clinton administration should ask Congress for a special aid package of up to $17 billion, allowing Israel to build up and modernize the IDF to compensate for the loss of the Golan.[11] This was a staggering amount that would be difficult to get endorsed by any Congress, let alone a Republican one explicitly hostile to Syria and reluctant to assist the Clinton administration in attaining its foreign policy objectives. Moreover, during the brief period of high expectations of an Israeli-Syrian breakthrough, the Golan Lobby in Israel and its allies in the American-Jewish community launched a campaign against U.S. support of a would-be Israeli-Syrian agreement. The campaign was reminiscent of the one conducted in the mid-1990s. As it turned out, the campaign was superfluous—cut short by the collapse of the negotiations in March 2000.

In contradistinction to the familiar arguments of Israeli and American opponents of a Syrian-Israeli settlement were the novel voices of a domestic Syrian opposition to accommodation with Israel. There were some indications of such opposition in the early and mid-1990s, but at that time they seemed marginal and muted. The domestic criticism of Assad's policies that surfaced in late 1999 and early 2000, however, was systematic and sustained. He and his regime were taken to task for their very willingness to accept the state of Israel, as well as for their apparent readiness to withdraw from some of Syria's original positions in negotiations. An article published by Aqleh Arsan, a Ba'ath Party member and chairman of the Arab

Writers Union headquartered in Damascus, was a particularly harsh example of such criticism. Arsan stated, "We
reject and will continue to reject any recognition of Zionism."[12] Echoing the bitter tone of Syria's greatest poet,
Nizar Qabrani, Arsan asked rhetorically, "Are we to remain with nothing but a sense of despair and possibly the
bitter memories of our defeat? Will the ghosts of millions
of Palestinians who were expelled from their homes dis-
appear?" He asserted that he and his colleagues saw the
struggle against the "Zionist enemy" as an "existential"
conflict—and not as a conflict over borders—in a clear,
sardonic reference to Faruq al-Shara's statement.

On February 13, Shara appeared before the members
of the Arab Writers Union and delivered a speech ex-
plaining and defending Syria's policy toward Israel. It was
an uncharacteristic speech for a foreign minister to make.
In ordinary circumstances, it would have been Assad's responsibility to offer an authoritative exposition of his regime's policy. But Assad's health had deteriorated to the
point that he was incapable of exercising his customary
leadership role.

Shara's speech was not a coherent, focused text but
rather a patchwork of ideas and arguments that constituted an effort to address different constituencies—and
was therefore full of contradictions. In defense of the regime's policies, he explained that the Arabs had been defeated by Israel, and Syria had been abandoned by its Arab
partners. Therefore there was no choice but to make
peace with Israel. In a similar apologetic vein, Shara repeated in a modified version the statement he had made
in Washington in December 1999 that the conflict with
Israel had been transformed from an existential to a terri-

torial dispute and was accordingly ripe for resolution. The foreign minister also repeated another motif from his Washington speech in stating that peace, in fact, meant a transformation of the military conflict to a political, economic, and cultural competition—one in which the Arabs stood a better chance.

However, in other segments of the February 13 speech Shara denounced Israel and Zionism, pledging his allegiance to the original vision and long-term goals of the Ba'ath. In response to a question from the audience, Shara went so far as to revive the "phased approach" of the 1970s: "The Ba'ath Party believes that regaining the whole of Palestine is a long term strategic goal that could not be implemented in one phase . . . the Ba'ath Party's doctrine draws a distinction between the different phases of the struggle for the liberation of Palestine."[13]

The failure of the Shepherdstown talks resulted in a stalemate that lasted for about two months. Both the Clinton administration and the Barak government were worried by this passage of time. The date of Israel's withdrawal from Lebanon was getting closer and Assad's health continued to deteriorate, exacerbating the Israeli debate on a prospective agreement with Syria. Proponents argued that it was preferable to conclude the agreement with a leader who commanded the stature and authority necessary to both make and implement the agreement. They also believed that the majority of Syria's political system and public had come to accept the notion of peace with Israel, so an agreement made by Assad would be kept by his successors even if he died shortly after signing. They further argued that if an agreement failed to be signed during Assad's lifetime, it would take his successor a long time to establish enough sway to complete the peace process with Israel. On the other side of the debate, opponents of a settlement with Syria reinforced their original criticism by arguing that handing over the Golan to a dying autocratic ruler would be an egregiously reckless act.

In any event, the United States and Israel reached the conclusion that a face-to-face meeting between Presidents Clinton and Assad was the only possible way to break the deadlock and reach a swift agreement. Washington and Jerusalem therefore acted on the assumption that Assad alone possessed the authority to make crucial decisions for breakthrough and accommodation, and that absent the prospect of a meeting between Barak and Assad, the closest approximation to an Israeli-Syrian summit was an American-Syrian one. Clinton was familiar with Barak's position and could be trusted to present and represent it well. And furthermore, Assad was believed to be more interested in a dialogue with Washington than in making peace with Israel.

This technique constituted a new version of Rabin's position with Warren Christopher in August 1993. Like that original deposit of Israel's willingness to withdraw from the Golan, Barak's reliance on Clinton reflected his exasperation by his repeated failure to reach Assad directly. He learned from the Lauder episode that it was easier to persuade Assad to make concessions when negotiating with him in person. But Christopher's meeting with Assad in August 1993 was a first step calculated to set a process in motion. The Clinton-Assad meeting in March 2000 was rather a final measure, a last-ditch effort to prevent total collapse of the Israeli-Syrian negotiation.

The March 26 meeting in Geneva ended in swift, reso-
nant failure. We have yet to find out the extent of the
efforts invested to secure the success of the meeting and
to save Clinton from another embarrassment. Clearly, the
U.S. president acted on the assumption (derived from
statements made by Faruq al-Shara in earlier discussions)
that Assad would be willing to show flexibility in drawing
the lines of June 4, 1967, and to allow a strip of land along
Lake Tiberias and the Upper Jordan to remain under Israeli sovereignty. The strip would be wider than the ten
meters stipulated by the 1923 agreement, which established the boundary between the British Mandate in Syria
and the French Mandate in Syria.

In Geneva, Assad rejected these ideas out of hand. He
made it amply clear that if Shara had spoken to that effect,
he had exceeded his authority. And so the ten-month effort launched in May 1999 collapsed—under Assad's insistence on obtaining part of the Lake Tiberias shore, and
under Barak's insistence that even if Israel agreed to
withdraw from the Golan Heights and to give up the al-
Himmeh enclave, it could not and would not give up full
sovereignty over the lake. Barak viewed full control of
Lake Tiberias as key to Israel's water regime; he also
sensed that this represented a political red line that the
Israeli electorate would not cross in a referendum or a
fresh election.[14]

The collapse of the fourth effort of Israeli-Syrian resolution in the final decade of the twentieth century had
several causes. Assad's uncompromising position and
Washington's and Jerusalem's tactical errors were two of
them. But the prime reason seems to have been Assad's
physical and mental decline. During the last months of

his life, Assad focused his residual powers on securing the succession to his son. He felt weak, and vulnerable, and was sensitive to criticism that he was willing to sacrifice his principles for a compromise with Israel. This criticism may well have reflected a minority view and was probably also an expression of opposition to the introduction of the dynastic principle into the political system of a formerly revolutionary republic. Nonetheless, on the eve of a problematic transition, Assad and his loyalist core were defensive. Had Israel succumbed to all his demands and provided him with "the peace of the victors," he might have signed an agreement—but for Ehud Barak this was not a viable option.

The failure of the Geneva summit provided fresh ammunition to those who had argued since the early and mid-1990s that Assad never intended to consummate the negotiations with Israel, and that he was merely interested in the political dividends accruing to participants in the peace process. For advocates of this interpretation, the Geneva meeting in March 2000 was a moment of truth that illuminated Assad's conduct throughout the previous decade. An entirely different interpretation argues that the failure of the 1999–2000 negotiation could have been avoided altogether. My own view is that the spring of 2000 cannot necessarily explain the previous decade owing to the profound change in Assad's outlook once he realized that his death was imminent.

Several attempts were made to revive negotiations in the aftermath of the failed summit in Geneva, but they were nipped in the bud by two developments: Israel's withdrawal from Lebanon in May and Assad's death in June.

Israel's withdrawal from South Lebanon ended a nine-year link between the Israeli-Syrian negotiations and the security issues along the Israeli-Lebanese border. Israel no longer expected an agreement with Syria to also provide a fundamental solution to its Lebanese dilemma. It also reached, independently, the conclusion that large-scale military operations in Lebanon, attacks on Hizballah, and exercising indirect pressure on Beirut were all ineffective strategies. Syria was the hegemonic power in Lebanon, and Israel's quest for security along its northern border would now rest on a classic deterrence equation. Attacks on Israel across an internationally recognized border would lead—it was suggested—to a full-fledged Israeli-Syrian collision.[15]

From Barak's point of view, the unilateral withdrawal from Lebanon was a risky gamble. There was no guarantee that either Syria or Hizballah would act cautiously. However, in reality it proved to be at least a short-term success. Hafez al-Assad died on June 10. Bashar's succession proceeded smoothly, and the new president was clearly interested in consolidating his position rather than in risky adventures. Nor were Teheran and Hizballah interested in a wave of violence in South Lebanon at that time. For them, Israel's withdrawal was a great victory—a vindication—and they were determined to exploit it politically by bolstering Hizballah's standing in Lebanon.

For nearly five months, Hizballah's leadership did indeed refrain from initiating dramatic attacks against Israel. Instead, it settled on digging in along the border and encouraging Lebanese civilians to come to the fence in an effort to defy and provoke IDF guards. While Israel claimed that its withdrawal from Lebanon was final and definitive, Hizballah argued that the issue remained open as long as Israel continued to hold Lebanese prisoners and failed to withdraw from the Shaba Farms. According to Israel (and the UN), the Shaba Farms were Syrian territory and should be dealt with by Israel and Syria. Hizballah (and eventually other Lebanese actors), however, saw fit to argue that this was Lebanese territory and that Israel's refusal to withdraw from it constituted an act of occupation and aggression. The organization was thus laying the groundwork for new attacks on Israel at some future date.

That future date came in early October 2000. After the outbreak of Palestinian-Israeli violence in late September, Hizballah was confronted with both opportunity and pressure to join the fray. From Iran's and Hizballah's perspective, the Palestinians were inspired by their exploits in Lebanon and applied the lesson that there was no need to make concessions to Israel. If one stood one's ground and fought for one's rights, the Israelis would pack up and leave. How could Hizballah's leadership remain an idle spectator under these circumstances? Hizballah's radical proclivities were reinforced by two developments: its poor performance in Lebanese elections and Bashar al-Assad's weakness. Bashar not only failed to restrain the organization but seemed to be under its leadership's spell. For Hafez al-Assad, Hizballah had been an actor on the Lebanese scene, an arm of the Iranian government, and an occasional ally of Syria's policy. But while he had sought to use and manipulate the organization, his son seemed to admire it.

With this backdrop of events spurring them on, Hizballah launched an offensive against Israel by abducting three Israeli soldiers who were patrolling the border on October 7. A week later it abducted an Israeli businessman in Europe. Other attempts did not materialize. Israel, reluctant to open a second front, decided to refrain from a military response.

Israel's policy changed after the formation of Sharon's government in February 2001. Hizballah attacked twice, and on both occasions Israel retaliated by attacking Syrian positions. Sharon thus implemented the deterrence equation established by Barak and underscored the view that Syria was the effective address for Israel's deterrence. In both cases Syria refrained from responding despite pressures that were reportedly exerted on Bashar al-Assad by his more radical associates.

The calming effect of Israel's actions evaporated after a few months. The Palestinian-Israeli war of attrition intensified, as did Iran's determination to destabilize the region. Hizballah's attacks grew in scope and boldness.

The tension and violence along Israel's northern border in 2001 and 2002 provided yet another manifestation of the "shifting horizon" phenomenon in Arab-Israeli relations. Even when Israel withdrew to the international border—and did so in cooperation with the United States—Hizballah (and subsequently Lebanon's government) have argued that Israel's withdrawal was less than complete. Furthermore, the Arab summit conference in Beirut in March 2002, meeting to adopt the Saudi "peace initiative," endorsed this position as well.

It was only in the early summer of 2000, after the final collapse of the Syrian negotiations and his unilateral withdrawal from Lebanon, that Barak devoted his full attention to negotiations with the Palestinians—protestations notwithstanding. It had been to the detriment of Israel's dealings with the Palestinians that Barak had focused primarily on the Syrian track during his first year in office. These new dealings consisted of several meetings with Arafat, of give-and-take with him through a discreet channel, and of a formal negotiation on the implementation of the Wye Agreement signed by Netanyahu's government in October 1998. Barak confronted a double dilemma: how to preserve Arafat's and the Palestinians' goodwill while assigning a clear priority to the Syrian track, and how to proceed with the implementation of the Wye Agreement without spending territorial assets that he would rather use in the final-status negotiations. Barak viewed himself as a leader possessed of capabilities and style different from those of Netanyahu and believed in his ability to accomplish final-status agreements with both Syria and the Palestinians. The agreement with the Palestinians would perhaps be reached and implemented in phases, but Barak was reluctant to offer massive concessions during the interim phases. (As a member in Rabin's cabinet in the summit of 1995 he abstained during the vote on the Oslo II Accord in disagreement with the phased withdrawals that were built into it.)

In any event, on September 4, 1999, Barak signed the Sharm al-Sheikh agreement for the implementation of the Wye Agreement that had been signed by Netanyahu in October 1998. The withdrawal that had originally been envisaged in two phases was now to be implemented in three, but the Palestinians were compensated by a verbal promise that they would be given contiguous "quality" territory. Agreement was also reached regarding a familiar set of issues including the port in Gaza, safe passage between the West Bank and the Gaza Strip, and prisoner release. The parties agreed on a continuous accelerated negotiation with a view to reaching agreement in two phases: a framework agreement within 2000 and a final-status agreement within a year.

The final-status negotiations were conducted in a secret channel. The Palestinian delegation was headed by Abu Alaa, chairman of the Legislative Council and Arafat's chief negotiator in Oslo. Barak was represented by Shlomo Ben-Ami, minister of domestic security, and Gilead Sher, an attorney who negotiated the Sharm al-Sheikh agreement on Israel's behalf. In May 2000, details of the secret Israeli-Palestinian negotiation began to leak. Natan Sharanski, minister of the interior in Barak's government and a prominent member of the right wing of the coalition, publicized these details and began to build up opposition to what he saw as excessive concessions on Israel's part.[16]

The formulas which underlay the understandings that coalesced in Stockholm were reminiscent of the core of the Beilin–Abu Mazen draft agreement put together in the fall of 1995: Israeli readiness to withdraw from the bulk of the West Bank and the Gaza Strip, and Palestinian acceptance of Israeli annexation of the large settlement blocs in return for an asymmetrical exchange of territories. Barak felt that a swift final-status agreement with Arafat was within reach on the basis of this formula, and he began to urge President Clinton to summon the parties to a summit modeled on the 1978 Camp David Conference, in order to reach such an agreement.

Barak was acting under the pressure of two ticking political clocks. In the United States, President Clinton's second term was drawing to a close. The presidential election was scheduled for early November, and Clinton's own assessment was that he could be effective only through September in helping the parties reach agreement and mobilizing support in Congress for the financial aid packages indispensable for its implementation. In Israel, Barak was acutely aware that his coalition was shrinking with the passage of time and a hostile majority was coalescing in the Knesset. These calculations were reinforced by the prime minister's sense that tensions were building up and that, barring an agreement, Israel and the Palestinians were on a collision course. The eruption of violence on "*Nakba* Day" (the term used by the Palestinians to designate Israel's independence and their defeat) in May 2000 lit a significant red light. The level and intensity of the violence were an indication of the potential for greater conflict, as well as of the fact that Arafat did not fully control the Palestinian "street," and that the popular rage was directed in part at him and at the Palestinian Authority.

In the summer of 2000, an intricate and intriguing link developed between the dynamics of Israeli domestic politics and Israel's conduct in its negotiation with the Palestinians.

As mentioned above, the elections of May 1999 produced a discrepancy between Barak's impressive personal achievement and the further fragmentation of the Knesset and weakening of the two large parties. In the two-ballot election, Barak won 56 percent of the vote; the list composed of the Labor Party and its partners won 26 seats in the Knesset (as compared to 34 in the 1996 elections). The Likud list was decimated to a mere 19 (as compared to 32). The ultra-Orthodox Sephardi Shas rose from 10 to 17, the left-wing Meretz from 9 to 10, and the new Shinuy (defined by an assertive secularist platform) won 6 seats. Several Arab members were elected, most of them through anti-Zionist lists.

From this fragmented picture, three major conclusions could be drawn. First, the Israeli public gave Barak an impressive personal victory but denied him the possibility of forming a stable coalition government. Second, Netanyahu was personally defeated, but "Netanyahu's coalition" suffered only a minor loss and commanded 58 seats in the new Knesset. And last, with regard to the principal issue on the national agenda—Israel's relationship with the Arab world—the Israeli body politic remained more or less evenly divided.

With these conclusions setting the stage, it is quite possible that Barak's choice of Shas as a principal partner to his "peace coalition" was doomed to fail. This inherent difficulty was then compounded by Barak's failure to learn from Rabin's mistake in 1992. At the time, Rabin had formed a coalition government with Shas and Meretz, and assigned the education portfolio to the latter's leader, Shulamit Aloni. Friction soon erupted over the budgeting of Shas's independent educational system (one of the party's principal mainstays). This was one of the main reasons for Shas's decision to withdraw from the coalition in 1993. In 1999, it was Meretz's new leader, Yossi Sarid, who became the minister of education. A tug-of-war soon started between Sarid and Shas, exacerbating the party's relationship with Barak and keeping their relationship on the edge of a permanent crisis. In June 2000, Meretz withdrew from the coalition, promising to sup-

port the government "from the outside." By this point
Barak's relationship with Shas was beyond all repair.

Nor did Barak fare well in his relations with the other
coalition partners. The ultra-Orthodox Yahadut Hatorah
left the coalition as early as 1999; Natan Sharanski, the
former anti-Soviet activist, was openly critical of Barak's
style of governance and his willingness to offer far-reaching concessions in order to reach agreements with Syria
and the Palestinians. The effect of these tensions in the
coalition's ranks was magnified by endemic criticism and
challenges to Barak's leadership in his own party.[17]

The disintegration of Barak's coalition was accelerated
by the decision to go the Camp David Conference. Shas,
the National Religious Party, and Sharanski and his fac-
tion were all opposed to the anticipated concessions and
left the coalition. Foreign Minister David Levy was of-
fended by the fact that the minister of domestic security,
Shlomo Ben-Ami, was put in charge of the negotiations
and was accompanied by his brother Maxim. Barak was
left with a coalition of 30. He managed to keep his government afloat for several more months, through parliamentary maneuvers and owing to the reluctance of several
Knesset members to end their term and face a new election. But by late November, Barak had reached the end
of his rope and called for a new election. On December
9, he formally resigned and became the prime minister of
a transitional government.

One important outcome of this chain of events was that
Barak conducted both the negotiations at Camp David
and the crisis that broke out at the end of September 2000
without parliamentary majority and through a diminished
cabinet. It was an extraordinary set of affairs. A prime

minister preoccupied with his own political survival and devoid of parliamentary support could hardly be expected to manage a profound and sustained national security crisis.

When Barak lost his coalition on the eve of his departure for Camp David, he established an unhealthy connection between his own political future and the success of the negotiations. The conventional wisdom at the time stated that a majority of Israelis supported an agreement with the Palestinians but opposed the concessions that such an agreement entailed. It was widely assumed that the Knesset would approve neither an agreement based on massive concessions nor a referendum that would endorse such an agreement. To facilitate one of these scenarios, Barak would have had to dissolve the Knesset and bring about a fresh election. Barak's supporters and opponents alike estimated that in that situation, he would be reelected. However, as the Camp David Conference failed, the issue remained moot.

The expectations generated by the very term "Camp David," as well as the changes in Israel's position in the negotiations, turned the second Camp David Conference in July 2000 into the high (and eventually low) point of Ehud Barak's effort to reach an accord with the Palestinians. Despite its saliency, the July summit should be seen as a phase in a negotiation that lasted for almost a year—from the spring of 2000 to the eve of the February 2001 elections.

As time goes by and accounts of that negotiation accumulate, it increasingly appears to have been a journey by Barak and his government from the center-right of the Israeli political spectrum to its left wing. This journey did

not produce a comparable shift on the Palestinian side
and did not obtain an agreement. Furthermore, since the
end of September, the effort had been overshadowed by
Arafat's attempt to exploit the outbreak of violence as another means of pressure on Israel. The Barak government's journey unfolded through five main phases.

## THE STOCKHOLM TALKS

After the final collapse of his negotiations with Syria,
Barak decided to accelerate the Palestinian track. Barak
chose to negotiate through Shlomo Ben-Ami and Gilead
Sher, with Abu Alaa as their counterpart. The chief venue
for the negotiations was near Stockholm, under the auspices of a Swedish government inspired by Norway's successful role in the 1993 Oslo breakthrough. Barak did not
adopt the Beilin–Abu Mazen formula, but its essential
components were clearly reflected in the understandings
reached in Sweden. According to Shlomo Ben-Ami's own
testimony, he and Barak quickly abandoned Israel's opening position ("sort of an Alon Plan . . . if I am not wrong
it would offer the Palestinians a mere 66% . . .). Instead,
the Israelis presented a map in Stockholm partitioning
the West Bank at a 12–88 percent ratio (the Gaza Strip
was to be fully or almost fully evacuated). Israel insisted
on keeping the three large settlement blocs and on holding on to the Jordan Valley for twenty years. Barak did
not authorize his negotiators to speak about territorial exchanges—he was wary of leaks that could jeopardize his
government's survival. Nothing was formally agreed, but
the Israeli negotiators felt that their Palestinian counter-

parts understood the need for Israel to keep the large settlement blocs and for flexible security arrangements.

With regard to the refugee issue, "a whole concept was
constructed for finding the solution in host countries, in
the Palestinian state and in third countries and family re-
unification in Israel." Ben Ami and Sher spoke of ten to
fifteen thousand refugees who would be absorbed in Israel
over the years. Abu Alaa and his associate, Hasan Asfoor,
did not agree to figures but were willing to enter into a
businesslike discussion of this particular issue.[18]

The negotiations continued through the period leading up to the Camp David Summit. In a meeting in Jerusalem, Abu Alaa agreed to give up 4 percent of the West
Bank. In the preparatory talks with the U.S. team, the
Palestinians gave President Clinton a 2 percent deposit.
Ben-Ami, in turn, further reduced Israel's territorial demand to 8–10 percent of the West Bank. It was felt that
a compromise could be reached somewhere between 4
and 8 percent. Regarding the Jordan Valley—or the future Palestinian state's eastern border—the Palestinians
rejected any notion of concession.

At the same time, an "informal discussion" of the Jerusalem issue began. In a meeting held in Nablus, Arafat
promised Ben-Ami that "the Wailing Wall and the Jewish
Quarter were ours [Israel's]." Other Palestinian spokesmen alluded to potential flexibility on Jewish neighbor-
hoods in East Jerusalem. But with regard to the refugees,
the Palestinians seemed to have taken a step back. According to Ben-Ami's detailed account, "Abu Mazen persuaded Abu Alaa not to discuss any numbers and to insist
on the principle of the Right of Return."[19]

## CAMP DAVID

At the Camp David Conference, Israel endowed its earlier concessions with a greater formality. It also accepted
the principle of exchange of territories (though not at a
1:1 ratio), and, most significantly, it agreed to far-reaching
concessions in Jerusalem (as compared to its original positions). These concessions were not made formally but
were offered in simulation games, or given as a "deposit"
that could be revoked in the absence of an appropriate
response. At this point, Israelis and Palestinians alike
knew that once a concession was laid on the table, the
impact of that idea could not be obliterated even if the
concession was formally withdrawn.

Barak's greatest concessions at Camp David concerned
Jerusalem and the Jordan Valley. He discarded one of the
sacred slogans of Israeli politics ("One Jerusalem, unified,
under Israeli sovereignty") and agreed to partition and
compromise, not only in East Jerusalem, but also in the
Old City and the Temple Mount. By agreeing to give up
permanent Israeli presence in the Jordan Valley, he
crossed both an Israeli and a Jordanian red line. Jordan
would rather have had Israel continue to postpone the
establishment of a Palestinian state; however, if this were
to change, Jordan would prefer Israeli presence in the Jordan Valley as a buffer.

Barak was more willing to cross these lines after Arafat's promise to Clinton on July 16 that he was ready to
give up 8–10 percent of the West Bank and to display
flexibility on other main issues. But Arafat retracted his
promise the next day, and this left Barak vulnerable. The
question of whether Arafat made his statement to Clinton

merely in order to extricate himself from a tight corner—
or whether it was a more sophisticated maneuver designed to lead Barak to open up the Jerusalem issue for
discussion—still remains unresolved.

The second Camp David conference ended in failure
and left the Israeli participants with the sense that Arafat
rejected Barak's gambit of agreeing to an "end of conflict"
and "end of claims" in return for the compromise formula
on Jerusalem. Arafat also refused to withdraw the Palestinian demand for the "right of return" in return for
the compromise formula for a resolution of the refugee
problem.[20]

## NEGOTIATIONS UNDER FIRE—
## SEPTEMBER–DECEMBER 2000

The limited Palestinian-Israeli war—often (but inappro-
priately) called the "second *intifada*" or the "*al-Aqsa intifada*"—broke out on September 28. It was triggered by
the visit of Ariel Sharon (then head of the opposition) to
the Temple Mount and the ensuing Palestinian riots.

The question of responsibility for the outbreak of the
violence is as controversial as the debate over the collapse
of the negotiations. Sharon's decision to visit the Temple
Mount had more to do with his rivalry with Benjamin
Netanyahu than with a quest to embarrass Ehud Barak.
Sharon advised the government of his plan, and the government, in turn, notified the Palestinian Authority. In
the tense atmosphere of those days it was clearly an un-
called-for visit. But by the same token, there was no real
reason to respond to it with violence. Did Arafat plan the
violence in advance, as some of his Israeli critics argue?

It was apparent that Arafat had prepared for a violent confrontation for some time. The events of the "Day of the *Nakba*" in May 2000 revealed the potential violence threatening to erupt in the Israeli-Palestinian relationship. According to his own testimony, Barak had acted in the shadow of such impending violence—whether spontaneous or organized—since his election. The available evidence suggests that Arafat did not order the violence, but once it broke out he chose to mount "the tiger's back" rather than try to calm things down. He undoubtedly saw the tactical advantages offered by the new turn of events: he could extract himself from a tight diplomatic corner as the apparent culprit in the collapse of the peace process, mobilize Arab and Islamic opinion over the Temple Mount, and expect a meek Israeli response and further concessions.

The spreading of violence into Israel proper, the large-scale confrontation between the Israeli-Arab population and police, and the killing of thirteen Arab citizens of Israel added a particularly ominous dimension to the ongoing Israeli-Palestinian crisis. It took a statement by Ehud Barak that a judicial commission of inquiry would be formed to investigate the events of October to restore calm.

It was at that very same time that Hizballah tried to ignite the conflict on the Lebanese-Israeli border. Barak, as we saw, decided to ignore the new rules that he himself had set after the withdrawal from Lebanon so as not to open a third front in the midst of crisis.

During the first few weeks of this mounting crisis, several attempts to settle were made through direct Israeli-Palestinian discussions and in two international meetings, in Paris on October 4 and in Sharm al-Sheikh on October 16. Although these attempts failed, the Sharm al-Sheikh meeting did produce the Mitchell Commission. The commission, named for the former U.S. senator who headed it, was established in response to the Palestinian demand that an international commission of inquiry be formed to investigate the outbreak of violence. The mission of the Mitchell Commission was transformed by the United States and Israel into an effort to chart a course out of the crisis.

The most dramatic attempt to reach an Israeli-Palestinian cease-fire was Shimon Peres's nocturnal visit to Gaza. Barak was initially reluctant to engage his rival, Peres, but eventually yielded to public pressure. On October 31, Minister Amnon Shahak and Israel's unofficial envoy to Arafat, Yossi Ginosar, held a preparatory visit to Gaza. On November 1, Peres was accompanied to Gaza by Gilead Sher, who had in the meantime become Barak's chief of staff. Their meeting with Arafat ended with a set of understandings and a joint communiqué. Despite this, the violence continued and was in fact intensified.

In December, Barak announced his resignation. New elections for prime minister (but not the Knesset) were set for February 6, 2001. In the United States the presidential election took place on November 7, but it wasn't until five weeks later that the Supreme Court finally ratified the election of George W. Bush. During this confused global scenario, an Israeli-Palestinian conference met in Taba, Egypt. It was a last-ditch effort to reach an agreement on the eve of the Israeli elections, in which the right-wing candidate was expected to win.

## PRESIDENT CLINTON'S BRIDGING PROPOSALS

Despite the glaring failure of the Camp David conference, the negotiations continued in an effort to consolidate and formalize points of agreement. The negotiations
were not interrupted by the outbreak of violence, despite
Israel's formal refusal to negotiate under fire. On December 23, a month before the end of his term, President
Clinton took an unusual step and "laid on the table a
bridging proposal of sorts." Clinton emphasized that this
was not an American proposal but "a presentation of my
own understanding as to how an agreement could be
reached within two weeks. These ideas go off the table
once I leave the White House." According to Sher's version, Clinton's ideas concerned five areas:

1. *Borders and Territory*. Eighty percent of the settlers would
   remain in the settlement blocs annexed by Israel. Israel
   would annex 4–6 percent of the West Bank unless an
   agreement was reached on the leasing of additional territories by Israel. Israel would transfer to the Palestinians
   1–3 percent of its own territory, probably close to the
   Gaza Strip, and would provide safe passage between the
   Gaza Strip and the West Bank.
2. *Jerusalem*. The underlying idea in this issue was that Arab
   areas were to have Palestinian sovereignty and Jewish
   areas to have Israeli sovereignty. The idea would be applied to the Old City as well. A special sovereignty arrangement would be developed for the Old City and the
   larger "holy basin." The Haram al-Sharif (the Muslim
   term for the Temple Mount) would be placed under Palestinian sovereignty, while the Wailing Wall and the area
   around it would be placed under Israeli sovereignty.

3. *Security*. In order to balance Israel's security needs with the Palestinian quest for maximum sovereignty, Clinton proposed that the future Palestinian state would be "non-militarized"; the only military forces on its soil would be the Palestinian police, security services, and an international force that could not be withdrawn without Israel's consent. The IDF would continue to hold positions in the Jordan Valley for an additional period of six years, and Israel would be permitted to retain three early-warning stations in the Palestinian state's territory. The status of these stations would be reexamined after ten years. In the event of a concrete threat to Israel's national security, it would be permissible for Israel to deploy additional forces in the Jordan Valley upon notifying the international force. Arrangements would be made to negotiate the Israeli Air Force's use of Palestinian airspace. Israel would have three years to complete the evacuation of those settlements and army bases designated for evacuation.

4. *The Refugees*. The refugee settlement was governed by the notion of two states for two peoples: Israel is the homeland of the Jewish people, and Palestine is the homeland of the Palestinian people. This means that the settlement must not affect Israel's Jewish identity or its sovereign decision making in matters of immigration into the country. According to Clinton's ideas, the principle of "the right of return" would be addressed by the Palestinians' right to return to "historic Palestine" or their "homeland." With regard to the refugees' ultimate place of residence, Clinton proposed five alternatives: the Palestinian state, the territories offered by Israel as part of an exchange, the host states, third parties, and Israel proper. With regard to the first two categories, no quantitative limits would be set.

5. *End of Conflict and End of Claims.* President Clinton stated explicitly that the signing of the agreement would signify an end to the conflict, and its implementation would terminate all claims.

The Israeli cabinet held a formal discussion of Clinton's ideas and decided to respond with a "yes, but . . ." In other words, it accepted them in principle but submitted a list of reservations and proposed modifications. Arafat in turn took his time equivocating between his reluctance to respond with a blunt rejection and his unwillingness to give a positive—albeit reserved—answer.

This, then, was the state of affairs in early January, just days before the end of Clinton's presidency. Israel's relationship with the Palestinians was in crisis—negotiations were deadlocked and there was violent confrontation; Barak's coalition and government had disintegrated and were practically bound to be defeated in the February 6 elections. Diplomatically, efforts continued to negotiate an end to the violence and to establish at least a measure of political understanding, a sine qua non for a durable cease-fire. It was against this backdrop that the Taba Conference was opened on January 21, 2001.[21]

## THE TABA CONFERENCE

Within the tortuous course of events in the July 2000–January 2001 period, the Israeli-Palestinian meeting in Taba stands out as a particularly peculiar and controversial episode. Was there a chance to reach an agreement on the eve of an Israeli election in which Barak was expected to be defeated owing to the collapse of his negotiations with the same Palestinian partners and the ensuing violence? Was Arafat likely to moderate his position in this context? And what could be expected as a new president, who emphasized his intention to keep away from Clinton's legacy in the Middle East, entered the White House? Was the Taba meeting an attempt to confront the Bush administration and the new Israeli government with a fait accompli? And if so, how valid would that attempt be?

Memoirs of Israeli policy-makers depict a pathetic picture of a sinking political boat. The acting foreign minister, Shlomo Ben-Ami, shared a surprising secret with the readers of *Ha'aretz*: Ehud Barak was blackmailed by one of his ministers. "There was a minister who threatened Barak that if he failed to go to Taba, he would publicly denounce him as refraining from making peace," he wrote. Barak's chief of staff complained about the license taken by some of the Israeli participants in Taba: "In the meantime, it transpired that in other rooms Israel's positions as given orally to the heads of the delegations were being eroded."[22]

The actual course of events in Taba is equally contested. Barak's present position claims that the meeting had no importance. Gilead Sher argues that little progress was made in Taba, while Yossi Beilin claims that much was accomplished and more could have been. Beilin himself was criticized for ceding too much ground regarding "the right of return." The European Union's special emissary to the Middle East published an optimistic summary of the discussions, but it is not at all clear how he arrived at his conclusions. Political considerations led the Israeli and Palestinian delegations to publish an unusually upbeat final communiqué: "[The Taba Talks] were unprecedented with regard to the positive atmosphere . . . but given the circumstances and the time constraints, it was not possible to reach an understanding on all issues, despite the substantive progress reached in all matters under discussion. The parties declare that they were never closer to reaching an agreement."[23]

This clearly was an attempt by both parties to provide Ehud Barak with some assets for the imminent election. But in the ensuing internal Israeli debate, the argument was made that in the months following the Camp David Conference and particularly in Taba, gaps in fact were closed, and "had the negotiators had a few more days . . ." thus Yossi Beilin in a press interview.[24]

Be that as it may, if Abu Alaa and his colleagues tried to generate a sense of optimism to help Ehud Barak, Arafat certainly chose to do the opposite—and did so dramatically and effectively. He appeared with Shimon Peres at the World Economic Forum in Davos and blasted Ehud Barak and Israel's policies before international cameras, inflicting a deadly blow to the effort to salvage a ray of hope from the debris of the stormy Israeli-Palestinian negotiations.

The preceding narrative became a matter of acute controversy in the immediate aftermath of the Camp David Summit. The numerous published accounts of the collapse of the peace process and the ensuing violence fall into four main categories.

## THE ORTHODOX SCHOOL

This version can be defined as "orthodox" owing both to its early dominance and to the fact that it was first articulated by President Clinton and Prime Minister Barak. After the collapse of the Camp David Summit, Clinton broke a long-standing American diplomatic tradition and placed the blame squarely in Arafat's court. He contrasted Arafat's refusal to budge with Barak's boldness and willingness to cross red lines in order to reach an accord. Clinton later moderated his statements, either because of the criticism he received for pushing Arafat into a corner or because he wanted to preserve his position as a patron of the peace process and a leader who could communicate with both sides. But in closed forums, Clinton continued to criticize Arafat. Thus at a party held at the home of Richard Holbrook, his former ambassador to the UN, Clinton is reported to have spoken at length and freely about his failure to broker an Israeli-Palestinian agreement. According to a *Newsweek* account, Clinton, during a telephone conversation three days prior to his departure from the White House, told Arafat that he had turned Clinton into a "colossal failure" and "told Arafat that by turning down the best peace deal he was ever going to get . . . the Palestinian leader was only guaranteeing the election of the hawkish Ariel Sharon. . . . He described Arafat as an aging leader who relishes his own sense of victimhood and seems incapable of making a final peace deal. . . . Clinton also revealed that the key issue that torpedoed the talks was not the division of East Jerusalem . . . but the Palestinian demand for a 'right of return' of refugees into Israel. . . ."[25]

In contrast to Clinton, Barak intensified his public criticism of Arafat with the passage of time. He did continue to negotiate with him up until the eve of the February 2001 elections and conducted his election campaign on a platform supporting the peace process. But Barak had argued from the outset that Arafat was responsible for the

negotiations' failure. Barak justified his willingness to offer
concessions by the need to establish whether Arafat was a
genuine partner, and thus felt vindicated by the fact that
"the mask has been removed from Arafat's face." Later
Barak came to argue that Arafat was not a partner for a
negotiated settlement, that Israel should draw the conclusion and opt for a unilateral separation from the Palestinians. In Israeli journalist Ran Edelist's book *Ehud Barak
and His War against the Demons*, drawn from long conversations with Barak, the author explains that Barak felt that
he had to test whether Palestinians under Arafat's leadership were ready for a final-status agreement that would
renounce the "right of return" and would include an explicit commitment to "the end of conflict." His conclusion
at the end of the Camp David Conference was clear: Arafat does not want such an agreement and certainly did not
come to Camp David in order to conclude one.[26]

A similar version of events was presented by Shlomo
Ben-Ami, Barak's chief negotiator with the Palestinians
and eventually his acting foreign minister. Ben-Ami,
though, drew different policy conclusions from the same
interpretation. In an eloquent and revealing interview
granted to the Israeli journalist Ari Shavit, Ben-Ami
joined those who argue that Arafat did not sign the Oslo
Accords with clean hands:

> It transpired that for Arafat, Oslo was a sort of a huge camou-
> flage act behind which he has been exercising political pres-
> sure and terror in varying portions in order to undermine
> the very idea of two states for two peoples.

According to Ben Ami, the Camp David Summit and
the whole process of negotiations was doomed to failure
because of Arafat:

At the end of the day, Camp David failed because Arafat refused to make his own proposals and because he failed to
indicate to us that there was a terminal point to his demands. . . . One of the important things we did at Camp
David was to define the very core of our vital interests: To
emerge out of the deceitful discourse of Israeli politics and
to define to ourselves what was really crucial. . . . We therefore did not expect to meet the Palestinians halfway, not even
two-thirds of the way, but we expected to meet them somewhere. . . . Barak is a rational, Cartesian man and in Camp
David we found out that Arafat was a mythological man.
Today, I am of the opinion that no rational Israeli leader
could have reached an accommodation in such a meeting.
Arafat is not a leader connected to the ground, he is a religious man. . . . In Camp David it was clear that he was not
looking for practical solutions but was focused on the mythological issues: the "right of return," Jerusalem, the Temple
Mount. He is hovering in the heights of the Islamic ethos,
the ethos of refugeeism and the Palestinian ethos. . . .

Dennis Ross, the coordinator of the peace process in
the State Department (in the Clinton administration)
spoke and wrote in a similar vein on several occasions.
Soon after he left the State Department after the formation of the Bush administration, Ross granted an
interview to Clyde Haberman for the *New York Times
Magazine.*

Ross feels, writes Haberman, that "when all is said
and done . . . those negotiations failed because they ran
into a brick wall called Yasser Arafat. 'Barak was willing
to give up a lot, including virtually the entire West Bank
and sovereignty over the Temple Mount . . . He was willing to yield so much that it cost him his job in February
. . . some senior Palestinian officials were not blind to the

opportunity of statehood that was within their grasp—
I had one Palestinian negotiator say to me if we can't
do an agreement under these circumstances we ought to
be fired.' "

"Ross is convinced," Haberman proceeded, "that in his
own heart of hearts, Arafat wants peace. 'But I have come
to the conclusion that he is not capable of negotiating
an end to the conflict because what is required of him is
something he is not able to do. It is simply not in him to
go the extra yard.' "[27]

Several months later, in another press interview, Ross
elaborated further and also explained Arafat's rejection of
Clinton's bridging proposals:

> He had, frankly, an unprecedented opportunity, given the
> ideas President Clinton put on the table. He had a historic
> moment and he could not seize it . . . even though he had
> the possibility of having the essence of Palestinian needs
> being met on every issue . . . on borders, on Jerusalem, on
> security arrangements, and even of refugees, he couldn't do
> it. Now I will say he had to make some hard decisions him-
> self. Arafat had to give up one of the animating beliefs of his
> movement and that was the right of return to Israel . . . now
> in 1988 he adopted a two state solution . . . the idea of a two
> state solution and the right of return, not just to your own
> state, but to Israel: those two ideas are contradictory. . . .
>
> You had an Israeli government prepared to stretch further
> than anybody thought possible and many in Israel thought
> wise," continues Ross, "but they were prepared to live with
> it. You had an American President prepared to put his ideas
> on the table. And he also made it clear that those ideas would
> be withdrawn if they were not accepted. So I don't think you
> can recreate those circumstances so easily.[28]

In the summer of 2001 after the publication of Malley and Agha's revisionist account of events (see below), Ross spearheaded a counteroffensive. In a letter to the editor of the *New York Review of Books*, Ross wrote that he had read the piece by Malley and Agha with "some dismay." He found their account "glaring in its omission of Chairman Arafat's mistakes. One is left with the impression that only Barak did not fulfill commitments. But that is both wrong and unfair, particularly given Arafat's poor record in compliance. However, while striving to prove that the reality was far more complicated than Israel offering and Palestinians rejecting, they equate tactical mistakes with strategic errors." Clinton and Barak made mistakes, but they were not responsible for the failure to make a deal.

While Clinton and Barak rose to the occasion and took risks, says Ross, Arafat failed to respond in kind. His conduct at Camp David—and in its aftermath—cannot be explained merely by suspicion and fear of entrapment. Arafat refused to prepare for the conference, or to initiate or react during the conference, and he even went so far as to invent a new myth: that the Jewish Temple's site had not been in Jerusalem but in Nablus.

According to Ross, as the United States was about to submit bridging ideas at the end of September, Arafat refrained from restraining the outbreak of violence. He knew it was imminent and yet did nothing. In brief: "I simply do not believe he is capable of doing a permanent status deal."[29]

In March 2003, the Orthodox School was joined by an unexpected member—Prince Bandar bin Sultan, Saudi Arabia's ambassador to Washington. Speaking to Elsa

Walsh for a *New Yorker* profile, Bandar complained about Arafat's refusal to complete a deal with Barak: "Clinton ... really tried his best ... and Barak's position was so avant-garde that it was equal to Prime Minister Rabin ... it broke my heart that Arafat did not take that offer."

## THE REVISIONIST SCHOOL

This school rejects the "orthodoxy" 's main assertions. It lays the burden of responsibility for the negotiation's failure on Israel and its policies, criticizes the conduct of the negotiations by Israel and the United States, and presents the Palestinian side and its actions in a more positive light. This version is held by the Palestinians and by part of the Israeli left, but its principal articulation can be found in an essay published in the *New York Review of Books* by Robert Malley and Hussein Agha. Malley was a member of Clinton's National Security Council's staff in charge of Arab-Israeli affairs; Hussein Agha is a Lebanese intellectual living in England who had helped Abu Mazen during his negotiations with Yossi Beilin. Their essay was published in August 2001 under the title "Camp David: The Tragedy of Errors." Its main points were published in a shorter, blunter version in the *New York Times*.[30]

Malley and Agha open their essay with a statement of intent. Their purpose is to undermine the version of events at Camp David in which "Israel is said to have made a historic, generous proposal which the Palestinians once again, seizing the opportunity to miss an opportunity, turned down. In short, the failure to reach a final agreement is attributed, without notable dissent, to Yasser Arafat."

For the authors "as orthodoxies go, this is a dangerous one," because it leads to policy conclusions such as "that there is no peace partner" and that Arafat is an obstacle to a "possible end to the conflict."

In order to discredit this interpretation, Malley and Agha offer an apologetic view of Arafat's conduct and devote the bulk of their essay to criticism of Barak, his policies, and Clinton's uneven attitude to the parties when he should have been an honest broker.

Any defense of Arafat's policies at the time must deal with the argument that even if Barak did not put a clear proposal on the table in Camp David, Clinton didpresent a compromise formula on December 23 that Arafat rejected.

Thus, Malley and Agha argue, "unlike at Camp David as shown both by the time it took him to react and by the ambiguity of his reactions, Arafat thought hard before providing his response. But in the end, many of the features that troubled him in July came back to haunt him in December. As at Camp David, Arafat felt under pressure, with both Clinton and Barak announcing that the ideas would be off the table—would 'depart with the President'—unless they were accepted by both sides. With only thirty days left in Clinton's presidency and hardly more in Barak's premiership, the likelihood of reaching a deal was remote at best; if no deal could be made, the Palestinians feared they would be left with principles that were detailed enough to supersede international (UN) resolutions yet too fuzzy to constitute an agreement."

The most telling paragraph in Malley and Agha's essay is the one seeking to explain the Palestinians' passive stance at Camp David and their refusal to offer counterproposals:

For all the talk about peace and reconciliation, most Palestinians were more resigned to the two-state solution than they were willing to embrace it; they were willing to accept Israel's existence, but not its moral legitimacy. The war for the whole of Palestine was over because it had been lost. Oslo, as they saw it, was not about negotiating peace terms, but terms of surrender. Bearing this perspective in mind explains the Palestinians' view that Oslo itself is the historic compromise—an agreement to concede 78 percent of mandatory Palestine to Israel.

The Israeli version of the Revisionist School derives from two sources—the segment of the Israeli public left who hold Israel responsible for the collapse of the negotiations and for the outbreak of violence and, in a different vein, most Israeli authors of the Oslo Accords who criticize Ehud Barak for the substance of his policies as well as for his conduct of the negotiations. The latter group is quite naturally preoccupied with the argument that the events of 2000–2001 revealed deep flaws in the Oslo Accords. Their theory is twofold: the failure was the result of Barak's policy, style, and specific decisions, and the cumulative effect of Israel's policies since the mid-1990s. This criticism is sometimes tempered by mild criticism of Arafat and Palestinian policy.

The two senior figures identified with the Oslo Accords were not direct contributors to this version of the story. Shimon Peres made no secret of his criticism of Ehud Barak and his policies, or of Peres's own preference for a different approach. He did, however, refrain from coming out with a full-fledged direct critique. Yossi Beilin, a member in Barak's cabinet and a partner to his policies some of the time, offers a more complex and nuanced explanation for the failure in his book *Guide for a Wounded Dove*.[31] Unlike Peres and Beilin, Uri Savir vented his frustration with Barak and his policy in a press interview.

The most comprehensive articulation of the Israeli revisionist school can be found in Ron Pundak's essay in the British journal *Survival* under the title "From Oslo to Taba: What Went Wrong?" Pundak participated in the early phase of the Oslo negotiations together with Yair Hirschsfeld and under Yossi Beilin's supervision. He then worked for an Israeli NGO, ECF, and is presently the director of the Peres Peace Center (whose president is Uri Savir).

In his essay, Pundak states that "there was in fact an opportunity for peace, but it was squandered through miscalculations and mismanagement of the entire process." As a result of the policies conducted by Netanyahu and Barak, the Palestinian public and "street"—as reflected in the Fatah movement—reached the conclusion that "Israel did not in fact want to end the occupation and grant the Palestinian people their legitimate rights."[32]

According to Pundak, the clock began ticking toward an explosion with the expiration of the interim agreement in May 1999. The only way to avoid that explosion would have been to swiftly and seriously implement signed agreements, but "Barak failed to understand this. . . . His error was twofold: he decided not to implement the third redeployment . . . which represented the most important element in the Interim Agreement; and although he entered into permanent status negotiations currently and in good faith, he did so on the basis of a faulty basic assumption and in a dilettante fashion which caused their collapse."

Pundak agrees that the Palestinian leadership "shares considerable blame for the crisis," but like Malley and Agha, he argues that "the story of the Camp David Summit that is often told in Israel and the U.S.—of a near perfect Israeli offer which . . . Arafat lacked the courage to grasp—is too simple and misleading."

Pundak, while also critical of the Palestinians, is crystal clear with his bottom line in his conclusion: "The insincere and incomplete implementation during Netanyahu's administration and the mismanagement of permanent status negotiations under Barak were the two main obstacles to reaching an agreement."

Uri Savir's criticism in his press interview was wide ranging—from his former partner Yossi Beilin, who found a place on Barak's team, through Sharon and Netanyahu, who acted overtly against the Oslo Accords, and culminating with Ehud Barak.

> . . . Then came someone who was supposed to represent Oslo, Ehud Barak, but he was opposed to the agreement, spoke against the agreement, acted against it, wasted a year on the Syrian track and when he finally came to deal with the issue, refused to speak to the Palestinians. Barak conducted the negotiations with the Americans. . . . He acted in an arrogant fashion, no one would tolerate such behavior. . . . With regard to Camp David, there was a huge campaign of disinformation . . . and yet today the story breaks out from all directions . . . the root of the problem is our attempt to keep educating them [the Palestinians]. We left Gaza, we left the West Bank, we did not leave the occupation . . . the bulk of Palestinian society in return for genuine freedom and independence is willing to give up the bulk of the right of return. . . .[33]

## THE DETERMINISTIC SCHOOL

This position is dominated by the critics of the Oslo agreement, who tend to come from the right wing of Israeli, American, and American-Jewish politics. Those who argued as early as 1993 that the Oslo Accords were flawed, that it was a terrible mistake on Israel's part to sign them, could quite naturally argue in 2001 that the collapse of the Oslo process was predictable and in fact inevitable. This is one of the principal themes of "Oslo— The Peacemongers Return" by Norman Podhoretz, one of the American Jewish Right's most eloquent spokesmen (*Commentary*, October 2001).

Podhoretz asserts, "the inescapable conclusion reached by many (most?) Israelis was that Camp David and its violent aftermath exposed the fraudulence of Arafat's expressed desire for coexistence between Israel and a new Palestinian state. He had no intention of making peace with Israel and never had. . . . Entering into the 'peace process' had been nothing more than a change of tactics in the overall strategy of destroying Israel."

Podhoretz offers a detailed analysis of the Palestinians' tactics at Camp David and during the subsequent months. To reinforce his argument, he quotes from an (indeed puzzling) interview granted by the most prominent Palestinian leader in Jerusalem, Faysal Husseini, shortly before his death. Husseini referred to Oslo as a "Trojan horse." It, "or any other agreement, is just a temporary procedure or just a step toward something bigger," namely, the liberation of all historical Palestine from the river to the sea. "Palestine in its entirety is an Arab land, the land of the Arab nation, a land no one can sell or buy."

In a more nuanced fashion, part of Israel's national security establishment has maintained that in 1993, Arafat had not budged from the "red lines" of his own definition of what constituted a legitimate and satisfactory resolution of the Palestinian issue. According to this view, Arafat signed the Oslo agreement (and by the same token the Oslo II agreement in 1995 and the Wye Agreement in 1998) because by signing interim agreements, he was not required to cross red lines. But when it came to negotiating and signing a final-status agreement, there was no escaping the final dilemma. Since Arafat could not and would not give up his principles, the negotiation was doomed to fail. This analysis leads to conclusions similar to those of Ben Ami and Ross, but it was presented much earlier. Gilead Sher's book tells us that in the corridors of the Israeli government, this view was dubbed "The Military Intelligence's concept (or mindset)."

The chief and most consistent articulator of this view was General Amos Gilead, who, since the signing of the Oslo Accords, continued to argue that Arafat had not relinquished his four basic principles: a Palestinian state in the June 4, 1967, lines; a capital in Jerusalem; sovereignty over and control of the Temple Mount; and implementation of "the right of return." This being the case, Gilead continued, stalemate and crisis should be expected once the moment of truth (namely, final-status negotiations) came, unless Israel was willing to concede.[34]

Gilead also warned that Arafat was actually preparing for such an inevitable clash. Positions similar to those of Gilead were expressed, though less systematically, by Israel's current defense minister, Shaul Mofaz, and Israel's current chief of staff, General Moshe Ya'alom. An Israeli

journalist, Ronen Bergman, was given access to a large
volume of captured Palestinian documents, some of them
taken from Arafat's headquarters in the Muqataah. Based
on these documents Bergman wrote a book denouncing
the Palestinian Authority and its chairman's corruption
and arguing that they had no real intention of settling the
conflict with Israel.

A deterministic element can also be found on a different level, in Henry Kissinger's book *Does American Need
a Foreign Policy?*.[35] In Kissinger's view, "a conflict defined
in this manner is rarely subject to compromises—at least
not within the short time limits of an American election
year; in fact it is generally concluded by exhaustion, either
physical or psychological. It is unlikely to be settled de-
finitively by an agreement (even if there should be one).
The most realistic proposal is for a definition of coexistence. To seek to go further is to tempt violence, as was
experienced by the July 2000 Camp David Summit. . . ."

Kissinger goes on to state that "the prime obstacle to
culmination of the peace diplomacy is the differing con-
ceptions of it held by the parties. Israeli and American
leaders define peace as a normality that ends claims and
determines a permanent legal status—in other words
they apply the concepts of twentieth century liberal democracy. But the Arabs and especially the Palestinians
consider the very existence of Israel an intrusion into
'Holy' Arab territory. They may accept territorial compromises for lack of a better alternative, but they will
treat it in the same way that France acquiesced in the Ger-
man annexation of Alsace-Lorraine in 1870—as a necessity leavened by the determination to regain what has
been lost (to be fair, sacred rhetoric has been part of the

Israeli discourse as well—for example regarding the indivisibility of Jerusalem)."

Having reviewed the history of Israeli-Arab peacemaking, Kissinger notes that "once Arab-Israeli negotiations reached the subject of Palestine, however, the different perceptions of peace emerged as a nearly insuperable obstacle. . . . in the negotiations with the Palestinians the Israeli perception of peace became like a mirage that evaporates the more one appears to approach it. . . . After Ehud Barak had made concessions inconceivable by any previous Israeli Prime Minister . . . Arafat found it impossible to accept the Israeli *quid pro quo* without inflaming his own constituencies. Another obstacle was the Israeli insistence that, after regaining the offered territories, the Palestinians would make no further demands. However reasonable that might sound to Americans and Israelis, Arafat shrank from its finality. He might have been willing to defer some demands for quite some time, but he could not bring himself to abandon them altogether and forever."

Kissinger supplemented these pessimistic fundamental observations with a critical analysis of Clinton's and Barak's policy during the year preceding the Camp David Conference, during the conference itself, and in its aftermath. He characterizes the relationship between the two leaders as a "symbiotic psychological analysis," in which Clinton was exercising pressure in order to extract concessions and Barak was anxious to demonstrate Israel's cooperation. Kissinger agrees with the decision to relinquish the phased approach but criticizes the sense of urgency and eagerness displayed by both Washington and Jerusalem. This conduct, in turn, served only to whet the appetite of Yasser Arafat, who found Israel's insistence on finality and end of claims unacceptable. Camp David thus became "a dialogue of the deaf."

## THE ECLECTIC SCHOOL

This category refers to a number of authors who, for various reasons, refrained from expressing the distinctive and pointed judgments that would have placed them in one of the first three categories. One such author is Yossi Beilin, whose book *A Handbook for a Wounded Dove* is marked by dissonance. The book is dedicated to Ehud Barak, "who acted boldly for peace," but Beilin is in fact critical of Barak's actual conduct and policies. The book was published soon after the February 2001 elections. As time went by and Barak escalated his criticism of Arafat, Beilin drew further from him and became more critical.

Another critic who can be placed in the same category is Dr. Menachem Klein. His book, *Breaking a Taboo*, deals primarily with the specific effort to resolve the issue of Jerusalem. But in his book and press interviews granted at the time of its publication, two larger themes were also given prominence: criticism of Israel's two senior negotiators, Barak and Ben-Ami (Klein served as adviser to the latter), and the idea that the "*al'Aqsa intifada*" had a significant intra-Palestinian dimension which was the product of frustration and antagonism directed at the corrupt, authoritarian leadership that had been accumulating since 1994. Klein subsequently applied Darby and MacGinxy's model for analyzing peace processes, and demonstrates that most of the criteria they identified as determining success (in South Africa and Northern Ireland) are absent

from the Israeli-Palestinian conflict. Thus, in a "deterministic" mood, Klein implies that the Israeli-Palestinian
negotiation was doomed to failure.[36]

Ironically, the memoir published by Gilead Sher—
Ehud Barak's confidant, negotiator, and, briefly, chief of
staff—can also be placed in the eclectic school. Sher's
book offers a detailed "Sher version" very different from
a "Barak version" and is critical of several of the principal
Israeli actors, including Barak. Sher's book is an invalu-
able source for the history of this period but does not
offer a clear-cut thesis.

In the coming months and years several important memoirs can be expected—by President Clinton and Secretary
of State Albright, by Dennis Ross and Martin Indyk, and
by Shlomo Ben Ami—and that will undoubtedly alter our
perspective. At this point, the following integrated analysis of the events of the summer of 2000 can be offered.

Ehud Barak presented to the Palestinians a far-reaching offer that could serve as the basis for a mutually
acceptable final-status agreement. It cannot be argued
that there was no "real" or "binding" offer; after all,
even if the offer was not made in this fashion at Camp
David, it was laid on the table in a clear and concrete
manner through President Clinton's bridging proposal in
December.

There were undoubtedly significant flaws in the conduct of the negotiations by Israel and the United States.
The Camp David Conference convened without adequate preparation and was held too close to the U.S. presidential election. In the circumstances surrounding the

summer of 2000, a final-status agreement was simply not within reach. It would have been preferable to prepare another interim agreement as a fallback option—or at least an exit strategy.

Ehud Barak's sense that the negotiating parties were on a collision course was truly perceptive. He was right to try to establish whether Arafat was a sincere partner in brokering a final-status agreement. However, once he found out that Arafat was not, Barak's adoption of an "all or nothing" approach was erroneous. Also, by arguing that he "tore the mask off his [Arafat's] face," he cast a shadow on the sincerity of his own (genuine) quest for a definitive agreement.

Yasser Arafat failed the test of statesmanship. A statesman is defined by his ability to read correctly the trends of unfolding history, to make the right decisions in that context and to build the requisite support for implementing those decisions. If Arafat had been guided primarily by the desire to establish a Palestinian state on reasonable terms, he should have exploited the "window of opportunity" that was opened between July and December 2000. There is no way to ascertain the veracity of the claims of Shlomo Ben-Ami and Dennis Ross, who argue that Arafat failed to "cross the Rubicon" for lack of will or capacity. Regardless, Arafat's conduct can be explained without reference to this underlying question.

It is certain that Arafat's and his associates' concept of the time dimension in Arab-Israeli relations changed between August 1993 and July 2000. In 1993, and through the mid-1990s, they acted on the assumption that for the first time in decades time was on Israel's side. This change in perspective derived from several developments: the collapse of the Soviet Union, the U.S. victory in the Cold War, the first Gulf War, and the wave of immigration to Israel from the former Soviet Union.

But by the decade's end, perspective had changed again. The impact of the dramatic events of the late '80s and early '90s faded. The United States acted softly in its conduct toward Iraq, Syria, and the Palestinians, and the demographic gap between Palestinians and Israelis was reopened.

The Israel of the late 1990s was perceived by many Palestinians as a rich, soft society that had lost the will to fight. Leafing through the Israeli press of the period, one is easily impressed by the meek and passive response to daily break-ins or car thefts. A. B. Yehoshua's *The Liberating Daughter-in-Law*, a novel dealing with Arab-Israeli and Palestinian-Israeli relations, offers a vivid literary expression of the encounter between an eager, hungry society and a soft, tired one.

In this context two events assumed a particular significance. One was the Hasmonean Tunnel crisis in September 1996, when a few days of rioting and shooting transformed Netanyahu's attitude toward Arafat. Another was Israel's unilateral withdrawal from Lebanon in the spring of 2000. Hizballah, Iran, and many Palestinians drew the lesson that it was wrong to make concessions to Israel; that Israel, when confronted with durable opposition, will blink first. This sensibility was reinforced by the Israeli-Palestinian negotiations of 2000, often described as a journey in which Israel made most of the concessions and at a rapid pace without adequate reciprocity. If Israeli moved within such a brief span of time from 66 percent to nearly 100 percent, why not keep pressing for additional concessions? And why conclude a complex final-status agreement with an outgoing U.S. president and an Israeli prime minister who had lost his coalition?

The effort to reach an Israeli-Palestinian agreement was also set back by the interplay between the Syrian and Palestinian tracks as it developed in 2000. The United States and Israel spent too much time in a futile effort to come to terms with Hafez al-Assad and were late to arrive at a crucial phase in the negotiation with the Palestinians. By that point, Clinton was too close to the end of his term and Barak had lost his coalition. The fact that Assad rebuffed Clinton's gambit in Geneva and did so with impunity was not lost on Arafat and emboldened him to do the same four months later. Israel's willingness to accept the principle of withdrawal to the lines of June 4, 1967, on the Syrian front reinforced the Palestinian demand for a full withdrawal in the West Bank. If Israel believed that the Palestinian case was different from those of its neighboring Arab states, it should have been clear and assertive in formulating its position. A single attempt, by the government's legal adviser, to argue that Security Council Resolution 242 did not apply to the territory of Mandate Palestine ended lamely. An Israeli claim for a portion of the West Bank should have been predicated on a sound basis.

Israel also erred in accepting the very term "right of return" as a legitimate part of the vocabulary used to address the refugee problem during the effort to reach a final-status agreement. There can be no final-status agreement without a mutually acceptable formula regarding refugees. The formula included in Clinton's bridging proposals of December 2000 may well be or come close to being the "magic formula." But by accepting this term, Israel acquiesces implicitly in the Palestinian and Arab claim of an "original sin" and leaves the door open for fresh demands in the future. In the conduct of negotiations, it is important to be flexible and inventive at most times, but it is equally important for both sides to clarify what their red lines are.

# 5

# SHARON, BUSH, AND ARAFAT

At the core of this chapter lie three interlocking personal-political narratives. The first belongs to Ariel Sharon, whose passage from marginality and controversy to the center of Israeli politics brought him to a point where choices that ran against the grain of his biography had to be made. The second is that of Yasser Arafat, who for thirty-five years had been successful in building and keeping for himself the position of both symbol and interpreter of Palestinian nationalism. Throughout this period he was able to impose his vision of the goals of that nationalism, discarding several opportunities to settle for less. The years 2000–2003 put that personal role into particularly stark relief. And the third is that of George W. Bush, who began his presidency reluctant to deal with Arab-Israeli affairs but soon found himself immersed in the politics of the Middle East and in the effort to resolve the Palestinian-Israeli conflict.

Ariel Sharon became the sixth Israeli prime minister within a decade who sought to grapple with the dual challenge of managing both the Israeli political system and Israel's relationship with the Arab world. Of those predecessors, Yitzhak Rabin was assassinated by an Israeli fanatic and the four other prime ministers—Yitzhak Shamir, Shimon Peres, Benjamin Netanyahu, and Ehud Barak—were all defeated at the ballot box.

The very fact of Sharon's election and subsequent three years in office as prime minister provides several layers of significance and irony. Sharon, who for decades had been knocking on the inner doors of Israel's political establishment, finally reached the ultimate position of power when he defeated Ehud Barak on February 6, 2001, winning 62.38 percent of the vote under the slogan "Sharon alone will bring peace." This was the culmination of a political career for the officer-politician, who had once failed to become chief of staff of the IDF and was removed from the post of minister of defense. Sharon's election was the product of the failure of Barak's policy and the ensuing crisis of the Israeli left and moderate left, his own political skills, and his cunning exploitation of Benjamin Netanyahu's miscalculations. After six years of leadership by two prime ministers who represented a new generation and a new style in Israeli politics, power shifted back to a member of the 1948 generation.

Sharon, whose visit to the Temple Mount had sparked the outbreak of the "al-Aqsa intifada," now obtained from the Israeli public a sweeping mandate to end the intifada and restore normal life in Israel. Sharon came into office as the patron of the West Bank settlements, possessed of a distinctive concept of Israeli national and national security agendas.[1] He had the aura of a bold, creative military commander from the 1950s and 1960s—the general who had also quelled Palestinian violence in Gaza in the early 1970s and crossed the Suez Canal in October 1973. Sharon viewed the Arab-Israeli conflict in terms of a war against terrorism, often referring to "a century of Arab terrorism." He believed in diplomacy backed by force and power, and was opposed to the Oslo Accords and to the course they charted for Israel.

But a pragmatic strand could also be identified in Sharon's career. This pragmatism was manifested in his role in the evacuation of the Israeli settlements in the northern Sinai (as Menachem Begin's defense minister); in the signing of the Wye River Agreement in October 1998 (as Netanyahu's foreign minister); and when, true to his preelection promise, he formed a national-unity government and made Shimon Peres—the man most identified with the Oslo Accords—his chief partner.

Shortly after his coming to power, it became clear that although Sharon had no magic formula himself for defeating the Palestinians, he would still check the efforts of his foreign minister (Peres) to reach an interim agreement with the Palestinian Authority. Sharon's proclivity for radical choices was checked by two principal considerations: his determination to preserve the partnership with the Labor Party in the National Unity Government, and the constraints imposed by Israel's international relations—primarily the relationship with the United States. As a consequence of this dynamic, Sharon was ironically positioned in the middle of the political spectrum, on the one hand restraining the extreme right wing's pressure to conduct an all-out war against the Palestinian Authority, and on the other hand blocking (at least temporarily) a return to negotiations.

Every so often, Sharon spoke of his readiness for "painful concessions" at the right time and of accepting the idea of a Palestinian state—without elaborating on its size and character. This rhetoric has not yet been tested, and the question remains as to whether Sharon has a vision for resolving the long-festering conflict, or whether he feigns a conciliatory posture as a sophisticated strategy for preserving his legacy and his government. Regardless, the man who for many years had been perceived as a fighter, leader of Israel's radical right, advocate of radical change and power-oriented thinking—a leader who "does not stop at the red light"[2]—was able to transform himself into the patriarch of Israeli politics. He managed this by both ably navigating Israel's political currents and building a close and effective relationship with the Bush administration. In January 2003, despite continuing violent confrontations with the Palestinians and a lingering economic crisis, Sharon was reelected by a huge majority, owing largely to two perceptions held by the Israeli public: that Arafat was not a credible partner for a political settlement, and that Sharon was unusually successful in managing what was seen as Israel's most important relationship—with the United States.

## THE BUSH ADMINISTRATION
## AND THE MIDDLE EAST

George W. Bush's election to the presidency and the formation of his administration, combined with the collapse of the peace process, the outbreak of the "second *intifada*," and Ariel Sharon's election in February 2001, changed the landscape of Arab-Israeli relations dramatically.

When Bill Clinton replaced George Bush in the White House, he chose to adopt the essence of George Bush's Middle Eastern policy—"dual containment" vis-à-vis Iran and Iraq and the "Madrid framework" to promote an Arab-Israeli settlement. Eight years later, George W. Bush and his team did their utmost to disown Clinton's legacy. The new administration made it abundantly clear that it had no intention of becoming immersed in Israeli-Palestinian peacemaking. The Bush administration believed America's efforts in the Middle East should be invested in the region's eastern flank, where the job—begun in Iraq in 1990—had yet to be completed. Iraq and Iran, they felt, should be denied access to weapons of mass destruction. This was a goal that could most likely not be reached without regime change in both countries. This new trend in the administration was demonstrated bluntly in a directive issued by Secretary of State Colin Powell to his subordinates: they were no longer to use the term "peace process"—a term that was particularly current (and somewhat overused) in the vocabulary of the Clinton administration. The post of special Middle East coordinator was abolished, the term "peace process" was discarded, and the conduct of the State Department's Middle Eastern policy shifted back to the Bureau of Near Eastern Affairs.

If Yasser Arafat and other Arab leaders had expected the new president to distance himself from Israel and draw closer to the Arab world, they were disappointed. The forty-first president had been tied to Republican groups identified with "Arabist" policies, oil interests, and oil-producing Arab countries, all with a view of the Middle East that perceived Israel as an obstacle to a natural friendship with most of the Arab world. His son, however, was connected to other Republican groups—namely, the party's conservative right wing and fundamentalist Christians—who were very supportive of Israel. And with Bush having barely won the election of 2000, the new president and his advisers were particularly mindful of the "Jewish vote."

Elected shortly after George W. Bush, Ariel Sharon skillfully exploited these trends in the administration and built a good rapport with the new president and his staff. But this auspicious beginning was replaced by a more complex relationship during Bush's first months in office. Some of Washington's traditional Arab friends, headed by Saudi Arabia, began to exert pressure on the administration to distance itself from Israel, publicize its criticism of Israel's policy toward the Palestinians, and become more actively involved in efforts to resolve the Israeli-Palestinian conflict. Their argument was quite familiar: a policy that is perceived as pro-Israeli undermines America's position in the Middle East and threatens the stability of "moderate" regimes—regimes already hard put to deal with an agitated Arab "street" galvanized by images of Israeli-Palestinian violence broadcast by the ubiquitous Arab satellite television channels.

Under this pressure in the early summer of 2001, the Bush administration took a series of measures designed to demonstrate some distancing from Israel, a rapprochement with Washington's traditional Arab friends, and support for the idea of a Palestinian state. During Sharon's visit to Washington in June 2001, the White House made a special effort to display a measure of tension in its relationship with Israel.

These trends, however, were suddenly both checked and reversed by al-Qaeda's terrorist attack on September 11, 2001. The "war on terror" became not just a major but the "defining" issue on the administration's agenda. A presidency that was initially seen as passive and unfocused was immediately transformed. George W. Bush began to radiate leadership, turning crisis and adversity to his advantage. Prior to September 11, his tendency to reduce a complex reality into black-and-white issues had been seen as a flaw; this now proved most useful as a huge public had to be mobilized for the struggle against an unfamiliar and ill-defined enemy.

The interplay between this development after September 11 and Washington's policy toward the lingering Israeli-Palestinian conflict was complex. The emergence of the war on terror as the major issue on America's national agenda immediately generated a debate between two distinct schools. The first argued that Palestinian terrorism and al-Qaeda's terrorism were of the same family, even if a direct organizational or operational link did not exist between them. Therefore, now that the United States had been attacked by a terrorist organization, it should understand the nature of the challenge Israel faces. It should be clear that the attack made on the United States by a group of Arab-Muslim terrorists was unrelated to its support for Israel. Israel and the Palestinian issue were occasionally mentioned by al-Qaeda's leaders, but the organization's hostility to the United States was rooted in its hatred of the Egyptian and Saudi regimes buttressed by the United

States, in its opposition to the presence of the American military in the Arabian Peninsula, and, broadly speaking, in radical Islam's grudge against the West and the leader and embodiment of the West—America.

The other school of thought produced by September 11 was a near mirror image of these arguments—that is, there is no comparison nor connection between terrorist acts perpetrated by al-Qaeda and those that represent the Palestinian "struggle for national liberation"; that there is no doubting the fact that the United States' support for Israel is a major source of anger and restlessness in the Arab world, and of the rage directed at Washington; and that there are no inherent reasons for anti-Americanism in the world of Islam. The supposition is therefore that, once the United States ceases its sweeping support of Israel, it should be able to establish sound relations with Muslim states.

The debate soon shifted from the theoretical to the practical level. The Bush administration began to plan a military campaign in Afghanistan, and the planning process raised numerous tactical questions. Did the United States want to build a coalition similar to the one assembled in 1990? If so, what Arab states could be expected to join it and what would the United States expect of them? Direct participation or logistical and political support, or both? And what could be done to avoid popular protest in the Arab world when the United States attacked a Muslim country such as Afghanistan, and possibly, at a second stage, an Arab country like Iraq?[3]

The early phase in the planning of the campaign in Afghanistan placed Israel in an awkward position. The Bush administration was clearly not interested in Israel as

a partner in the campaign, nor did it wish to have an Israeli association in the attack on a Muslim country. At the
same time, the United States was seeking the cooperation
of states like Iran and Syria and of the Palestinian Authority—all seen by Israel (and many others) as intimately
linked to terrorist networks and activities. From the Bush
administration's point of view, at that stage, everything
was subordinate to the success of the anticipated military
campaign. The administration tried to gloss over the inherent contradictions and dissonance of that policy by
drawing a distinction between "local terrorism" and "terrorism with a global reach." In other words, a suicide
bombing in the Israeli town of Netanya was a "local"
event, while an attack on New York or Washington was a
"global" matter.

The Bush administration also decided to move forward
with some of the measures discussed earlier in the summer to obtain the Arab world's cooperation or at least a
calm atmosphere in the "Arab street." In early October
2001, Secretary of State Powell let it be known that he
was contemplating when and how the U.S. plan for an
Israeli-Palestinian settlement should be publicly introduced. Originally, it was to be brought to the UN's
General Assembly in September, but that gathering was
postponed owing to the events of September 11. The
U.S. plan was reportedly designed to manifest support for
the idea of a Palestinian state, and to address the major
final-status issues: borders, Jerusalem, and "the right of
return."

Powell's intimation provoked a particularly sharp response from Sharon. On October 6, he called upon the
"Western states" to learn a lesson from the failure of the

"appeasement policy toward Germany on the eve of World War II," and asserted, "Israel will not be [a second] Czechoslovakia." The White House was irritated by the allusion to Neville Chamberlain but chose to refrain from a public retort.[4]

In any event, this phase ended swiftly. The United States reached the conclusion that its military and technological capabilities were such that it could topple the Taliban regime in Afghanistan without the help of Middle Eastern allies. Furthermore, alarm bells notwithstanding, there were no signs of agitation in the "Arab street." As the military campaign in Afghanistan was unfolding successfully and the administration's self-confidence continued to grow, some voices in the Pentagon began to mention transitioning to the second and third phases of the "war on terror." Tension between the United States and the Arab world now centered on two issues: (1) which Arab state or states could become a target in the next phase (Iraq, Syria, and Yemen were all mentioned); and (2) the American anger—both official and public—directed at Egypt and Saudi Arabia for the roles Egyptian and Saudi nationals had played on September 11. These developments facilitated a mending of fences between Bush and Sharon and contributed to the decision to delay publication of the American plan Powell had first mentioned in October 2001.

Yasser Arafat's growing identification with "the other side" in the war on terror reinforced this dynamic. In the immediate aftermath of September 11, Arafat made a series of moves designed to placate American opinion, denouncing the attack and publishing repeated public directives to cease fire against Israel. But as time went by, these efforts petered out. Attacks on Israel—including suicide attacks—continued, and the distinction between "local" terrorism and "terrorism with a global reach" began to lose its significance. The Israeli capture in January 2002 of *Karin A*, a ship carrying weapons from Iran to Gaza, was of particular importance. It clearly was an event of "global reach" and therefore a great embarrassment to Arafat, who began by denying any connection to the ship and ended by informing the secretary of state that, as president of the Palestinian Authority, he would take responsibility. On other occasions, Israel and the U.S. intelligence community provided President Bush with evidence linking Arafat directly to the financing of specific terrorist acts. These occurrences were all important links in the chain of events leading President Bush to the conclusion that unless Arafat was removed from power, there would be no prospect for a political settlement.

On June 24, 2002, President Bush presented the U.S. plan for an Israeli-Palestinian settlement. He was the harbinger of good news in the long term for the Palestinians: the plan outlined the establishment of a Palestinian state alongside Israel; Israeli withdrawal; and resolution of the major issues of borders, Jerusalem, and refugees through a final-status agreement. Bush also reiterated Washington's commitment to the Mitchell Commission's plan that once progress was achieved regarding Israeli security, the IDF would be required to withdraw to pre–September 28 lines, and that in any event, Israel should stop all settlement activity in "occupied territories." But in the short term, the main challenge belonged to the Palestinians: they should halt and fight terrorism, as well as replace their current leadership. "In order to achieve peace and for a Palestinian state to be established, a different leadership is required. I call upon the Palestinian people to choose new leaders who do not compromise on the issue of terror," said Bush. He went on to anchor his statement in a position associated with both American and Israeli conservative right wings. Bush asserted that the emergence of a viable Palestinian state depended on fundamental rather than cosmetic changes, meaning a democratic government, a market economy, and opposition to terror. In practical terms, he drew a distinction between the establishment of a Palestinian state, whose borders and other aspects of sovereignty would be provisional, and subsequent permanent arrangements.

The course of events can now be reviewed and analyzed against this backdrop in four major areas: the Israeli-Palestinian war of attrition; the attempts to reach a settlement; the road to war and the war in Iraq; and the effort to renew the Israeli-Palestinian negotiations in its aftermath.

## THE PALESTINIAN-ISRAELI
## WAR OF ATTRITION

The term *intifada* implies a spontaneous popular uprising. A spontaneous element can, indeed, be discerned in the violent confrontation that erupted between Israel and the Palestinians in late September 2000, as well as popular anger and criticism at the Palestinian Authority. But the confrontation was quickly transformed into an organized campaign orchestrated (at least in part) by the Palestinian Authority. With the passage of time, the Palestinian Authority lost both power and authority to the radical opposition and to local groups. The outbreak of violence pitted the Palestinians, who sought to extract additional concessions, against an Israel determined to show that its resolve had not been eroded and to use its overwhelming military advantage for a clear victory. The conflict has so far unfolded through six phases.

The first phase, during the fall of 2000, lasted for several weeks. It was characterized by such distinctive manifestations of a popular uprising as demonstrations and marches toward Israeli roadblocks. But the calculated use of firearms was integrated into these activities in order to provoke an Israeli response as well as create casualties. Israel was, in fact, well prepared for this initiative, having predicted it by intelligence assessments, and the IDF correctly applied the lessons derived from the violent clashes in September 1996. During this early phase, Israel suffered a small number of casualties; the Palestinians' casualty rate was high. This had two principal outcomes: (1) significant improvement in the international standing of the Palestinians, who were once again perceived as victims and the weaker party to the conflict, rather than as the political party that had just rejected Israel's offers at Camp David; and (2) increased Palestinian motivation to press on and escalate the combat.

During the second phase, which began at the end of 2000, manifestations of Palestinian "popular resistance" were virtually abandoned and the conflict began to be conducted between two armed (though uneven) entities. Among the Palestinians, two main groups emerged. The first included the radical Islamic groups Hamas and Islamic Jihad, later joined by the Popular Front for the Liberation of Palestine. This group sought to undermine the

quest for a settlement by initiating attacks—including suicide bombings—in Israel proper. The second group, led
by the Tanzim (a radical offshoot of the Fatah), focused
their activities in the West Bank and Gaza, attacking both
the IDF and Jewish settlers. Their definition of victory
was a settlement on their terms. The distinction between
these two groups remained clear until the spring of 2001.

In the third phase of the conflict, which can be placed
in the second half of 2001, the distinction between these
two Palestinian groups became increasingly blurred. This
change reflected a new approach from Arafat and his
associates. The quest for improved terms in a negotiated
settlement was replaced by the assessment that the Palestinians could drive Israel by force from the West Bank
and Gaza, without relinquishing the notion of a two-state
solution. Escalation on the Palestinian side bred corres-
ponding escalation of Israel's activities, including incur-
sions into Arab territories, "targeted assassinations," and
longer stays in Arab territories. Still, as prime minister,
Sharon displayed an unexpected degree of pragmatism
and restraint. This restraint stemmed from the considerations mentioned above—his sense of ultimate responsibility, his partnership with the Labor Party, the importance
of Israel's relationship with Washington—as well as from
Sharon's reluctance to play into the Palestinians' attempts
to "internationalize" the conflict by inviting the European Union or the UN to play an active role or seek an
imposed solution.

The fourth phase was defined by the terrorist attack on
the United States on September 11, 2001, and the wave
of attacks inside Israel in the spring of 2002. The events

of September 11, America's declaration of a war on terror, and the central position assigned to the issue of terrorism on the international agenda all had a complex impact on the Palestinian-Israeli war. Yasser Arafat and his associates immediately (and correctly) sensed that it was important to establish a clear distinction between their war against Israel and organizations such as al-Qaeda and Hizballah that were seen by the United States as the chief instruments of "international terrorism." This Palestinian recognition, however, was not consistently applied in practice.

Arafat did initially act to lessen the violence in the Palestinian-Israeli conflict, but only to limited effect. To begin with, he failed to impose his authority on the Islamic organizations. Israel, in turn, felt that the weakening of Arafat's position (and, more broadly, the Palestinian position) enhanced its freedom of action. It thus chose to eliminate Raid Karmi, the head of the Tanzim in Tul Karam, on January 14. After a comparatively long lull, this decision renewed the radical groups' quest to heighten the escalation.

The fifth phase of the conflict unfolded from late March 2002 to December 2002. A wave of suicide bombings led to an Israeli counteroffensive that culminated in two massive operations: "Defensive Shield" and "Determined Way." The Israeli offensive resulted in renewed control over most of the West Bank, and emasculated the control and presence of the Palestinian Authority in the region. Israel refrained from reoccupying the main cities and chose instead to dispatch army units for longer stays. The Palestinian Authority's physical emasculation was notably demonstrated in the virtual destruction of the Muqataah, Arafat's headquarters. Israel was less active in the Gaza Strip. The security fence separating the Gaza Strip from Israel proved very effective in preventing suicide bombings. Even if Israel had contemplated military action in Gaza, it was deterred by the difficulty of operating in one of the world's most densely populated areas.

Israel's consistent pressure reduced the operational capacity of the terrorist groups, but their residual capabilities allowed them to continue occasional suicide bombings and other attacks. The level of violence was kept below that of March 2002, but even this volume sufficed to keep the conflict going and exact a heavy price from both societies. The virtual collapse of the Palestinian Authority and the renewal of Israeli military control over most of the West Bank raised the question of whether it might be necessary to rebuild the Israeli military administration, previously dismantled with the implementation of the Oslo Accords. Thus far, Israel has not been forced to make a decision regarding this complex matter. International aid organizations and the remnants of the Palestinian Authority's apparatus provide the population with a minimum level of service. The sixth and current phase is described in the final part of this chapter.

In Israel, the continuing conflict has created growing pressure for "separation" from the Palestinians—a fence between the two societies—in both the territorial and the physical sense of the term. As a rule, Israel's right wing has opposed the construction of a fence along the "green line" (on the pre-1967 maps), arguing that it would be tantamount to a renunciation of Israel's claim to the West Bank (or at least a sizable portion of it). The net result of this counterpressure was slowly paced construction along segments of the green line.

Meanwhile, criticism of Yasser Arafat and the Palestinian Authority intensified among the Palestinians. The familiar complaints of corruption and arbitrary government were reinforced by the public critique of a strategy that was exacting a high cost from society, leading to the loss of autonomous rule, and that seemed to go nowhere. One particularly strident example of such criticism was the speech Mahmud Abbas (Abu Mazen) delivered in a closed session in mid-November 2002. The text, eventually made public and published in the Arab press, included statements such as the following:

> ... We should have sat down to the negotiations table and pushed him [Sharon] to a corner where we are more able to act than he is, rather than allowing him to drag us into an arena in which he excels and outshines not only us but the entire Arab world, namely that of military power and the force of arms.[5]

Demands by Palestinian intellectuals and political activists for an end to the authoritarianism and corruption of Yasser Arafat and the Palestinian Authority preceded the Bush administration's own demand (in June 2002) for Palestinian reform and for Arafat's removal from power. In fact, the pressure the United States exerted actually played into Arafat's hands. Arafat was adroit enough to both evade it and exploit it to embarrass his critics (who, he charged, were accomplices of the Bush administration). One critic, Dr. Khalil Shikadi, a political scientist and pollster from Nablus, vented his exasperation in a *New York Times* op-ed piece entitled "How to Reform Palestinian Politics":

> If you were Mr. Arafat, you would certainly have no incentive to step down. After all, he would be doing nothing more than leaving his people with a despicably corrupt and rightly friendless Palestinian Authority, keeping for himself only a political farewell colored by shameful defeat. He might also be leaving his people to the mercies of a politically strengthened fundamentalism. These do not have to be our alternatives. Mr. Arafat does need to give up some power and a great many Palestinians want him to. But neither he nor they will yield to curt demands from Washington or anywhere else.[6]

## THE ONGOING QUEST
## FOR A SETTLEMENT

Efforts to establish a cease-fire and to renew the Israeli-Palestinian negotiation did continue under the shadow of the violent conflict, albeit in an intermittent and indeterminate fashion. But these efforts were doomed throughout this period. Sharon's concept of a settlement was modest. He was determined to replace the terms established by the negotiation of 2000 with a framework that was acceptable to parts of the Israeli right wing, and preferred to obtain such a settlement after a clear victory. Arafat, in turn, insisted on finding hope within the ebb and flow of the Israeli-Palestinian conflict and was not willing to offer the concessions that would have forced Sharon's hand.

Furthermore, it became quite evident during the latter half of 2002 and the early months of 2003 that the Bush administration was determined to go to war against Iraq. It was therefore widely assumed that a serious effort to seek a political solution to the Palestinian-Israeli war would have to wait for the larger changes in the region that could be expected in the war's aftermath.

The quest for settlement during this period was pushed forward by four principal actors: Shimon Peres, as foreign minister in the National Unity Government, along with a small part of the Israeli political spectrum holding on to the idea that a settlement was still feasible and still Israel's best option; the UN, a number of European states led by France, and, to some extent, the State Department; Arab states such as Egypt, Jordan, and Saudi Arabia; and that segment of the Palestinian political establishment which felt that the armed struggle had failed and that the public was paying an unacceptable price for the continuation of a futile effort.

The quest for settlement was resisted by an array of both vocal and tacit opponents. At the height of its success, the Palestinian radical camp was swept into believing in its ability to expel Israel from the West Bank and Gaza; a larger number of Palestinian militants sought more temperate goals, hoping to wear Israel down or garner enough support for an imposed settlement in the international arena. Israel's right wing argued in a number of different ways that the events of 2000–2002 demonstrated the failure of the "Oslo Concept," that there was no point in renewing the negotiations and certainly not within the Oslo framework, and that in any event it was essential for Israel to emerge victorious from the confrontation initiated by the Palestinians. The Bush administration, as will be described below, did not speak in a single voice nor pursue a coherent line.

What mattered most, however, was Yasser Arafat's failure to cope effectively with the cardinal importance George W. Bush assigned to the "war on terror" after September 11. As we saw, a series of mistakes by Arafat led the president and several of his aides to view him as part of "the terror camp," and to endorse Sharon's view that he was not a legitimate partner for a renewed negotiation.

During 2001 and 2002, four main efforts were made to reach a cease-fire or an agreement. The first was a U.S.-led effort to find a formula for a cease-fire and the resumption of the negotiations. This effort began with an international commission formed after the Sharm al-Sheikh conference of October 2000, headed by Senator George Mitchell (whose report was submitted in May 2001). It was continued by the director of the CIA, George Tenet, who in June 2001 had submitted a "recipe" for achieving a cease-fire and renewing Israeli-Palestinian security coordination, and had culminated in the appointment of General Anthony Zinni as a special envoy.

The Mitchell Commission was a well-balanced group whose report analyzed the crisis of late September and offered a reasonable scenario for ending it. George Tenet's mission had been predicated on the experience and credit assembled by the CIA in the 1990s when it helped build the Palestinian security services and mechanisms for coordinating with their Israeli counterparts. General Zinni was expected to translate his predecessors' recommendations into an actual course of action. All three efforts were essentially technical in nature, rather than a quest for a fundamental, political resolution. These were to end violence, renew security coordination, get the IDF to withdraw from the positions captured after September 28, 2000, and (in a more political vein) halt new settlement activity by Israel. His mission collapsed in March 2002 under the wave of Palestinian suicide bombings in several Israeli cities. It was not until June 2002 that President Bush presented a comprehensive plan for an Israeli-Palestinian settlement.

The second main effort was the negotiation conducted between Shimon Peres and Abu Alaa throughout 2001 in an attempt to reach an interim agreement that would be linked to an ensuing permanent-status negotiation. In December, the "Peres–Abu Alaa Understandings" were assembled. The main points were these: cease-fire within six weeks; Israeli recognition of a Palestinian state of over 40 percent of the West Bank; and a negotiation on final-status issues to be completed within one year and implemented within two.

It is not known how much support Abu Alaa had for this plan, but Sharon, who had authorized his foreign minister's give-and-take with Abu Alaa, rejected out of hand the product of their negotiations, in public on December 23, 2001.[7] Sharon was not opposed to the linkage to a final-status negotiation nor to the notion of a Palestinian state. But he had in mind a slower pace and a more modest concept of a future Palestinian state.

Third, in February 2002, Prince Abdullah, Saudi Arabia's crown prince and virtual ruler, came out with a Saudi initiative that offered a simple formula for a comprehensive Arab-Israeli settlement: full Israeli withdrawal to the lines of June 4, 1967, in return for full peace and normalization. His initiative reflected the growing anxiety of Arab states such as Saudi Arabia, Jordan, and Egypt that the lingering Israeli-Palestinian conflict would undermine their stability. It also demonstrated Saudi Arabia's desire to end the tension that had developed in its relationship with the United States post–September 11. The plan had two main advantages: simplicity, and Saudi Arabia's willingness to endorse the notion of "normalization." (During the heyday of the Arab-Israeli peace process in the 1990s, the Saudis had taken exception to the idea of normalizing relations with Israel.) But these advantages were overshadowed by several problems. For one thing, Ariel Sharon and most Israelis were opposed to full withdrawal to the lines of June 4, 1967. And the Saudi initiative would have to be converted into a plan of action that could be endorsed by the Arab world (or at least by the relevant Arab parties). Would Syria sign on to the idea of full normalization with Israel? Would the Palestinians give up the demand for the "right of return" not included in the Saudi plan?

After investing a strenuous diplomatic effort, the Saudis were successful in persuading the other participants to endorse a modified version of their initiative and turn it into an "All-Arab Initiative" at the Arab summit meeting in Beirut in late March 2002. The new version included an indirect reference to the "right of return," referring to resolution of the refugee problem in accordance with UN Resolution 194 (on which the Palestinian insistence on a "right of return" relies as a source of "international legitimacy"). Furthermore, a second communiqué that specifically mentioned the "right of return" was issued at the conclusion of the summit. Despite these efforts, however, the Saudi initiative was not pursued and eventually evaporated.

Finally, in April 2002, a new international forum called "the Quartet" was launched at a meeting in Madrid as yet another mechanism for bringing about a resolution. As the term implies, it was attended by four major actors: the United States, the European Union, the UN, and Russia. The Quartet was not a product of U.S. diplomacy. It was formed at the initiative of its three other partners and reflected their desire to shape Arab-Israeli diplomacy as well as the failure of the efforts led by Mitchell, Tenet, and Zinni.

Washington's willingness to join this forum stemmed from the need to reduce tensions with partner-rivals— whose collaboration Washington required in the offensive against Saddam Hussein—as well as the need to close ranks after the recent exacerbation of Israeli-Palestinian fighting. The "Madrid Declaration" reflected a shift in Washington's position toward that of the Quartet's other members.

The Quartet's second meeting took place in New York in July 2002, a month after President Bush called for Arafat's removal from power. The decisions adopted at the New York meeting were a compromise: the end result of give-and-take between the United States and its three partners. It was agreed that the Palestinian Authority would undergo a reform, elections would take place, Arafat would be elected to a symbolic position, and a Palestinian state would be formed within three years. In September 2002, the Quartet published a "road map" for an Israeli-Palestinian settlement, to proceed in three phases: (1) reform within the Palestinian Authority, Israeli withdrawal to the lines of September 2000, and Palestinian elections; (2) the formation of a Palestinian state in provisional borders and a Palestinian constitution in the course of 2003; and (3) in the course of 2004 and during the first half of 2005, final-status negotiations.

On October 15, 2002, President Bush released the text of his version of the "road map." These moves were not meant to have an immediate impact; their main importance was in laying guiding principles on the table for the anticipated resumption of the Israeli-Palestinian negotiations once the Iraqi crisis had been resolved. Sharon's government was opposed to the "road map" but chose not to confront the Bush administration over an issue that seemed hypothetical and remote.

## THE UNITED STATES AND
## THE WAR IN IRAQ

The Bush administration established a link between U.S. policy in Iraq and the Israeli-Palestinian crisis in its very early days. Several spokespersons deprecated the Clinton administration's previous massive investment in Arab-Israeli diplomacy, particularly in view of its meager accomplishments. For the Bush administration, the critical issues of the Middle East lay in the region's eastern part. The administration felt that when an effective U.S. policy was developed to restrain Iraq and Iran, it would have a calming effect on the whole region—Israelis and Palestinians included.

The sense that the United States had "to complete the job" in Iraq and topple Saddam Hussein's regime had deep roots in the Bush administration, beginning with the president's determination to settle the political—and, indeed, a personal, familial—score. This sense rested on the doctrines and arguments of a group of neo-conservative intellectuals and Republican activists, some of whom were now appointed to senior positions in the new administration. This group had been sharply critical of Clinton's policies in the Middle East during the latter part of the 1990s, denouncing what they saw as a weak stance taken vis-à-vis Saddam Hussein. From their perspective, beyond eliminating the dangers posed directly by his regime, toppling Saddam would become the cornerstone of a new policy that would weaken and perhaps even eliminate the radical elements in the region. This would then enable the United States to reorganize the Middle East, relying on such trusted allies as Israel, Turkey, Jordan, and, according to one version, "the new Iraq" as well.

During its first months in power, the Bush administration did not assign much importance to this issue. The energy saved in the region's western front was not invested in the east. But this state of affairs changed radically on September 11. The Bush administration understood that it had to come up with an impressive response, but it was hard put to identify a suitable target in the immediate aftermath of the terrorist attack. During the discussions held at the administration's senior level, the Pentagon's team, spearheaded by Deputy Secretary Paul Wolfowitz, advocated attacking Iraq. They argued that it was difficult to target an organization such as al-Qaeda, whereas Iraq was more readily accessible and was replete with targets that should be destroyed in any event. There was no proof of a "direct connection" between Iraq and al-Qaeda, but a strong case could be made that Iraq was a terrorist-supporting state and that it was crucial to ensure that unconventional weapons were not transmitted to any terrorist group. Beyond these arguments lay the conviction that a change in Iraq was the key to a larger change within the region.[8] This drive exacerbated the tension that had earlier appeared, separating Secretary Powell from Vice President Cheney and Secretary Rumsfeld, with their respective teams in the White House and the Pentagon. In the end Wolfowitz's initiative was rebuffed and the United States chose to go to war against al-Qaeda and the Taliban regime in Afghanistan.

But the idea of an attack on Iraq and its link to the new principal theme of the Bush administration was not shelved. Iraq was mentioned as a potential target of the second phase of the war; in 2002, President Bush reached the conclusion that he had to act against Iraq before it developed a nuclear weapon. The administration endorsed this view, which put together two separate issues: the war on terror and the effort to deny "dangerous" states, such as the members of "the axis of evil" (Iran, Iraq, and North Korea), possession of weapons of mass destruction—nuclear weapons in particular. This view was made possible by the presupposition that states like Iraq were liable to transmit unconventional weapons to terrorist organizations, thereby exposing the United States and its allies to a new level of risk. Once Iraq obtained a nuclear weapon or a delivery system for the biological and chemical weapons already in its possession, it would be difficult and perhaps impossible to act against that nation. It was, therefore, crucial for the United States to act early.

Later, a third angle was added to this line of argument: in the spirit of President Bush's speech on June 24, 2002, the idea that war in Iraq could serve as a key to profound change in the region and as an important step on the road to democracy in the Middle East.[9] A few weeks after that speech, the White House released another important document: a reformulation of the national security doctrine of the United States. In this document, the United States explicitly endorsed a doctrine of "preventive strikes" in the event of an emerging threat deriving from the accumulation of unconventional weapons and ballistic missiles or from a terrorist threat to national security. The president stipulated that the United States would act against such emerging threats before they were fully formed.

The road to war in Iraq was rich in mistakes and complications, many of which derived from internecine conflict or from the need to persuade multiple constituencies that the war was warranted. The main line of conflict within the administration was by now familiar—between Colin Powell and the State Department, on the one hand, and, on the other, Vice President Cheney and Secretary Rumsfeld and their teams.

As chairman of the joint chiefs of staff, Colin Powell had been reluctant to use American military power overseas. As secretary of state seeking to affect—if not shape—policy toward Iraq, he insisted that the political-diplomatic route be fully explored before a military action was undertaken. Powell and the State Department took exception to the vision of toppling Saddam's regime in order to effect change in the region; they advocated continued cooperation with Washington's traditional friends. Within the Israeli-Palestinian context, they supported a return to negotiations rather than Arafat's removal.

In the public arena, a clear tension now arose: between the need to mobilize American opinion by positioning Saddam in stark terms as an immediate threat, and the need to obtain international support—or at least to mute criticism—by resorting to the Security Council and to the mechanisms established by the UN in the 1990s to neutralize Iraq's capacity to develop weapons of mass destruction and delivery systems. With this end in mind, the Bush administration had to change the definition of its policy goals from changing the regime in Iraq to the enforcement of Security Council resolutions, thereby dismantling Iraq's unconventional capabilities and forcing it to collaborate with the international system.

Powell finally succeeded in persuading President Bush to act through the Security Council. True, it was a longer route and full of potential obstacles; the United States was exposed to the risk of a veto that France, Russia, or China could cast at any point. But Powell persuaded the president that international endorsement was important for swaying Congress and American public opinion. These diplomatic moves and the process of military buildup close to Iraq delayed the preparations for war until the late winter and early spring of 2003. This also meant that serious decisions regarding the Israeli-Palestinian conflict were postponed again; whatever one's view in this matter, there was no point in making any serious decisions before the end of the anticipated campaign in Iraq.

Powell's policy had an early success when the Security Council adopted Resolution 1441 on November 8, 2002. This seemed to pave the way for a possible war against Iraq with the Security Council's support. Even Syria voted for the resolution. But the next phase was less auspicious. The new inspection mechanism, installed by the UN under the Swedish diplomat Hans Blix, reported that it found no evidence that Iraq either possessed or was developing weapons of mass destruction. A dramatic appearance by Colin Powell, in which he used intelligence material in an effort to undermine Blix's case, failed to help. France and Germany led an international campaign against Washington's quest to go to war against Saddam Hussein. They transformed the issue into the focal point of what was virtually a crusade against unacceptable American hegemony and domination in a unipolar world. A mass protest movement was forming, both around the world and in the United States itself, against America's intention to go to war.

Israel occupied an important place in two contexts in this controversy, which culminated in the early months of 2003. One was the claim that the United States was being dragged to war not for "reasons of state" but rather in order to help Israel. The authors of this thesis seized on the fact that several advocates of the war were Jewish. Such arguments were made by a number of European politicians, by marginal figures in the United States, and by the archconservative politician Pat Buchanan and Congressman Jim Moran. Of greater significance was the fact that President Bush decided to assign much weight, in the winter of 2003, to the argument that a victory in Iraq would pave the way for launching the "road map" and effecting an Israeli-Palestinian agreement. Bush continued to stress the importance of destroying Saddam's weapons of mass destruction, and of bringing democracy to Iraq and to the region, but he put special emphasis on the link between the war in Iraq and the "road map." To some extent, Bush was motivated by the need to help his closest ally, Tony Blair, who was facing sharp criticism at home and in Europe for his support of the war. But Bush's statements also reflected a determination to use the anticipated victory in Iraq as a way of restarting an Israeli-Palestinian negotiation.

A parallel debate was also taking place in the Israeli public and political arenas. One school of thought, clearly right-wing in orientation, held a position similar to that of the Pentagon and argued that the war in Iraq and Saddam's fall would weaken Arafat; a path would then be opened for negotiating a settlement with the Palestinians on lines different from those of Clinton's bridging proposal of 2000. The Israeli left, on the other hand, argued that once the war in Iraq was over, the United States would find the time and the will (and perhaps would be forced) to deal with the Israeli-Palestinian issue, to the point of imposing a settlement on the parties.

On March 19, the United States finally went to war with Iraq, aided by a small international coalition. The war ended formally on May 1 with a clear-cut military victory. The United States and its allies suffered relatively few casualties. Saddam's regime was toppled without heavy civilian casualties and without considerable damage to Iraq's economy and infrastructure. Dire predictions to the contrary notwithstanding, the Arab world responded calmly to the attack on Iraq and to the toppling of Saddam's regime.

But there was a darker side to the picture. Saddam, most of his family, and the hard core of his regime were not captured. The United States failed to find weapons of mass destruction or persuasive evidence that they had ever existed. The opposition groups cultivated prior to the war by the United States failed to provide a base for the rapid construction of a new government. The United States encountered problems in the effort to reestablish normal life in Iraq and has been sustaining a steady stream of casualties. The mirage of a liberating army welcomed by a grateful population did not materialize.

It will take years before the outcome of the war in Iraq and its repercussions can be fully assessed, but the conflict certainly had a considerable immediate impact on Israel and on its relations with its neighbors. The destruction of Saddam's regime and army, and the removal of the threat—ambiguous as it was—of Iraq's arsenal had a dramatic effect on the balance of Israel's national security. The lesson of the Iraq campaign was the victory of a modern army, enjoying air superiority and equipped with precision-guided munitions, over a large army encumbered with outdated weapons systems. This victory cast a new light on the Israeli-Syrian military equilibrium. The notion of an eastern front could now be removed from Israel's national security calculus for at least a few years. Furthermore, as described in detail in the next chapter, at the war's end Syria found itself in a state of unprecedented confrontation with the United States.

America's relationship with Syria and the state of affairs in Lebanon continue to be significantly influenced by Washington's relations with Teheran. George W. Bush included Iran in the "axis of evil," and Iran, in fact, represented a far more ominous threat. But Iraq was a much easier target. Saddam had already been demonized, and U.S. military planners knew full well that despite its formidable image, Iraq's army was no match for the coalition

forces. Regarding Iran, the Bush administration adopted
the line that Iranian society was in turmoil and that Saddam's ouster might very well accelerate a domestic
change in Iran. Should this prediction fail to materialize,
the United States will have to formulate a more effective
strategy toward Iran. Iran continues to develop nuclear
weapons and ballistic missiles, and to serve as patron to
both Hizballah and Hamas.

These are open questions. Thus far, the one short-lived
regional ramification of the war in Iraq was the launching
of the "road map" for an Israeli-Palestinian settlement.

## THE WAR IN IRAQ
## AND THE "ROAD MAP"

On January 28, 2003, Ariel Sharon was reelected as Israel's prime minister. Israel's original electoral system having been restored, Sharon was elected by a single ballot
and led his party, the Likud, to an impressive achievement—40 members of the Knesset as opposed to the 19
elected in 1999. It took Sharon nearly a month to put
together a coalition of 66 members of the Knesset.

Sharon's major coalition partner was Shinuy, a secularist middle-class party that now had 15 seats. It was
joined by two right-wing parties: the National Religious
Party and the National Union. The Labor Party was
reduced to 19 seats and chose to remain outside the
coalition.

These developments created a dissonance between the
platform Sharon presented on the eve of his reelection
and the position held by a sizable portion of the coalition

and of the Likud's MKs. We saw that during his first term Sharon maintained a considerable degree of ambiguity regarding the issue of a political settlement with the Palestinians. He spoke in favor of settlement, and of his readiness for "painful concessions" in order to reach it, but refrained from any elaboration on the nature and scope of such concessions. He nurtured the dialogue with the Bush administration but maintained a parallel dialogue with the leadership of the West Bank and Gaza settlers. This dialogue, and the determination he showed in fighting the Palestinian Authority, raised questions as to the nature of his true position. Did Sharon seek to please all parties? Did he cling to his traditional positions while coaching them in softer rhetoric? Or did he come to the conclusion that "painful concessions" were indeed inevitable—but felt that one's hand should not be played too soon?

As the election date approached, Sharon's position grew more concrete. He announced his acceptance of the idea of a Palestinian state and held on to that position even when it was rejected by the Likud's Party Center. The most complete public articulation of Sharon's position took place on December 4, 2002, in the "Herzliya Gathering." Regarding the American plan (as distinguished from the "road map") the prime minister said:

> In the second phase of President Bush's outline, Israel will enable the establishment of a Palestinian state within provisional boundaries coinciding with Areas A and B with the exception of vital security areas. A Palestinian state would be completely demilitarized. It would be permitted to have police and domestic security forces equipped with light weap-

ons. Israel would continue to control all entry and exit points
of the Palestinian state and its air space. It would not be
permitted to enter into agreements or alliances with Israel's
enemies.

In the final phase of President Bush's outline, a negotiation would begin for determining the final status of the Palestinian state and its borders. As I have emphasized, we will
not move to this phase before a proven state of quieter relations, a change in Palestinian patterns of governance, and an
even stronger coexistence are established. . . .

The tensions and contradictions inherent in Sharon's
position, the composition of his own party and coalition,
and his relationship with George W. Bush could be managed only as long as two essential elements of the status
quo remained: the uncertainty concerning the war in Iraq
and Arafat's hegemonic position in Palestinian politics.
Once the war in Iraq was formally concluded and Mahmud Abbas became the Palestinian Authority's prime
minister, the situation was transformed. From Washington's perspective, the groundwork had been laid for a resumption of the Israeli-Palestinian negotiations. It also
became politically important to calm the Israeli-Palestinian arena, and therefore to be able to present the anticipated breakthrough as an American achievement and a
by-product of the war in Iraq.

Sharon, in turn, was busy preparing Israel's political
system and public opinion for the concessions that would
have to be made once the Bush administration launched
the effort to resume the Israeli-Palestinian negotiations.
The prime minister's efforts were conducted through a
maze of political and verbal maneuvers. Politically, he
managed to avoid a head-on collision with the settlers and

their allies. Rhetorically, he was careful to balance statements concerning anticipated concessions with contradictory pronouncements. And yet, in word and deed (the
adoption of the "road map"), he led Israel—albeit grudgingly—in a clear direction, toward an interim agreement,
predicated on the establishment of a provisional Palestinian state, and linked to a subsequent agreement on the
permanent borders and status of that state.

On April 13, *Ha'aretz* published a particularly significant interview of Sharon by the columnist Ari Shavit.
This was Sharon's first public statement going beyond
vague general references to "painful concessions." Sharon's message, moreover, was embedded in a set of arguments that ran against the grain of both his image and his
heritage. Among other things, he said:

> I think that this [the idea of two states for two peoples and
> the partition of the Land of Israel west of the Jordan] is going
> to happen. The situation must be viewed in a realistic fash-
> ion: at the end of the day there will be a Palestinian state. I
> look at things primarily from our perspective. I do not think
> that we should control another people and manage its life. I
> don't think we have the strength for this. It is a very heavy
> burden on the public and raises heavy moral and economic
> problems.

He went on to say:

> I am determined to make a true effort to reach a true
> agreement. I think that those who saw this awesome entity
> called the state of Israel taking shape perhaps have a better
> understanding of things and a better understanding of the
> road to a solution. I therefore think that this task is for my
> generation to fulfill. . . . I am seventy-five, I have no political

ambitions beyond my current position. And I regard it as a
goal and a purpose to bring peace and security to this nation.
I will therefore invest great efforts. I believe that this is something I should leave [as a legacy]: to try to come to an
agreement.

On April 16, Sharon once again spoke differently in an
interview granted to two other journalists, Nahum Bar-
nea and Shimon Shiffer.[10] But on May 26, having agreed
to the "road map" and having absorbed sharp criticism
from the right, Sharon dug in further with his moral and
ideological justification. "It is important to come to a political settlement," he said to the Likud caucus in the
Knesset. "The idea that one could hold 3.5 million Palestinians under occupation is hard for Israel. . . . What is
happening now is that three million Palestinians are kept
under occupation. In my mind this is bad for Israel, for
the Palestinians, for Israel's economy. Do you want to stay
permanently in Jenin, in Nablus, in Ramallah, and in
Bethlehem?"[11]

These developments in Israel were matched by a parallel set of developments in the Palestinian Authority. The
United States reached the conclusion that it could not
facilitate Arafat's removal and decided to settle on the formation of a cabinet headed by Mahmud Abbas (Abu
Mazen). This cabinet would reduce Arafat's direct control
and create an additional power center with an aim of promoting three interrelated tasks: political reform and a
campaign against corruption, renewal of the negotiations
with Israel, and (as a prerequisite) combating terrorism.

Washington promoted its candidates for key positions
in Abu Mazen's cabinet. These were Salam Fayyad, as

minister of finance (to advance financial efficiency and accountability), and Muhammad Dahlan, who was seen as the person with the ability to rebuild the Palestinian Authority's security apparatus and use it effectively against terrorism.

Abu Mazen's cabinet was formed in late April. Washington's pressure led the Israeli cabinet to endorse the "road map" on May 25 and to a show of Arab and international support in the Sharm al-Sheikh and Aqaba conferences on June 3 and 4, 2003. In June the World Economic Forum held an economic conference in Jordan in which Arabs and Israelis took part. These moves were designed to help Abu Mazen through a transitional period during which he had to establish his legitimacy and harness the resources that would enable him to act as an effective negotiating partner with Israel.

But the edifice constructed in April and May collapsed in the summer of 2003. In the territories of the Palestinian Authority, a de facto alliance between Yasser Arafat and Hamas was created in order to obstruct Abu Mazen and the U.S. plan. Arafat had no intention of becoming a "symbolic figure," powerless and "irrelevant." He fought for control of the security apparatus and financial resources. Hamas signed a cease-fire (*hudna*) with the Palestinian Authority but was determined to undermine the new diplomatic efforts by using the method that had proven so effective in the 1990s—terrorist acts in Israel proper. Sharon's government, never quite enthusiastic about the "road map," continued to fight Hamas through "targeted killings," among other ways. It complained—correctly—that Abu Mazen's government had failed to take on the terrorist infrastructure. In June 2003, a new vicious cycle was created, as terrorist acts by Hamas were followed by Israeli preemptive action, and vice versa. The Bush administration found itself ever more deeply immersed in Iraq, and its senior echelons significantly reduced their investment of time and attention in the Israeli-Palestinian arena.

In September 2003, Abu Mazen resigned. Arafat nominated Abu Alaa to replace him. If Abu Mazen and Muhammad Dahlan were seen from May to September as the alternative to Arafat's erstwhile domination of Palestinian politics, Abu Alaa and another security chief, Jabril Rajub, were conjured up by Arafat in September as the manifestation of his success in overcoming yet another adversity.

In mid-September, after a new cycle of suicide bombings and targeted killings, the Israeli cabinet decided "in principle" to expel Arafat. It was a declaratory act, allowing Sharon—should he decide at some future point to expel Arafat—to do so without having to convene his cabinet and obtain its approval. The decision was a compromise between those right-wing members of the cabinet and coalition who felt that Arafat's immediate expulsion was indispensable to any progress, and another group, headed by Sharon himself, who realized that this would not be acceptable to the Bush administration. The net effect was that Arafat was kept in the Muqataah, his position enhanced by manifestations of Palestinian and international solidarity. It is hardly surprising that the war in Iraq failed to break the Israeli-Palestinian deadlock. Whatever its long-term effects may be, it failed to create an instant functioning political order in Iraq or to transform political patterns in the larger region. The Bush administration found itself mired in Iraq, its will and ability to sustain the "road map" launched in May seriously curtailed. In the absence of U.S. chaperoning, the "road map" was doomed—Arafat and the Islamic organizations were determined to block it; Sharon endorsed it without real conviction or enthusiasm but rather as another compliance with Washington's wishes. He was subsequently criticized by several prominent Israelis, among them the chief of staff of the IDF, for failing to extend real support to Abu Mazen. And so, three years after the outbreak of violence on September 28, the parties were still engaged in an all too familiar vicious cycle without any apparent exit.

# 6

# THE WEB OF
# RELATIONSHIPS

As we have seen throughout this exploration of the Arab-Israeli conflict, the very term is somewhat misleading—implying as it does the notion that a single conflict pits Israel against the Arab world, that the ebb and flow of Israel's relations with the Palestinians are linked organically to, say, its rivalry with Iraq or its complex relationship with Morocco. To a considerable extent, this has indeed been true: broad trends have applied across the region; after all, the Arabs collectively rallied against Israel in 1948, participated in the conflict when it festered and swelled, was devastated by the defeat of 1967, condemned Sadat in 1977 for moving toward peace, and adopted his formula only a decade later. But under the umbrella of unity, there have always been exceptions, rivalries, and tensions within the Arab world.[1]

## EGYPT

For the thirty years between its participation in the Arab invasion of the young Jewish state in 1948 and the Camp

David Accords of 1978, Egypt was Israel's most formidable foe. Its decision to enter the war in 1948 had not been a matter of course. It was preceded by a policy debate between two principal schools of thought, one upholding the *raison d'état* of the Egyptian state, and the other stressing Egypt's Arab and Islamic commitments, as well as the political imperatives of Egyptian leadership and hegemony.[2] The issue was decided at the eleventh hour by King Farouk, who was motivated by dynastic considerations and personal ambition. His decision's momentous consequences included the monarchy's own downfall four years later, and it added the humiliation of defeat to Egypt's already complex attitude toward Israel.[3]

The 1948 war launched a quarter-century-long cycle of violence that included four full-fledged wars and a war of attrition. On the Egyptian side, the interplay of ideological commitment, state interests, and personal ambition was given new scope and new intensity by the rise of Gamal Abdel Nasser's revolutionary regime. As the leader of a messianic pan-Arab nationalism, as the head of a military regime, as Moscow's ally, and as the president of the Egyptian state, angry at the wedge Israel had driven between Egypt and the eastern Arab world, Nasser mobilized hitherto unfamiliar resources against Israel. Israel viewed Egypt as the key to a peaceful settlement with the Arab world. Yet during most of the Nasserite period the prospect of a settlement seemed remote, and Israel remained deeply concerned that Egypt's power alone was a threat; in addition, it could carry large parts of the Arab world with it. In the May 1967 crisis that deteriorated into the Six-Day War, Egyptian and Israeli misperceptions and misreadings of intentions and capabilities were gross.[4]

Six more years and two more wars were required before Israel and Egypt could move to peaceful settlement
and reconciliation, but the foundations for these were laid
in the war, in which Israel demonstrated an overwhelming
military advantage, acquired territorial assets for a land-
for-peace deal, and dealt a devastating blow to Nasser and
his regime. When Nasser died in September 1970, his
heir apparent, Anwar al-Sadat, was seen by other contenders for power in Egypt as a harmless transitional figure. But Sadat showed himself an astute politician, who
outwitted his rivals and emerged as a true international
statesman—a dramatic evolution that set the stage for
Egypt's reconciliation with Israel.

As part of his comprehensive reorientation of his country's politics and policies, Sadat decided that Egypt must
disengage from the conflict with Israel. This agenda and
that of Prime Minister Menachem Begin overlapped in
1977 enough to enable them to conclude the Camp David
Accords in 1978 and a peace treaty in 1979. For Sadat,
peace with Israel was necessary in order to regain the
Sinai Peninsula and to build a new relationship with the
United States. He was willing to dispute with the other
Arab states over his and Egypt's right to follow this policy
to give priority to Egypt's own interests over its commitment to the Arab and Palestinian causes. But at no time
was Sadat willing to make a separate deal with Israel or
to "divorce" his country from its Arab context. Begin, in
turn, came to agree to a complete Israeli withdrawal from
the Sinai so as to have peace with this most important
Arab state. But he also presumed that Egypt would willingly acquiesce in a perpetuation of Israel's control of the
West Bank, that somehow the Palestinian autonomy plan

that was part of the peace treaty could be finessed.[5] This certainly was not the Egyptian view of things.

Though implementation of the bilateral part of the Israeli-Egyptian agreement proceeded smoothly, the collapse of the autonomy negotiations, the continuation of the Israeli-Palestinian conflict, and Israel's decision to go to war in Lebanon in 1982 had a very negative effect on the fledgling peace between Egypt and Israel. This was reinforced by Egyptian considerations—domestic Islamic opposition and Nasserite criticism, and a desire for conciliation with the rest of the Arab world. Over the years, as the result not of a conscious early decision but, rather, of a murky trial-and-error process, Egypt, first under Sadat and then under his successor, Hosni Mubarak, adopted a policy of "cold peace." It kept its principal commitments toward Israel—diplomatic relations, an agreed-on security regime in the Sinai, Israeli tourism permitted in Egypt—but also kept economic and trade relations to a minimum, discouraged visits by Egyptians to Israel and cultural relations of all kinds, and signaled to the critics of peace with Israel that the regime did not really frown upon them. Nor did the government curtail virulent verbal attacks on Israel and Jews, invoking its commitment to freedom of the peace.

This policy, which Israel and occasionally the United States criticized, on the whole functioned reasonably well, and by the late 1980s Egypt's reconciliation with the Arab world was completed. With the Soviet Union's decline, even Sadat's most bitter critic, Hafez al-Assad in Syria, eventually renewed his country's diplomatic relations with Egypt and indicated his readiness to try to resolve its conflict with Israel.

The inauguration of the Madrid process and, even more, the formation of the Rabin-Peres government should have dramatically improved Israeli-Egyptian relations. The separate peace with Israel was not part of a comprehensive peace process; the new Israeli government used Egyptian help to advance its negotiations with the Palestinians, and eventually signed an agreement with them that was much more attractive than the original autonomy plan had been. Yet a real improvement in relations with Egypt failed to happen. It was obviously difficult for Mubarak's regime to dissociate itself from the policy of "cold peace," for it was dealing with a radical Islamic opposition, pursuing an occasionally neo-Nasserist regional and foreign policy, and wanting to signal that it was not Washington's captive. But the additional, larger dimension to Egypt's coolness was its renewed sense of Israel as a competitor. This was given a new urgency by the very success of the peace process. It certainly did not wish to see Israel as a regional superpower enjoying a special relationship with the United States, flexing its military and economic muscles throughout the region and beyond.

There was a time, before the Oslo Accords and for a few months after them, when Egypt appeared reasonably pleased to mediate between Israel and Arab parties. But when Israel signed a peace with Jordan, began to normalize its relations with the Gulf States and in North Africa, and developed new concepts for regional cooperation, this satisfaction was replaced by alarm.[6] And the principal means it used to articulate its unhappiness was the issue of nuclear weapons. Egypt, like the rest of the Arab world, had taken it for granted that Israel had a nuclear arsenal, even though Israel adhered to a policy of studied ambiguity in this matter. For years Israeli governments had been using the convenient formula that "Israel will not be the first nation to introduce nuclear weapons to the Middle East," and had consistently refused to sign the Non-Proliferation Treaty, arguing that it was not willing to undertake its commitments while countries like Iraq and Iran might develop nuclear weapons regardless of having signed the treaty. In the late 1960s, after considerable tension with the United States over this issue, Israel finally arrived at a modus vivendi with Washington; also, its destruction of Iraq's nuclear reactor in 1981 displayed its determination to deny the nuclear option to other Middle Eastern countries.

As the senior Arab state, Egypt traditionally led the Arab world's campaign at the United Nations and elsewhere against Israel's nuclear option. Egypt, as a populous country with a large conventional army, was genuinely opposed to the introduction of nuclear weapons to the Middle East, and resented Israel's quest for nuclear deterrence and nuclear monopoly, considering these as symptoms of Israel's hegemonic and exclusivist ambitions. When the security regime for the Sinai was negotiated at Camp David, Egypt raised questions on this issue and was rebuffed. Sadat chose not to insist so as not to obstruct his main goal—regaining the Sinai. But for the next fifteen years, Egypt continued to raise the issue in the familiar diplomatic settings. When the working group on arms control and regional security (ACRES) began to meet in 1992 (part of the multilateral track of the Madrid process), Egyptian-Israeli disagreements over this issue soon emerged, naturally enough. But by late 1994, a qual-

itative change had occurred: Egypt began to use the issue
in order to slow the diplomacy down—first in ACRES,
then in the working group on environmental issues (given
the issue of nuclear waste), and finally in the multilateral
steering group.

The change was to some extent due to the approaching
Non-Proliferation Treaty Review and Extension Conference in April 1995. The United States wanted the treaty
to be renewed indefinitely, and to Egypt this seemed like
the last opportunity to bring pressure on Israel to sign
the treaty. Israel recognized the genuine concern, but it
calculated also that Cairo had a much broader agenda:
Rabin and Peres could not quite understand why, after
fifteen years of passive opposition to Israel's nuclear option, Egypt was shifting to active and vociferous opposition precisely when Arab-Israeli peace seemed to be in
reach. As they and their advisers saw it, this was part of a
deliberate effort to slow down Israel's "normalization" in
the Middle East.

Puzzled and angry as they were, Rabin and Peres chose
to moderate their reaction to this Egyptian policy. Israel's
relationship with Egypt was too precious and fragile to
be guided by emotions. They also understood that when
conflict between the two countries ended it would be replaced not by friendship but by peaceful competition. In-
cidentally, it was convenient for both Egypt and Israel to
pretend that Cairo's anti-Israel moves had been initiated
by Foreign Minister Musa, an ambitious man subscribing
to a new version of pan-Arabism; this allowed President
Mubarak to stay above the fray as a supreme leader arbi-
trating between rival factions in his government and
nonetheless preserving Egypt's relationship with Israel.[7]

Egypt shared some of Jordan's discomfort with Peres's view of the peace to come, but its criticism was milder, concerned principally with Peres's quest for a new regional order. It was also skeptical of his determination to have Israel come quickly to a far-reaching agreement with Syria, about which Egypt was full of ambiguities. Syria's definition of a "dignified settlement" was expressed in terms that were in contradistinction to the Camp David Accords, and when Syria was discussed as the key to a comprehensive Arab-Israeli settlement, Egypt felt put in second place. But, unlike the Jordanians, the Egyptians still hoped to see Peres win in May 1996, its unhappiness with some aspects of the Labor government's peace policies being minor compared with the prospect of a Netanyahu victory.

Despite Mubarak's open unhappiness with Israel's new prime minister and his policies, a dialogue was maintained with Netanyahu's government. The Egyptian government also allowed further degrees of cultural normalization with Israel. Clearly, Mubarak and his aides had come to realize that the policy of cold peace was playing into the hands of the Israeli right wing. At the same time, Egypt took advantage of the political change in Israel to cut the peace process down to size: Egypt did not want this process to transform the regional politics of the Middle East. Having Israel come to a settlement with the Palestinians and eventually with Syria is one thing; watching Israel use these agreements to develop a network of political and economic relations across the Middle East, to construct new strategic relations with Turkey, and to continue special relations with Washington and a nuclear monopoly—that is another.

The formation of Barak's government in July 1999 and the revival of the peace process resulted in an improvement of Egypt's relationship with Israel but failed to transform it. Egypt resumed its familiar role as the Palestinians' patron in their negotiations with Israel, taking a critical view of two salient aspects of Barak's policy: the preference he gave to the negotiations with Syria and his quest for a comprehensive, dramatic final-status agreement at the expense of an incremental implementation of earlier commitments. In the same vein, Egypt took a skeptical view of the Camp David Summit in July 2000 and refrained from offering Arafat real support and encouragement to conclude a comprehensive agreement.

The eruption of Palestinian-Israeli violence in September 2000 confronted Egypt with a dual challenge—to maintain its "normal" relationship with Israel even at the "cold peace" level, and the conflict's immediate and potential impact on the Egyptian "street": like other Arab regimes, Mubarak's Egypt had to take into account the repercussions of the media revolution of the past few years. In marked contrast to earlier crises, the ubiquitous satellite television stations brought to numerous Egyptian homes graphic, vivid images of the Israeli-Palestinian conflict, thereby agitating Egyptian public opinion. The Mubarak regime's predicament was exacerbated by other, unexpected developments—the events of September 11, the general tenor of Bush's policies in the Middle East, and the long, tortuous road to the war in Iraq.

This complex reality bred a complex Egyptian policy toward Israel. The ambassador was recalled from Tel Aviv, but diplomatic relations were maintained; Egypt maintained its discreet channels of communication with Israel after Sharon's election and its parallel public dialogue with the Labor Party and the Israeli left. Another effort was invested in preserving Cairo's hegemonic position vis-à-vis the Palestinians. Egyptian mediators—the foreign minister, the president's foreign policy adviser, and the head of the Security Services—played an important role in persuading the various Palestinian factions to accept the arrangements that led to the cease-fire and resumption of dialogue in the spring of 2003.

## SYRIA

Israel's current relationship with Syria has been shaped by the legacy of nine years of unfinished negotiations, by lingering hostility and rivalry, and by new realities: Hafez al-Assad's death, his son Bashar's coming to power, Israel's departure from South Lebanon, and the war in Iraq.

Israel and Syria continue to disagree on the course of their negotiations—what was promised, what was agreed upon, and who is to blame for the failure to reach agreement when agreement seemed to be at hand. But the acrimonious debate of the Netanyahu years over the bottom line of the negotiations under Rabin and Peres evaporated during Barak's tenure. Once Barak said in a cabinet meeting that his three predecessors accepted the principle of withdrawal to the lines of June 4, 1967, and once he articulated his own acceptance of the same principle, the historical-political-legal controversy of the mid-90s lost its relevance. Today's debate—were opportunities missed? who is to blame?—is of marginal importance and could assume renewed significance only when negotiations are resumed at some future point.

Upon succeeding his father in June 2000, Bashar al-Assad focused on the consolidation of his position and rule. From this vantage point, Syria's new order chose to conduct a pragmatic policy toward Israel seeking to avoid escalation in South Lebanon. While holding on to his father's full territorial claims (including the shoreline of Lake Tiberias), Bashar made no real effort to renew the negotiations. He had yet to consolidate his hold on power, and after September 2000 he realized that the focus of Arab-Israeli relations had shifted to the Palestinian issue.

But Bashar al Assad's initial prudence was replaced several months later by a bold, sometimes reckless, policy that granted Hizballah occasional freedom of action, which led to two Israeli punitive actions against Syrian targets and brought Israel and Syria to the verge of a head-on collision. In 2000 and 2001, Secretary of State Albright and Vice President Cheney had to issue stern discreet warnings to Bashar al-Assad to restrain his Lebanese allies.

This change derived from several sources. The lingering Israeli-Palestinian fighting generated pressure on Syria to act as well. Israel's reluctance to open a second front in the north restrained its reactions and delayed the emergence of the deterrence equation envisaged by Barak when he decided to withdraw from Lebanon. In the absence of any political-diplomatic breakthrough, the focus of the Israeli-Syrian relationship shifted back from the quest for a settlement to conflict and confrontation. But the most important change had to do with the transition from a mature, experienced president to his inexperienced son. This was manifested in the Israel-Lebanese arena but even more so in the context of the Iraqi crisis.

Indeed, since the fall of 2002, when it transpired that the Bush administration was determined to go to war in Iraq, the Iraqi issue took precedence on Syria's agenda. Within a few months, Syria found itself confronting an American military presence on its eastern border and facing a hostile, critical attitude on the part of the Bush administration.

During the final phase of the war in Iraq, Washington's relationship with Damascus deteriorated to the point at which President Bush and several of his senior aides issued public strident threats to act against Syria. They were incensed by the assistance given by Syria to Iraq on the eve of and during the war and particularly by the assumption that several senior members of Saddam's regime and part of his unconventional arsenal were hidden in Syria.

For three decades, Hafez al-Assad conducted a complex relationship with successive U.S. presidents and administrations. He bargained with Washington and fought it simultaneously and, as a rule, emerged unscathed even when obstructing its policies. The ability to conduct a dual policy and to walk safely to the brink was indeed characteristic of Hafez al-Assad's style. He did the same with Israel in the '90s, negotiating a peace settlement while hosting Palestinian rejectionist groups and collaborating with Hizballah in Lebanon.

Bashar al-Assad was clearly incapable of coping successfully with such complexity. After September 11, he tried to placate the United States by sharing some intelligence on al-Qaeda but continued to support Palestinian and Lebanese terrorist groups. Syria voted for Security Council Resolution 1441 but also offered Saddam some clandestine aid. Military equipment bought by Iraq from Yugoslavia was transferred through Syria. But this double game collapsed at the war's end when the United States threatened to turn Syria into the "war on terror" 's next target.

On the agenda were four main issues:

1. Syria's conduct in Iraq, as described above, reinforced by the United States' anxiety that Syria may feed anti-American agitation in postwar Iraq.
2. Syria's own arsenal of weapons of mass destruction (primarily Scud missiles armed with chemical warheads).
3. Syria's hegemony in Lebanon and support of Hizballah.
4. Syria's support of the Palestinian "rejectionist" organizations, the fact that most of them have offices in and operate from Damascus, and Washington's and Jerusalem's concern that Syria would act to undermine the resumption of Israeli-Palestinian negotiations as long as it was excluded from the Middle Eastern "diplomatic game."

On May 3, 2003, Secretary of State Colin Powell visited Syria. The strident threats were replaced by a more subtle effort to persuade Syria to accommodate Washington's demands and wishes. Syria was indeed relieved. In response to Powell's demand, it instructed the Palestinian rejectionist organizations to close down their offices but in practice enabled them to continue their activity. This line was emblematic of the policy pursued by Bashar al-Assad:

1. A limited effort to placate Washington.
2. A parallel effort to persuade Washington that the best option for both countries was to develop a discreet channel.
3. A demand to draw a second "road map" for the Syrian-Israeli track, expression of willingness to renew the negotiation with Israel (at the point at which it was inter-

rupted), the spreading of rumors about Syrian-Israeli contacts, and, finally, an actual offer (through the UN's envoy to the Middle East, Terje Larsen) to renew the negotiations.

4. Continued covert support for anti-American and anti-Israeli activities.

In 2000, after the failure of the Clinton-Assad meeting in Geneva and prior to Hafez al-Assad's death, the Syrian intellectual Sadek al-'Azm published in the *New York Review of Books* an essay titled, "The View from Damascus."

Al-'Azm is well known as an independent, courageous intellectual and definitely does not speak for the Ba'ath regime, but his essay should be read with an awareness of the limits of free expression in Syria, particularly regarding such a sensitive issue as peacemaking with Israel.

Al-'Azm asserts that the Syrian public (by which he means primarily Damascene society) had accepted the notion of peace with Israel. The only remaining question is when. (Al-'Azm's concept of peace is a different matter; it is quite far from Israel's most modest concept of peace with Syria.)

Three years after its publication, al-'Azm's essay can be read with more than a touch of irony. It seems far removed from the present realities. But it remains significant. Present realities can change swiftly and dramatically, and the deep currents of Syrian opinion could once again become relevant.

## LEBANON

In the 1950s and 1960s, a political cliché was current in Israel to the effect that "Lebanon will be the second Arab state to sign a peace with Israel." The cliché, clearly not borne out by the course of events, was inspired by earlier contacts between Zionist diplomats and some Maronite Christian leaders in Lebanon and on a mistaken perception of the nature of Lebanese politics. Many Lebanese Christians thought of Israel as another non-Muslim state that was or could be a bulwark against pan-Arab nationalism, but most of them viewed Lebanon as a part of the Arab world and wanted to preserve the delicate domestic and external balances so indispensable to Lebanon's precarious survival.[8]

That balance was upset in the early 1970s, and the Lebanese state and political system collapsed in the 1975–76 civil war. From Israel's perspective, the civil war and lingering crisis in Lebanon had several negative results: the Lebanese state was incapable of exercising authority over Lebanese territory, Syria had become the paramount power and military presence in Lebanon, and the Palestinians built a territorial base in Beirut and southern Lebanon under PLO direction. Israel responded in various ways: a tactical indirect understanding with Syria to preclude a Syrian military presence in southern Lebanon, an Israeli "security strip" along the Lebanese border, and a strategic alliance with several Maronite groups in Lebanon. But the Lebanese front was the main arena of the PLO's armed conflict with Israel. The growing Palestinian and Syrian challenge and a misguided belief that Israel could place a friendly government in Beirut and change the strategic configuration in the region led Begin's government to launch the 1982 war.

For Lebanon and Israel both, the war had momentous, mostly unintended consequences. The PLO's leaders and groups moved to Tunisia; Syria's hold over Lebanon, after an initial setback, was reinforced; the Christian communities preserved some of their political privileges but lost much power. But the war's single most important outcome was the acceleration of a process that had been apparent earlier—the mobilization of the hitherto underprivileged Shi'ite community and its quest for a political position commensurate with its demographic strength in Lebanon. This trend was reinforced when Iran's Islamic revolution of 1979 was projected into Lebanon and its Shi'ite community—its only successful foreign destination.[9] The Shi'ite militias of Amal and Hizballah were propelled not by nationalism but by religion, and they introduced into the conflict such then-novel elements as suicide bombings.

By 1985, Israel gave up any claim to figure in Lebanon's national politics and focused on the defense of its northern frontier. It withdrew to an expanded security zone maintained by the Israeli Defense Force with the help of a local militia; since then, the security zone and occasionally Israel itself have been attacked primarily by Hizballah, under direction from Teheran and with the tacit cooperation of Syria.

In October 1989, an Arab conference held in Taif, in Saudi Arabia, tried to consolidate and formalize the situation. The compromise embodied in the Taif accord envisaged Syria's military withdrawal from Lebanon, albeit as a remote prospect. But the accord remained a dead letter. In fact, Syria took advantage of its participation in the American-led coalition during the Gulf crisis and Gulf War to consolidate its hold over Lebanon; fourteen years after its original invasion. Syria finally controlled Lebanon through a functioning local government, maintaining a significant military presence there not as an army of occupation but as a guarantor of its hegemony, as a defender of the western approaches to Damascus, and as a potential threat to Israel. Syria makes a point of acting as the guardian of the trappings of Lebanese statehood, but in subtle and less-than-subtle ways it ensures Lebanon's acquiescence with its will and interests. Thus, no progress should be made in Lebanese-Israeli negotiations so long as a breakthrough has not occurred in Syrian-Israeli relations; Syria has undertaken, once such a breakthrough occurs, to obtain a comparable agreement for Lebanon; and Lebanon's territory must be used to pressure Israel to come to terms with Syria.

In 1994, the broad lines of an understanding about Lebanon were, in fact, worked out between Israel and Syria in the "ambassadors' channel." Provided that a Syrian-Israeli agreement was reached, Syria was willing to endorse an Israeli-Lebanese peace agreement to be implemented within nine months—a time frame that coincided with the nine months that Rabin envisaged in his discussions with Christopher for the first phase of a prospective agreement with Syria. But no such agreement was reached.

Unfortunately, there was also a violent side to this story. Hizballah's offensive against Israel's security zone in southern Lebanon and occasional Katyusha rocket attacks on northern Israel kept up a permanent cycle of violence along the Lebanese-Israeli border. Twice—in July 1993 and April 1996—Israel launched large-scale land operations in Lebanon in an effort to break the cycle. Both operations led to "understandings" between

Israel and Hizballah that limited the violence but failed to end it.

Soon after the formation of his government in June 1996, Netanyahu sought to promote a "Lebanon first" initiative, which he hoped would win Syrian endorsement. But Syria suspected this was an attempt to drive a wedge between Damascus and Beirut, and it wasted no time in rebuffing the gambit. In September, a redeployment of Syrian troops in Lebanon led to a brief war-scare, since some in Israel wrongly interpreted it as a preparation for launching an attack, while Syrians wrongly interpreted Israel's statements and responsive movements as preparations for an attack. Eventually, reassuring messages were exchanged and a confrontation was averted, but the episode showed how explosive the Israeli-Syrian-Lebanese triangle was.

As the months went by and the number of Israeli casualties grew dramatically, so did public and political pressure to extricate Israeli soldiers from southern Lebanon. A mixed coalition of concerned parents, left-wing politicians, and Golan settlers who were eager to sever the link between southern Lebanon and the Golan Heights has led a movement calling for Israel's unilateral withdrawal from Lebanon. Netanyahu's government responded with a novel tactic—a conditional acceptance of Security Council Resolution 425, requiring Israel to leave Lebanon. This put Lebanon's President Harawi and Prime Minister Hariri in a difficult position: it was hard for them to explain why they were refusing to take Israel up on its offer to withdraw. Their predicament enhanced Syria's suspicions that they might seek accommodation with Israel on their own, and Syria made highly visible efforts to keep Lebanon's government in tow.

As has been described above, this state of affairs was transformed by Ehud Barak's decision to withdraw the IDF from South Lebanon that was implemented in June 2000. Barak took care to execute the withdrawal in close coordination with the United Nations (not a common practice in Israel's diplomatic tradition) and obtained the organization's stamp of approval for the completion of Israel's withdrawal to the international boundary. But Hizballah and subsequently the government of Lebanon complained that Israel's failure to withdraw from the Shaba Farms and the village of Ghajur (Syrian territory according to Israel and the U.D.) and Israeli overflights constitute ongoing acts of aggression. For Hizballah these complaints justify the maintenance of regular low-level pressure on Israel's northern borders with occasional outbursts of more spectacular attacks.

From Israel's perspective, this is yet another manifestation on the part of the Arab parties to the conflict serving to undercut the sense and substance of "end of conflict." It also feeds the debate on the pros and cons of the unilateral withdrawal from Lebanon. And, perhaps most significantly, it underlines Iran's pernicious impact on Israel's relationship with the Arab world.


## JORDAN

Israel shares its longest border with Jordan; the two countries have immense actual and potential impact on each other's national security and economy, but their relationship is, and for a long time has been, primarily affected by their respective and common relations with a third party—the Palestinians.

Jordan's very birth as a modern state was intimately linked to this issue. When Great Britain decided in 1921 to create ex nihilo a principality for the Hashemite monarch Amir Abdullah, it needed to placate him personally and the Hashemite family in general for what they considered a betrayal—for their receiving only a meager share in the postwar settlement in the Middle East—and so it detached the East Bank from the territory of Mandate Palestine and gave it to Jordan. In doing so, Britain was also trying to reduce the impact that the formation of a Jewish national home in Palestine would have on the region. During the next twenty-five years, Abdullah, with British help, developed a genuine polity in Jordan, and in 1946 the principality became a kingdom. At the same time, a significant political relationship grew between Abdullah and the leaders of the Jewish community in pre-state Israel, the Yishuv. This understanding was predicated on their common enmity to radical Palestinian Arab nationalism, as personified by Haj Amin al-Husayni, mufti of Jerusalem. Abdullah was hostile not merely to the mufti but to his political style and to the brand of Arab nationalism that he represented. And he was never satisfied with the desert principality assigned to him and was eager to extend his rule to more significant territories and cities—Syria and Damascus, or Palestine west of the Jordan and Jerusalem.

When the idea of partitioning Palestine into Jewish and Arab states came to the fore in 1937, a new dimension was added to Abdullah's relationship with the Yishuv. If this partition came to pass, he might annex the Arab part of Palestine to his kingdom and provide the stability and pragmatism that had been so glaringly absent from the scene. The term "Jordanian option" was coined later, but the concept originated then: the solution of Israel's Palestinian dilemma by means of Jordan. This became a viable option after the UN's partition resolution of November 1947.

The Jewish leaders had accepted the notion of Palestine's partition and were quite content to go along with part of Abdullah's annexation plan. But they disliked the other aspect of Abdullah's policy—his part in the Arab states' invasion of Palestine on May 15, 1948, which would facilitate his own takeover of the area assigned to be a Palestinian-Arab state in the partition plan.

During the war, Abdullah's army, the Arab Legion, was a resolute and effective enemy that inflicted on the young Israeli Defense Force some of its most painful defeats, and at the war's end Abdullah was indeed in control of what became known as the West Bank and East Jerusalem. His annexation of these territories was formally recognized by only two foreign governments, but, whatever the legal aspects, it transformed the Jordanian polity. (It was called Transjordan until 1964, and Jordan thereafter.) Palestinians now made up a majority of its population; many of them regarded Abdullah, his kingdom, and his act of annexation as illegitimate.[10] And in the years before Abdullah was assassinated by a Palestinian in 1951, the transformation of his kingdom's traditional politics as a consequence of the annexation of this large, better-educated, politically mobilized, and embittered Palestinian population had become apparent. In 1949–50, a treaty between Israel and Jordan was negotiated and initialed but it was not finalized, for Abdullah realized that he had neither the power nor the authority to carry his country with him to a peace settlement with Israel.[11]

During the next fifteen years, the issue was not annexation but survival. Following a brief regency period, the eighteen-year-old Hussein ascended the throne that he was to occupy for forty-five years. The young monarch proved to be extremely determined, astute in maintaining external support and facing down domestic opposition, and unusually skillful and lucky at aborting plots and evading assassination attempts. For revolutionary Arab nationalism held sway over much of the Middle East, and the king's Palestinian subjects were among its staunchest supporters. Yet at the same time Jordan, reflecting the new demographic realities and in keeping with its claim to embody the Palestinian issue, was the only Arab state that offered citizenship to Palestinians. In 1967, King Hussein paid dearly when he joined Egypt and Syria in their war against Israel, and he lost the West Bank and Jerusalem. Jordan now had no West Bank but a Palestinian majority in the East Bank; yet by then many Palestinians had been "Jordanized" and had come to accept Jordan as their country and state. Yearning for Palestinian self-determination is one thing, and the realization that life under the Hashemites is quite attractive is another.[12]

So the Six-Day War reopened "the question of Palestine." For the first time since 1949, all of what had been Mandate Palestine was placed under a single authority. Israel was in control of the sizable Palestinian population living in the West Bank and in the Gaza Strip, in addition to its own Palestinian Arab minority. The debate over the future of the West Bank and the Gaza Strip became the governing issue of Israeli politics. For Israel, three principal alternatives presented themselves: reviving the "Jordanian option"; seeking or accepting the creation of an independent or autonomous Palestinian entity; or perpetuating Israeli control, either as a deliberate policy or, more likely, by failing to make painful choices.

The Hashemite regime's initial preference was to come to an agreement with Israel, but the king insisted that he could do so only on the basis of Israel's full withdrawal from the occupied territories. With the passage of time, as Israel's attachment to the West Bank grew stronger and so did the PLO's stature and power, the prospects for this "Jordanian option" waned. Nor did various notions of a Jordanian-Palestinian federation turn into a magic formula.

Its protestations of formal support notwithstanding, Jordan has consistently opposed or at least been uneasy about the idea of a Palestinian state in the West Bank and the Gaza Strip. For Hashemite Jordan, a small Palestinian state in part of the West Bank and the Gaza Strip cannot be a durable, satisfactory solution to the Palestinian problem, and Palestinians are likely to direct their irredentist claims eastward and to seek the allegiance of Jordan's Palestinian majority. True, many of the kingdom's Palestinian subjects view themselves as Jordanians, but why expose their loyalty to such a challenge?[13] So, for many long years, staying with the status quo proved to be the easiest choice for Jordan, too. A channel of communication with the Israeli leadership was kept discreetly open, but not quite secret, for nearly three decades. Several attempts were made to reach a settlement, various practical issues were sorted out, and a dialogue was maintained between

King Hussein and most of Israel's prime ministers. A community of interests was established with both Labor and Likud leaders, based on shared opposition to the PLO and to the notion of Palestinian statehood.

One tenet of this relationship—the Israeli belief that the survival of the Hashemite regime and its control of the East Bank were important Israeli national interests—was shaken when, in 1970, Likud adopted the slogan "Jordan is Palestine" and took the position that there was no need to establish a second Palestinian state. The argument also presumed that, once the Palestinians took over the reins of government in Amman, their claim over the West Bank would weaken.[14] The issue came into stark relief in September, when Israel was key in facilitating King Hussein's victory over Syria and the PLO. Golda Meir and Yitzhak Rabin believed that his survival and American-Israeli strategic cooperation should be Israel's paramount considerations; their decision was subsequently criticized by Ariel Sharon, leader of Israel's radical right, who argued that the government had missed an opportunity "to let nature take its course."

In the rich chronology of Israeli-Jordanian history during these years, several defining events stand out: King Hussein's decision not to join the Arab war coalition in October 1973; Kissinger's inability to effect an Israeli-Jordanian interim agreement in the spring of 1974; the Arab summit's decision in October 1974 to designate the PLO as the legitimate claimant to the West Bank; the London Agreement of April 1987, which was Israel's last attempt to exercise the "Jordanian option," albeit in a modified version; Jordan's formal disengagement from the West Bank in 1988;[15] and the Gulf crisis and Gulf

War, which was the culmination of Iraq's threat to Jordan's independence.

The signing of the Oslo Accords affected this history paradoxically. The Hashemites resented Israel's choice of a "Palestinian option" but decided that they had to draw closer to Israel, the better to affect the course of events. The emergence of a Palestinian state, though it became more likely, was not a foregone conclusion, and Jordan and Israel still shared a significant agenda. But there was another side to the same developments. By signing the Oslo Accords with Israel, the PLO enabled Jordan and other Arab states to pursue their bilateral agendas with Israel. But at issue was a trilateral relationship, for the United States was involved; there were also regional issues (strategic cooperation with Turkey, the future of Iraq).

Meanwhile, Israel's commitment to the survival of King Hussein's regime was buttressed by a close personal relationship between King Hussein and Yitzhak Rabin. This relationship played a crucial role in enabling the two states to sign a peace agreement in October 1994 and to formalize their relationship. This changed during Peres's brief tenure as Rabin's successor. The king was worried that his policies would lead all too quickly to an independent Palestinian state and to Israeli-Syrian and Syrian-Lebanese agreements; these would jeopardize and dwarf Jordan's position. On the eve of the May 1996 elections, Jordan indicated its preference for Benjamin Netanyahu and a peace policy managed at a more deliberate pace.

Yet these hopes were not fulfilled. For, although Jordan is opposed to an accelerated peace process, it finds it essential to have a viable one, particularly vis-à-vis the Palestinians. The collapse of Israeli-Palestinian negotiations, let alone outbreaks of Israeli-Palestinian violence, would make Jordan's peace with Israel hardly tenable. This may be a tall order, but the Hashemites expect from Israel finesse and subtlety in the conduct of a delicate, fragile relationship. They soon came to believe that Netanyahu was a prime minister who could not manage that relationship, who could not keep the king's personal trust, and whose real intentions with regard to the peace process could not be divined. The king vented his frustration in a scathing letter to Netanyahu, the text of which became available to the international media. Yet the king kept the lid on: most of the interests that keep Jordan wanting a peace with Israel are still valid, and the cost of an open break with Israel still outweighs the benefits it might produce. And so, for the time being, Israeli-Jordanian peace has survived, but the expectations of a special relationship, a warm peace, and a mutually beneficial web of economic and development projects have failed to materialize.

In February 1999, King Hussein died of the cancer he had fought during the previous few years. On his deathbed he removed his brother Hassan, who had served as crown prince for more than thirty years, and appointed his oldest son, Abdullah, as his heir. After ascending the throne, the young king reassured Israel on several occasions that he was committed to the peace his father had signed. Yet Israeli apprehensions about Jordan's ability to contend with potential and external threats were exacerbated by the simultaneous loss of two experienced and familiar partners.

King Abdullah's early decisions and the change of government in Israel in the late spring of 1999 improved the atmosphere in the two countries' relationship, but the intimacy and special relations of the Rabin-Hussein years were not restored. Jordan followed anxiously Barak's swift apparent progress toward far-reaching agreements with Syria and the Palestinians (as it had under Peres). It was particularly alarmed by Barak's willingness to give up permanent presence in the Jordan Valley, thereby laying the groundwork for an uncomfortable contiguity with a future Palestinian state. But in keeping with a long-established tradition, Jordan did not express such concerns in public and chose to pay lip service to Palestinian nationalism.

Jordan must not have lamented the collapse of the Israeli-Palestinian negotiation in July 2000. But the outbreak in short order of the "*al-Aqsa intifada*" created new pressures on a state with a Palestinian majority that had made and maintained peace with Israel. Amman lowered the profile of its relations with Israel and took security precautions. Politically, it was a tacit source of inspiration for what eventually became known as the Saudi Initiative (see chapter 5).

## THE PALESTINIANS

In October 1975, a senior American Arabist, Harold Saunders, testified at a hearing held by the House of Representatives' Committee on Foreign Affairs. In his prepared written text, Saunders referred to the Palestinian issue as the core of the conflict between Arabs and Israelis in the Middle East.[16] At the time, little attention was paid to Saunders's testimony, but it subsequently drew considerable attention and animated objections from the Israel government. Israel was then in the midst of a complex diplomatic process orchestrated by the United States and predicated on the assumption that the key to the Arab-Israeli conflict lay in Israel's relations with the major Arab states. Saunders's argument ran against the grain of U.S.-Israeli policies and was, indeed, a harbinger of the change that came with the Carter presidency. If the Palestinian issue was the core question of the Arab-Israeli conflict, did it not make sense to predicate the quest for Arab-Israeli peace on a resolution of the problem that lay at its heart? Indeed, the Carter administration, and Saunders, acted in the Middle East on the dual assumption that it could resolve the Palestinian problem and that its success would offer the key to a comprehensive Arab-Israeli peace.

But was such a resolution feasible? Since 1948, Israeli attitudes toward Palestinians have to a large extent been shaped by a sense that the Israeli-Palestinian dispute is a zero-sum game, that Palestinian demands and expectations can be met only by intolerable terms. It was much easier for Israel and Israelis to think of Israeli-Arab reconciliation by means of negotiations and agreements with states like Egypt, Jordan, and Syria, which could focus on such issues as boundaries and water.[17]

This frame of mind was for many years reinforced by the course of Palestinian history and the drift of Palestinian politics. Between 1949 and 1964, the Palestinians were absent from the Middle Eastern arena as an independent force. They were crushed, fragmented, and dispersed. Their traditional leaders were discredited, and most young Palestinian activists invested their zeal in ideological parties that promised a remedy to the Palestinian predicament within a larger scheme. The Arab states, in turn, were eager to take charge of the Palestinian issue and to suppress the efforts made by Palestinian groups to take charge themselves. For more than a decade, the vast majority of them were under the spell of Gamal Abdel Nasser and his brand of messianic pan-Arab nationalism. When Nasser defeated the enemy—the unholy trinity of Western imperialism, Zionism, and domestic reactionary forces—and united the Arab homeland, Arab Palestine would be liberated and redeemed. It was only with Nasser's and Nasserism's decline that an authentic Palestinian national movement was born.

The PLO was founded by the Arab states as their instrument but was taken over in 1968 by the authentic Palestinian groups that had emerged a few years earlier. Yet, for another twenty-five years, most Israelis did not consider the PLO an acceptable interlocutor. It had drafted a charter that called for Israel's destruction, and it used terror as a principal instrument. All efforts to persuade Arafat to take positions that would enable the PLO to join the peace process in the 1970s were to no avail. The PLO only slowly adopted the formula of a "two-state solution." Nor was Israel, the more powerful party to the conflict, ready or willing to take the initiative.[18]

Thus, while Israel and Egypt went ahead toward their peace treaty of 1979, armed conflict between Israel and Palestinian nationalists and their struggle over the land of the West Bank continued. The ambivalence and equivocation that marked Israel's Labor governments about putting Jewish settlements in the West Bank was replaced after the Likud victory in 1977 with open encouragement to do so. These efforts created (mostly by design) a new reality under which a workable compromise with the Palestinians became ever more difficult to achieve, yet at the same time the sight of expanding Israeli settlements persuaded many Palestinians, particularly in the West Bank and the Gaza Strip, that time was not necessarily on their side and that it was imperative to reach a settlement.

In 1988, Arafat finally endorsed the principle of a two-state solution, and on that basis diplomacy began between the PLO and the United States. The changes in Washington's and the PLO's positions amplified the considerable impact of the *intifada*, and increased the pressure on Israel's second national-unity government to renew, after a seven-year hiatus, negotiations about Palestinian self-rule. The profound disagreement between the government's Labor and Likud components over this issue expedited its collapse in March 1990. When Israeli-Palestinian negotiations began again in 1991, they were part of the Madrid process, and they played out against the backdrop of other great changes: the Soviet Union's collapse, the end of the Cold War, the Gulf crisis and Gulf War, and a fresh wave of emigrants from the former Soviet Union to Israel.

In the course of putting the Madrid process together, Secretary of State Baker discovered that Prime Minister Shamir's resistance to the very notion of negotiating with the Palestinians could be mitigated by a shifting of emphasis from the Palestinian issue to having a parallel channel of diplomacy with Israel's Arab neighbors. This blunted the Palestinian edge of the Madrid process, which was further reduced by the formal incorporation of the Palestinian delegation into a Jordanian-Palestinian delegation. But the junior status thus assigned to the Palestinians, and the PLO's formal absence from the Madrid process, reflected the PLO's decline in the Arab world after

the Gulf War, though the effect of this humiliating turn
of events was limited at first, since no progress occurred
during the first nine months of the post-Madrid negotiations. But when the Rabin government was formed, the
PLO's hold over Palestinian politics acquired fresh significance. An Israeli-Palestinian agreement became a key
to any progress; whether Israel would come to such an
agreement without the PLO or deal with the PLO and
find an acceptable formula became a crucial issue on its
diplomatic agenda.

We have seen how Rabin pondered the comparative
advantages of the Syrian and Palestinian options. In early
August 1993, the hypothetical vacillation turned into an
actual policy choice. Then, by signing the Oslo Accords,
Israel predicated the new phase of the peace process on
its agreement with the PLO, and not with a major Arab
state such as Syria. This resulted in a radical change of
perspective. Having signed a framework agreement with
representatives of Palestinian nationalism, Israel now argued that the core issue of the Arab-Israeli conflict had
been addressed and the chief obstacle to Arab-Israeli reconciliation and normalization had been removed. This
created a hitherto unfamiliar mutual dependence between
the government of Israel and the PLO leaders.

The Oslo process was a very complex and fragile mechanism; genuine cooperation and a genuine sense of partnership were indispensable to its success. As we have seen,
these were accomplished to only a limited degree.

And the Israeli-Palestinian conflict was not over. In
both societies, powerful forces were opposed to reconciliation and continued to try to abort it. Competition for
control of the West Bank and Jerusalem continued, and

the leaders, cooperating as they did in implementing the agreements they had signed, were separated by their different visions of the final-status agreement. Both societies had yet to think through, separately or together, some fundamental issues. Were Israel and the Palestinians interested in separation, or in some form of cooperation or integration within the Israeli-Jordanian-Palestinian triangle? And if separation was what they wanted, was it feasible? And what sort of relationship could be envisaged between societies separated by such social and economic gaps? How would twelve or fifteen million Israelis and Arabs share the limited resources of land and water in the space between the Mediterranean and the Jordan early in the next century?

The Oslo process ran its course and the Israeli-Palestinian dispute had not been resolved. We have seen how Benjamin Netanyahu failed to maneuver among the forces that buffeted his Palestinian policy, and how Ehud Barak shifted from the preference he had assigned to the Syrian track to the boldest effort by any Israeli leader to reach a final, comprehensive agreement with the Palestinian national movement. The collapse of Barak's negotiations with Arafat and the outbreak of violence in September 2000 set the stage for a resumption of a full-blown conflict between the two protagonists.

## FROM "ISRAELI ARABS" TO "ISRAEL'S PALESTINIAN CITIZENS"

In the original terminology of the Arab-Israeli dispute, the conflict in and over British Mandate Palestine was conducted between an Arab side and a Jewish side. It was only after the establishment of the state of Israel and the conclusion of the 1948 war that a stark distinction was drawn between Israelis and Palestinians as the successors of the Jewish and Arab communities in Palestine. In Israeli usage, the term "Arab" came to refer to the people who lived in the larger Arab world beyond Israel's borders, while the term "Palestinian" referred to Palestinians residing outside Israel. Israel's own Arab or Palestinian citizens were strictly referred to as "Israeli Arabs," as members of Israel's "Arab minority" or "sector." This curious choice of terms well expressed Israelis' uneasiness about the Palestinian issue. It was, in a way, easier to cope with a national minority pertaining to an amorphous Arab world than with a people who laid specific claim to Israel's own land.[19] For twenty years or so, Israel's Arab citizens accepted this terminology and used it themselves, but by the 1970s, they began to refer to themselves as Palestinians or as Palestinians who happened to be Israeli citizens. This was but one of many profound changes in the complex relationship between the Israeli state and its Arab citizens.

When the 1948 war ended, some 130,000 Palestinian Arabs remained in the territory of the independent Jewish state and became its citizens. So the fledgling state of Israel had a population of just over a million, and its Arab citizens constituted a minority of about 11 percent. In the aftermath of a brutal war, the victorious Jews considered this Arab minority as a potential fifth column, liable to be used by a hostile Arab world in an inevitable, imminent "second round." This underlying attitude was translated into a policy of control embodied first and foremost by the imposition of a system of "military government" on the Arab population, which was abolished only in 1966 by Israel's third prime minister, Levi Eshkol.

This policy of control was carried out in an ambivalent context. Israel as a Jewish state was hard put to decide whether it wanted to separate the Arab minority from the mainstream of Israeli public life or whether, as a democratic state dominated by a social-democratic political establishment, to integrate it. Ironically, integration was first accomplished, after a fashion, in the political realm. As full-fledged citizens of the state of Israel (though not equal members of Israel's body politic and society), most Israeli Arabs voted for Zionist parties through satellite lists and in fact helped to perpetuate Labor's hegemony.

During these early years, the Arab minority, predominantly rural and Muslim, can best be described as powerless, traumatized, and confused. Its members had to adjust to defeat, to minority status, to isolation from the other parts of the fragmented Palestinian community, and from the larger Arab world. And there was an acute problem of leadership—the pre-1948 Palestinian Arab elites were now beyond Israel's borders, and those who had stayed tended to be poorer and less educated. Arab political opinion and activity in Israel spanned a spectrum that went from pragmatic acceptance of the reality of the Jewish state to nationalist opposition to and rejection of it. Pragmatism was manifested by most Arabs' voting for the major Zionist parties, and opposition was manifested primarily through the Communist Party. Attempts to form a local Arab nationalist party (notably a grouping called Al-Ard, "The Land") collapsed when faced with an insurmountable obstacle: in order to qualify as such, the party would adopt a platform negating Israel's very existence and legitimacy as a Jewish state, and then the government and courts would label it seditious. A subtler, politically easier way for members of the intellectual Arab elite in Israel to express their rejection of the Israeli state was in literary prose and verse.

As in so many other respects, 1967 was a watershed in the evolution of Israel's Arab minority. The reemergence of an authentic and effective Palestinian nationalist movement and the removal of the physical barrier that had once separated them from the Palestinian and Arab worlds beyond Israel's borders induced a process of Palestinization. But the balance that had been achieved in practice between Israeli and Arab nationalist components in the community was upset. It was a measure of this change that the term "Israeli Arab" was discarded, and Israel's Arab citizens came to refer to themselves as Palestinians. This nationalist awakening, coupled with socioeconomic improvements—a higher standard of living, a higher level of education, the partial breakdown of the extended-family system, the transformation of several villages into towns—led to a new phase of political activism. On March 30, 1976, a massive protest was organized under the title "The Day of the Land" against the expropriation of Arab-owned land in the Galilee. In clashes with security forces, six people were killed. March 30 became an annual day of protest for Palestinians in Israel and in the West Bank and Gaza.

Yasser Arafat and the PLO turned "The Day of the Land" into an all-Palestinian event, but as a rule the PLO did not view Israel's Arab minority as part of its constituency. Long before the PLO formally accepted the notion of a two-state solution, its leaders had presumed it, while the Arabs in Israel, though galvanized by Palestinian nationalism, continued to see their future within the state of Israel. Some Israeli Arabs crossed a physical and mental line and joined the PLO and its orbit, but the vast majority continued to live within the Israeli state and system. Israel's Arab minority did not join either the violent conflicts between the PLO and Israel or the *intifada*.

Still, the patterns of organization and activity in Israeli Arab political life after 1967 underwent profound changes. The Zionist parties' satellite lists disappeared, and nationalist Arab parties were formed that found a way of operating within the boundaries of Israeli law (most notably Abdel Wahab Darawshe's Arab Democratic Party, founded in 1988). Semipolitical civic groups like the Committee of Heads of Local Arab Councils emerged. In the late 1970s, a powerful fundamentalist movement appeared, partly as a reflection of regional trends and partly in response to particular local conditions. Muslim fundamentalists in Israel are primarily a religious and social phenomenon, but their potential political power is enormous.[20]

The Oslo and Washington Accords of 1993 were another watershed. On the one hand, the agreement between and mutual recognition of the state of Israel and the Palestinian national movement released Israel's Arab citizens, as it did other Arabs, from their all-embracing commitment to the Palestinian cause and enabled them to pursue their particular causes and interests. Most Arabs living in Israel now consider themselves Palestinians and support the ideas of Palestinian self-determination and statehood, but they are not interested in becoming part of that state. Rather, they view themselves as a Palestinian component of Israel and are primarily interested in their status and position within its systems. For Israel, encumbered with difficult problems of segmentation and coping with contending definitions of its political community, the Arab minority's new focus on its relationship with the state is not easy. Nor is the challenge alleviated by the diversity of Arab opinion. Most Arab citizens of Israel care about the mundane issues of integration and equality—educational opportunities, a larger slice of the national economic pie. But the intellectual and political elites address and challenge the very foundations of the Israeli state and system as presently constituted. Some demand that Israel "de-Zionize" itself and become "a state for all its citizens," or, in other words, cease to define and conduct itself as the national state of the Jewish people and become a state in which Arabs can be full members of the political community, rather than members of a national minority with less than full civil and political rights. Others speak of autonomy or a return to the old notion of a "binational state."

Such ideas are amplified by their converging with a "post-Zionist" ideology that has been adopted by parts of the Israeli left. Whether they argue that Zionism was or is inherently wrong, or whether they feel that Zionism has accomplished its original mission and should change, they, too, advocate a reformulation of the underlying ethos of the Israeli polity, and commensurate constitutional and political changes.[21]

But of far greater potential significance is the growing Arab vote in Israeli politics. At the end of 1996, there were 1,122,000 non-Jews in Israel, 19.5 percent of the total population. (This figure includes 180,000 Palestinian residents of East Jerusalem, who were annexed to Israel but have chosen not to vote in Israeli elections, and 50,000 non-Arab Christians. If these two figures are subtracted, there remain 900,000 Arab citizens of pre-1967 Israel, constituting 15.5 percent of the general population.) The fifteenth Knesset has 12 Arab members out of 120. Four of them were elected from Zionist lists (3 in the Labor Party's list, and 1 through the left-wing Meretz) and 8 through Arab, non- or anti-Zionist ones. (Formally speaking, the New Communist List is a non-sectarian Arab-Jewish party; it has Jewish members and activists, and sent one Jewish member to the Knesset, but essentially it is an Arab party.) It is also important to look at the breakdown of Arab votes for Knesset members in 1992 and 1996, as summarized in table 1. The change is striking. In 1992, a clear majority of Israel's Arabs voted for mainstream Zionist parties, and less than 40 percent voted for non- or anti-Zionist Arab lists. In 1996, the figures were reversed.

In weighing the significance of this change, one must consider the effect of the electoral system introduced in the 1996 elections. Like other groups in the Israeli electorate that could now split their vote, Arab voters tended to cast their "responsible" ballots for the prime minister's post and to "go ethnic" with their party-list ballots. So Arab voters gave overwhelming support to Peres against Netanyahu but drifted away from Zionist party lists to Arab nationalist ones when voting for local candidates. But the change in the electoral system clearly accelerated trends that had been set in motion much earlier.

The full impact of these trends has thus far been blunted by the fragmentation of the Arab vote, but the

Table 1
Breakdown of Arab Votes for Knesset Members, 1992 and 1996 (in percentage of Arab voters)

|                                                        | 1992 | 1996 |
|--------------------------------------------------------|------|------|
| Democratic Front for Peace and Equality                | 23.2 | 37.0 |
| United Arab List (Arab Democratic Party and Islamists) | 15.2 | 25.4 |
| Labor                                                  | 20.3 | 16.6 |
| Meretz                                                 | 9.7  | 10.5 |
| Likud and (Jewish) Religious Parties                   | 19.3 | 5.2  |
| Others                                                 | 12.3 | 5.3  |
| Subtotals                                              | 61.6 | 37.6 |

importance of the Arab vote and of Arab politicians and groups to Israeli politics is bound to increase dramatically in the coming years. In a deeply divided political system, in which national elections are often decided by only two or three percentage points, the Arab vote can become decisive. And when it is, vociferous complaints by the Jewish nationalist right wing will follow, for this group views the Arab vote as less than fully legitimate. The argument was raised in the early 1990s that the Rabin and Peres governments, relying as they did on the votes of Arab members of the Knesset, did not have a "Jewish majority." In the 1996 elections, Netanyahu defeated Peres by the slim edge of only some sixteen thousand votes, but Netanyahu had a clear majority of 55 percent among Jewish voters. Had Peres squeaked in, the right wing would probably have complained that he had been elected by "the Arab vote" and had no mandate to make concessions unacceptable to "the Jewish majority." These trends continued to

Table 2
Breakdown of Arab and Druze Knesset
Members (Fifteenth Knesset)

|        | Arab | Druze | Total |
|--------|------|-------|-------|
| Labor  | 1    | 1     | 2     |
| Meretz | 1    | —     | 1     |
| Likud  | —    | 1     | 1     |
| Hadash | 2    | —     | 2     |
| Balad  | 2    | —     | 2     |
| Ra'am  | 5    | —     | 5     |
| Total  | 11   | 2     | 13    |

unfold through the elections of May 1999, as the table 2 clearly demonstrates.

A year and a half later, the tensions that had accumulated in the Israeli state's relationship with its Arab citizens burst out in the wave of violence of October 1. In the clashes between Arab demonstrators and rioters and the Israeli police, thirteen Arab citizens of Israel were killed.

It is difficult to overstate the importance of an event that had a traumatizing effect on both sides of the Arab-Jewish divide. On the Jewish side, the violent clashes of early October joined the outbreak of the "*al-Aqsa intifada*" in creating the sense of the end of an era. If the peace process of the '90s generated expectations for the normalization of life in Israel, the events of the autumn of 2000 underscored the fact that such normalization remained a remote prospect.

In certain respects, the Arab-Jewish clashes inside Israel were more ominous than the outbreak of violence with the Palestinian Authority in that they exposed the pernicious potential of the tension between the Israeli state and a national minority of nearly 20 percent. Critical or even hostile rhetoric by an Arab intellectual or member of the Knesset can be seen as releasing tension and frustration in a legitimate fashion; but blocking roads or clashes of thousands of angry demonstrators with the police are a different matter. This produced a variety of responses on the Jewish side, from efforts to open new channels of communication to the percolation into the mainstream of the idea that in a future exchange of territories with the Palestinians, Israel would offer territories inhabited by part of its Arab population.

On the Arab side of the equation, apart from anger at the killing of thirteen fellow Arabs, the clashes served also to reinforce the criticism voiced earlier by various groups—academics, businessmen, municipal leaders—of radical political leaders and members of the Knesset. The critics felt—and argued—that if Israel's Arab citizens wanted to find their place in the Israeli polity, they would have to communicate effectively with the Jewish majority. But in more immediate terms, Israel's Arab citizens responded by boycotting the elections of February 2001, thereby contributing to Ariel Sharon's sweeping victory.

On the eve of the February elections, Ehud Barak formed a commission of inquiry headed by a Supreme Court Justice (the Orr Commission) to investigate the government's (particularly the police's) conduct during the October crisis. The formation of the Orr Commission served to calm the atmosphere and to suspend full discussion of Arab-Jewish relations in Israel for nearly three years—the time taken by the commission to complete its work.

But this anticipation of the commission's findings and recommendation did not mean suspension of unfolding trends. Two developments were of particular significance:

1. Steady increase in the involvement of Arab citizens of Israel in terrorist activities. The absolute numbers are still small but the percentages grew alarmingly: in 2002 there was an increase of 32 percent (74 Israeli Arabs were arrested for involvement in terror-related activities as against 56 in 2001). The number of terrorist cells rose from 8 in 2000 to 25 in 2001 and 32 in 2002.

2. Tension arose over the participation of Israeli Arab politicians and lists in the elections of January 2003. The Central Elections Committee (headed by a Supreme Court justice but made up of politicians) disqualified the list headed by Azmi Bishara and the personal candidacy of Ahmed Tibi. In response, voices were raised in the Arab sector calling for the establishment of a separate, alternative "Arab political system." Eventually, the Supreme Court overruled the previous decision, and the air was cleared at least temporarily. The number of actual Arab voters in January 2003 was low, but it sufficed to elect 8 Arab members in three Arab lists, as against 10 in the outgoing Knesset.

The Orr Commission published its report in September 2003. The bulky report chided political leaders (former Prime Minister Barak, Minister Shlomo Ben-Ami, and a number of Arab MKs) and the leadership of the police, and recommended sanctions against several police officers. But the importance of the report (coauthored by Professor Shimon Shamir and Justice Hashem Khatib) was in the thorough analysis of the relationship between

the state of Israel and its Arab citizens. Future governments will have to address this analysis or face consequences more ominous than the events of October 2000.

## ISRAEL AND IRAQ:
## CONFLICT WITHOUT RELATIONS

Iraq occupies a special place among all of Israel's relationships with Arab nations. Iraq is sufficiently remote from
Israel to have chosen to act as a "nonconfrontation" state,
but for a variety of reasons its rulers have preferred over
the years to participate in military conflict with Israel
even though it does not share a border with Israel. Indeed,
the absence of a common border has radicalized the Iraqi-
Israeli conflict. Arab-Israeli peace has mostly been predicated on these two foundations—that the cost of war is
prohibitive and that "land" can be exchanged for "peace."
Neither is an element in the Israeli-Iraqi equation, and
the conflict between the two countries has been nourished by other sources.

The pattern was established early. Iraq played an important part in the 1948 war, by pushing for Arab participation and by sending an expeditionary force to it. But,
unlike Israel's immediate neighbors, Iraq chose not to end
with an armistice agreement, and in similar fashion it dispatched expeditionary forces in 1967 and 1973 but took
no part in the diplomatic activities that brought these
wars to an end.[22]

Israel's conflict with the conservative Iraqi regime of
the decade after the 1948 war was muted. But the over-
throw of the Iraqi monarchy and its replacement by a succession of revolutionary and postrevolutionary regimes

changed the situation. Showing their own ambitions for Arab leadership and their competition with Egypt and Syria, Iraq's leaders from Qassem to Saddam Hussein tended to take the most radical positions and to pursue them from the comparative safety afforded by distance. Israel, in turn, was worried by the prospect of having to confront Iraq's full potential as a participant in future wars, as the linchpin of an eastern front comprising Iraq, Syria, and Jordan, or as an immediate neighbor if it took over Jordan. To keep such possibilities at bay, Israel pursued two principal policies: it helped the Kurdish secessionists in northern Iraq, and it cultivated a strategic alliance with the Shah's Iran. (This latter had a broader agenda, but common enmity with Iraq was an important component.) These Israeli actions, needless to say, were well known to the Iraqis and helped to develop further their view of Israel as a dangerous national enemy.[23]

This configuration was altered in the late 1970s, when the peace treaty with Israel was signed, when Israel lost its alliance with Iran, and when the Kurdish rebellion collapsed. Saddam Hussein's rise to power thus ushered in a period of domestic stability. Over time, Saddam built an army of sixty(!) divisions and also sought to obtain nuclear weapons and other weapons of mass destruction. Along with Hafez al-Assad, Saddam led the opposition to Sadat and Egyptian-Israeli peace, but he and his country were soon absorbed in Iraq's eight-year war with Iran.[24] Israel was worried not so much about Iraq's conventional military buildup as about its acquisition and development of weapons of mass destruction—chemical weapons, Scud missiles, and, most ominously, nuclear weapons. Israel was not necessarily the only likely target: Saddam's army used chemical weapons against Kurdish civilians, and Scud missiles were launched against Iran. But the notion that a regime like Saddam Hussein's might be in possession of nuclear weapons was unacceptable. When, in June 1981, an Israeli air raid destroyed Ossirak, Iraq's nuclear reactor, Iraq did not respond or retaliate, but Israel's action further exacerbated Iraq's hostility.[25]

The end of the war against Iraq had the effect of releasing the huge military machine that Saddam Hussein had constructed. He was determined to use it in order to aggrandize his regime, and he saw Israel as a principal foe and an obstacle to his schemes. In April 1990, he publicly warned that Iraq possessed "binary chemical weapons" and threatened to "make fire eat up half of Israel if it tries to do anything against Iraq." He may have been thinking of the conquest of Kuwait, or of Israel's anticipated opposition to any Iraqi act of aggrandizement, but he was also trying to deter Israel from interfering with his plans, and to couch his expansionist schemes in anti-Israeli terms.[26] In the event, Saddam chose to carry out his aggrandizement in the Gulf; he occupied Kuwait and threatened Saudi Arabia, thus triggering the crisis of 1990 and the war of 1991. He positioned himself as a latter-day Nasser fighting for the Arab cause against the West and against Israel, depicting his occupation of Kuwait as part of a broader challenge to the colonial order that had been imposed on the Arab world at the end of World War I. This was hollow posturing, and most of the Arab world saw it as such. But some mistakenly either accepted Saddam's claims or believed that he would somehow emerge victorious. The PLO's leaders and many Palestinians in the Gulf made these errors.[27]

During the Gulf War, Saddam fired about forty Scud missiles at Israel, primarily in order to draw Israel into the war and to split the Arab coalition the United States had organized against him. Shamir's government, partly of its own volition and partly under American pressure, did not respond—restraint that paid off handsomely. The U.S.-led coalition decimated Iraq's military machine, and the constraints imposed on Iraq by the United States through the UN at the war's end destroyed almost all, if not all, of Iraq's missiles and unconventional arsenal; a sanctions regime severely limited Iraq's oil exports and oil revenues. Washington's "containment" of Iraq has denied it any effective role in the Middle East since 1991.

In the 1980s, at the height of its war with Iran, and then in the 1990s, Iraq sent some indirect messages to Israel that it was interested in entering into a tacit dialogue. Some Israeli politicians and strategic planners supported this idea, arguing that it could balance the threat posed by Iran or provide leverage vis-à-vis Syria. Others argued that Saddam was not credible, that Israel should support U.S. policy and not subvert it, and that in any event Iraq was not seriously interested in dialogue but, at best, in buying some goodwill in the United States. The latter arguments prevailed, and a tacit dialogue, whether or not Saddam intended it, never developed.

Israel, alongside the United States, monitored closely Iraq's compliance with the regulations imposed on Baghdad at the end of the Gulf War. With almost all of Iraq's arsenal of weapons of mass destruction and ballistic missiles destroyed, as well as its capacity to reproduce them, and with Iraq's oil exports limited to the bare minimum, this edge of Iraq's offensive capabilities was blunted. Saddam's limited resources were invested instead in his regime's very survival. But he was also remarkably consistent in his drive to erode this situation, to erode Middle Eastern and international support for Washington's policies, and to maintain or restore at least a measure of Iraq's offensive capability. On several occasions the United States responded to these challenges with limited military action and in February 1998 prepared the ground for a large-scale operation.

We saw above how this dynamic was transformed by George W. Bush's election to the presidency and by the terrorist attack of September 11, 2001. The anticipated repercussions of the war in Iraq on Israel's relationship with the Arab world are analyzed in this volume's conclusion, "The New Agenda."

# 7

# PEACE AND NORMALIZATION

In the mid-1970s, an unusual book was published in Egypt under the title *After the Guns Fall Silent*, written by the Egyptian left-wing intellectual and journalist Muhammad Sid Ahmed.[1] It was the first presentation of an Arab vision of accommodation with Israel, the first Arab effort to spell out what the Middle East might look like after the establishment of Arab-Israeli peace. The author of this bold, pioneering work was roundly criticized in Egypt and elsewhere in the Arab world for breaking a taboo in his endorsing and propagating the idea of peaceful accommodation with Israel. This was so even though the book was written and published after the signing of the Israeli-Egyptian and Israeli-Syrian disengagement agreements, and after two Arab summit conferences had redefined the Arab consensus to embrace the principle of a political settlement with Israel. But a full-fledged vision of Arab-Israeli peace written by a major Egyptian intellectual with left-wing credentials was still difficult for those who remained ideologically and emotionally committed to the struggle against Israel.

In fact, there is a great deal of ambivalence and vacillation at the very core of Sid Ahmed's book. The author began by posing this question: "What shape will the Middle East take after a just and permanent peace?" He then explained that "among Arabs the topic is taboo, condemned as a notion by the bulk of public opinion as well as by most of the intelligentsia. It is condemned because there is a deep-rooted conviction in the Arab psyche that the only conceivable settlement would entail complete surrender." But, he argued, after the October War, which brought more balance to the Israeli-Arab equation, a change occurred in the Arab view of a political settlement. The Arab world decided to settle, "but as long as the settlement with Israel and the future of peace in the region is not embodied in a clearly defined vision, Israel will never admit that the Arab goal is genuine: it will continue to cast doubts on the sincerity of their overtures and maintain that the Arab position is basically unchanged."[2]

It is precisely that "clearly defined vision" that Sid Ahmed set forth. As he saw it, an enduring peace would require Israel to play a "functional role" in the Middle East, comparable to but different from that of Lebanon. "There is . . . more or less tacit acknowledgement that the existence of Israel within secure and recognized borders is unavoidable after the Arabs recover their occupied territories and after the establishment of some Palestinian entity." Then, once settlement is achieved along these lines, the chief psychological barrier to Israel's integration into the region could be addressed: "The stumbling block has always been the Arabs' fear of Israel's technological superiority and her ability, if peace came to the region, to dominate the Arabs economically and to prevent them from becoming masters of their own fate."[3]

But Arabs after the October War, buttressed by the use of the "oil weapon" and having accumulated huge revenues, "acquired a new confidence that Israeli superiority could no longer deprive them of their freedom of decision—even in the case of peace . . . Israeli quality could no longer neutralize Arab quantity. . . . For the first time some kind of match between Israeli technological know-how and Arab capital can be envisaged in certain quarters." Moreover, in the spirit of "complementarity" there need be no contradiction between security arrangements and economic interests. Security arrangements do not necessarily have to rely on "negative sanctions" (like demilitarized zones or areas policed by UN forces) but can actually go hand in hand with "positive incentives" to "promote the interest of the protagonists to abstain from war."

> Industrial projects could conceivably be set up in Sinai, in the Negev, the Gaza Strip, the West Bank, in various parts of a Palestinian state, and even on the borders separating Israel from Syria and South Lebanon. Possibly petrochemical plants could be erected in some of those regions and more and more of the crude oil that now goes to the West could be retained to feed these petrochemical complexes. This Arab asset could be exported not in the form of crude alone but also in the form of finished and semifinished products.[4]

Sid Ahmed saw several advantages in matching security arrangements with economic-development schemes. Capital could be mobilized for projects that might not be feasible otherwise. Countries like Egypt would benefit by shifting part of their population from densely populated regions to desert areas. Advanced industries in an area like the Sinai could also include "nuclear plants to desalinize sea water for irrigating wide areas of the desert to meet growing food requirements." Industrial projects "erected inside the Palestinian state will invalidate the argument that this state is not viable."

After a first phase of this kind, during which Israel would be reluctantly but inevitably absorbed into the life of the Middle East, a second phase could develop in which Arabs "could use Israeli human and technological assets to achieve a Middle East conglomerate able to stand up to the big geopolitical conglomerates expected to coalesce at the turn of the century." Curiously, some of Sid Ahmed's paragraphs read like the vision of Arab-Jewish coexistence that T. E. Lawrence had sketched out more than half a century earlier. Most of the time Sid Ahmed wrote and thought as a Marxist, dialectically—the course of events being determined by the interplay between "contradictions." It is thus fully in character that, after completing the presentation of his impressive ideas about Arab-Israeli peace, he argued the opposite case: that the obstacles inherent in the situation are such that implementation is quite unlikely; indeed, that another Arab-Israeli war may yet be launched.

Most of the "stumbling blocks" the author identified had to do with Israel itself. Muhammad Sid Ahmed had come to accept, in fact advocate, the idea of accommodation with Israel, but he retained a critical, not to say negative, attitude toward the Jewish state, anticipating Israeli attempts to break up the settlement into a number of separate agreements ... in the hope that partial agreements would allow it to neutralize the weaker links instead of dealing with all Arab parties as equals.

But even if a total settlement is achieved, there will be a problem concerning Israel itself. The only justification for its existence is as the embodiment of the Zionist design, and it would lose its *raison d'être* if its role is reduced to that of an economic instrument that the Arab environment would have digested and used for its own development.[5]

Furthermore, "if a settlement is reached, many Arab Jews will eventually return to their original homelands as Israeli emissaries or end up by resettling. Israel has always derived its strength by claiming that its very existence was at stake. Can it continue to obtain foreign aid once this argument loses credibility?" He concluded on a pessimistic note: "For all these reasons Israel will resist being absorbed into the region with all the means at its disposal. That is why a fifth war is likely."[6]

More than twenty years after its publication, *After the Guns Fall Silent* stands out as a unique and exceptionally prescient work in a number of ways. Not merely was it the first work in Arabic to offer and endorse a vision of Arab-Israeli peace, but for many years it remained the only work of its kind. (Not until recently was it supplemented by Hazem Sughria's *In Defense of Peace*.) Sid Ahmed understood correctly that beyond an agreement enabling Israelis and Arabs to sort out their differences and settle their conflicts lay complex and difficult questions regarding Israel's own essence, its view of itself, and its role in the region. For a peace settlement to be durable, Israel would have to become part of the Middle East and to have a "function," as he calls it, in its development. For that to happen, he assumed that Israel would have to undergo a transformation, and then he posed a legitimate question: could Israel become an integral part of the Middle East and retain its own character and cohesion? (Sid Ahmed held a view common in Egypt that Jews of Middle Eastern extraction are "Arab Jews" whose ultimate identity has yet to crystallize.)

Sid Ahmed's ideas regarding the actual cooperation possible between Israel and the Arab states—industrial zones in border areas, nuclear-powered desalinization plants in desert areas—are remarkably farsighted. But his ambivalence is as telling: the traces of lingering hostility to Israel, his doubts, his questions.

Yet the term "peace" has occupied a prominent place in the vocabulary of Arab-Israeli relations for more than fifty years. This had not been the case during the early decades of the Arab-Jewish conflict in and over Palestine, when the contenders sought victory, accommodation, or political settlement. The UN partition resolution, the establishment of the state of Israel, the 1948 war, and Israel's victory in it created an entirely different situation. The war consolidated Israel's existence, but it also expanded and exacerbated the conflict between the new state and its Arab surroundings. Yet, in order to normalize its position and to proceed with its agenda, the new state needed peace. And peace was for the Arabs to give or deny; this capacity, and the adamant and persistent refusal to extend it, soon became their principal weapon against Israel.

Recent scholarship has shown that Israeli and Arab attitudes toward the notion of a peaceful settlement during the very early stages of the conflict were more complex than had been assumed in subsequent decades, which were characterized by Israeli craving for and Arab rejection of the very idea. During the final phases of the 1948 war and immediately thereafter, several Arab protagonists were willing to discuss peace, but Israeli policy as shaped by David Ben-Gurion preferred armistice agreements to peace treaties. Israel thought the terms demanded by those prospective Arab partners were dangerous, unwarranted, and unacceptable. It preferred to consolidate its existence and preserve its achievements through a more modest series of armistice agreements, and to seek peace later, on a more secure base. Then, during late 1949, when Israel's calculus and policy changed, full-fledged peace agreements proved elusive. King Abdullah of Jordan was the only Arab leader then to conduct—and in fact complete—a peace negotiation with Israel, but when it came to implementation in early 1950, he discovered that he no longer had the authority or the political base for such a bold move.[7]

This brief quest for Arab-Israeli peace was followed by nearly two decades during which peace was an abstract, remote notion. On the Arab side, peace with Israel became equated with capitulation and betrayal. When the president of Tunisia, Habib Bourguiba, proposed in 1965 that the Arab world adopt a "phased strategy"—recognize Israel and continue the struggle through peaceful means—he was denounced as a traitor. Two years later, right after the Six-Day War, the Arab summit conference in Khartoum reiterated and reformulated Arab nationalism's categorical rejection of the very notion of peace with Israel.

On the Israeli side, peace was increasingly considered in mystical terms and as inaccessible, while actual policies focused on meeting Arab political and military challenges. The outcome of the 1967 war altered the situation. The United States shared Israel's view that its victory must be converted into nothing less than a full-fledged peace settlement, and initiated the "territories-for-peace" policy which, through several variations, has guided its conduct to this day. Yet the very idea was initially unacceptable to the defeated Arab states and their supporters and was never accepted by Israel. And, though it informs Security Council Resolution 242, given the UN's need to satisfy diverse and contradictory interests, references to territorial concessions and contractual peace were indirect or coded. Thus peace in the full sense of the term was postponed for another decade, and Middle Eastern diplomacy focused instead on more modest forms of accommodation. When, in February 1971, Egypt's new president, Anwar al-Sadat, communicated through the UN envoy, Gunnar Jarring, his willingness "to enter into a peace agreement with Israel," he probably did not have in mind the full-blown peace treaty he ended up signing in 1979, and Israel did not take his regime and his offer seriously.[8]

Only after the October War was serious thought given to, and work done for, a peaceful resolution of the Arab-Israeli conflict. On the Israeli side, the principal figure was Yitzhak Rabin during his first tenure as prime minister, in 1974–77. (Golda Meir and Moshe Dayan, whose policies collapsed during the war in 1973, saw through the disengagement agreements with Egypt and Syria, but Rabin was left to deal with the long-term consequences.)

Rabin's policy was based on two premises: that, at the height of Arab economic power and international political influence, it was not to Israel's advantage to seek a comprehensive settlement; and that Israel could not and should not accept one based on withdrawal to the June 4, 1967, lines. He therefore collaborated with Henry Kissinger in the "step-by-step" diplomacy that led to the September 1975 Israeli-Egyptian interim agreement. On the Arab side, the principle of settling the conflict politically was formally endorsed at the summit conference in Algiers in November 1973. But this meant, as the final communiqué expressed it, acceptance of the Arabs' two premises: that Israel had to withdraw from all Arab territories occupied in June 1967 (including Jerusalem); and that the Palestinians must recover their "established national rights." This was rather vague and could be and indeed was interpreted in more than one way. But Egypt kept edging toward a bolder concept of a peaceful settlement.[9]

Egypt's political and intellectual elite more or less agreed that Egypt must disengage from the policy it had followed vis-à-vis Israel for a quarter-century. Egypt had paid a terrible price for the Six-Day War and the war of attrition; the oil-producing states of the Gulf had accumulated wealth and influence while Egypt declined. So Cairo's priorities had to be altered. Thus a will to disengage from the conflict with Israel was clear, but it was not matched by a clear sense of how this could or should be achieved. Debates raged. Muhammad Sid Ahmed drew his bold scenario of peace and "complementarity," while others advocated a theory of Israel's "withering" with a more hostile edge: the Arabs would make peace with Israel if the latter withdrew from all territories occupied in June 1967. An Israel "reduced to its natural dimensions," a "second Lebanon," was an entity Egypt and the Arab world could accept; in any event, a shriveled Israel was not viable, would lose coherence and sense of purpose; internal contradictions would come to the fore; and the Israeli state would wither over time.[10] A slightly milder approach was offered by Boutros Boutros-Ghali, then a senior scholar and member of Egypt's foreign-policy establishment:

> In any case, the front-line states may in the near future accept a de jure recognition of Israel, but not the possibility of instituting diplomatic, commercial or cultural relations with it. This is not to say that such relations are inconceivable in the more distant future. It will remain for the State of Israel to prove to the interstate community of the Arab world that it wishes to and is able to integrate itself into the region. This willingness on Israel's part would have to include a vast program of Arabization in which Arabic would become a language of Israel on equal footing with Hebrew[, and] an active process of cultural and social decolonization, in which the policies of both immigration and emigration would be calculated to encourage the integration into the Israeli population only of elements that could adapt to this profound change in the nature of Israeli society. The author does not underestimate the difficulties that would be created in Israeli society by this sort of change[, but] only a change of this nature can incur the passage of the front-line states from a stage of confrontation to one of coexistence and, from there, to a level of active cooperation without which there can be no real or durable peace in the area.[11]

The debate ended with the direct Egyptian-Israeli negotiation predicated on the principle of "land for peace." The bilateral part of the Camp David Accords and the subsequent peace treaty rested on a clear formula: Israel's full withdrawal from the Sinai Peninsula in return for contractual peace, "normalized" relations, and a satisfactory security regime. But the same clarity did not apply to the "framework for peace." Disagreements over the implementation of the "autonomy plan" for Palestinians marred the new relationship, and the initial hopes that Israel's relations with the Arab world would be transformed were dashed.

Before this turn of events, Israelis had time to think seriously about the meaning of peace. It was no longer an abstract notion wrapped in mist but a concrete, accessible goal. Egypt was opened to Israeli tourists in 1979 and thousands traveled to Cairo, Alexandria, and Upper Egypt. Israelis were engaged in drawing up bold plans as well as in soul-searching. When borders were open and people could move in both directions, would Israel lose its coherence and identity? Would Israeli Jews of Middle Eastern extraction perhaps feel more comfortable in Egypt than in Israel's Westernized culture?[12]

But by 1981 it had become clear that the "framework for peace" was doomed. The "cold peace" meant that diplomatic relations and some elements of "normal relations" were implemented and maintained, that the security regime in the Sinai was adhered to, but a critical, negative tone came to characterize Cairo's attitude and policy toward Israel.

This selective policy enabled Egypt to maintain the basic, most important elements of its new relationship with Israel and to cultivate its new relationship with the United States while at the same time placating Islamist and leftist opposition and mending fences in the Arab world. But some Israelis criticized and complained: this was not the peace they had yearned for and envisioned. Among other Israelis, who had felt uncomfortable with the prospects of opening up to the Arab world, of losing the comfort of a familiar way of life, there was a lack of genuine interest in Arab social and cultural life. (It is significant that no correspondent for an Israeli newspaper or television station has been stationed over time in Cairo.) In January 1999, Ariel Sharon, addressing a closed session of Israeli diplomats in New York, expressed the atavistic discomfort most Israelis seem to have with the prospect of open borders between Israel and her Arab neighbors: "If we keep open borders—which may be a vision of this peace [process]—Israel would be swamped by many vehicles, would become a country of transit; hundreds of thousands of Arab visitors would come carrying not swords in their hands but olive leaves in their mouths . . . this is a very complex issue that will have to be thought through."[13]

This Israeli frame of mind might conceivably have been altered, with the gradual development of new ties, but that was not allowed to happen. Instead, both sides settled into the new reality of a limited selective relationship. Thousands of Israelis went to Egypt as tourists; very few Egyptians came to Israel. Curiously, an Israeli Academic Center was allowed to open in Cairo, but it was rendered controversial by the unruly media, and its effect was in any event limited because it was boycotted by Egypt's hostile intelligentsia and academic establishment.

The Israeli assumption that peace with the largest, most important, and most powerful Arab state would go a long way toward ending the Arab-Israeli conflict proved wrong. That Egypt had made a full peace with Israel had no profound immediate effect elsewhere in the Arab world. The termination of the military conflict between Egypt and Israel tended to telescope rather than limit the Arab-Israeli conflict. Indeed, resolution of the Israeli-Egyptian conflict only exacerbated the Palestinian, Syrian, and Lebanese dimensions of Israel's situation. Hardly less damaging was the realization that peace could be made and maintained without a genuine reconciliation. Menachem Begin had wanted a separate peace with Egypt, and at this he proved to be quite successful, but it fell short of being the peace Israelis yearned for.

The lengthy suspension of the peace process finally ended with the Madrid Conference in October 1991 and its new concept of four tracks of bilateral negotiations (with Israel's immediate neighbors: Syria, Lebanon, Jordan, and the Palestinians) and a parallel track of multilateral negotiations. As we have seen, the multilateral efforts were made by five working groups concerned with refugees, water, arms control and regional security, environmental problems, and economic development. Arab states from the Gulf and North Africa and interested states from other parts of the world were invited to join these working groups. By dealing with issues that were meant to be solved after the resolution of Israeli-Arab political disputes, the parties could glimpse the prospect of regional cooperation, and this in turn could facilitate the difficult bilateral negotiations. This proved to be a particularly productive idea. The multilateral talks were successful both in their own right and as a launch for the regional economic conferences that were the high-water mark of the peace process in the mid-1990s.

It was through these multilateral talks that a nation like Saudi Arabia came to participate in the peace process. The Saudis had been sharply critical of Sadat's original peacemaking with Israel, but time had changed their perspective and priorities. The Iranian revolution of 1979, the rise of a powerful Iraqi state, and the tidal wave of radical Islam all over the Middle East presented new and ominous threats to the kingdom's survival and prosperity. In the perspective afforded by these developments, the Israeli challenge lost much of its edge. In fact, Egyptian-Israeli peace and stabilization at the core of the Middle East came to be seen as a positive development, for it would help contain Iran, Iraq, and the radical tide in the Gulf. The signing of the Oslo Accords legitimized a significant measure of Saudi-Israeli normalization. It was a first step, still a far cry from the Arab definition of a "just peace," but if "the sole legitimate representative" of Palestinian nationalism had crossed the threshold and agreed to mutual recognition with Israel, why should Saudis, Omanis, and Tunisians refuse to discuss future regional projects with Israelis in a multilateral working group?

Rabin approached all these new developments in his customary pragmatic way. Israel faced both an opportunity and a duty. The availability of the Madrid framework, the evident changes in Arab attitudes, the hospitable regional and international arenas all offered unusual chances to move the peace process forward, and it was

Israel's duty to take advantage of them. But it was not at all clear how far and along which course the peace process could be moved. As Rabin saw it, Israel should indicate its willingness, explore the options, make progress where progress could be made, and make fresh decisions along the way.

Rabin's approach was incrementalist. As he had in the mid-1970s, he shied away from a sweeping approach to a comprehensive or swift settlement. A final resolution was not feasible, and whatever version of it was available came with a prohibitively high cost. Israel's first step should be made with either the Palestinians or the Syrians, and the next step should depend on that first breakthrough and be tailored to the circumstances. And so it was that the first agreement was with the PLO and that it was followed by peace with Jordan. Rabin was surprised by the willingness of other Arab states to normalize relations with Israel and to participate in the regional economic conferences in Casablanca and Amman. But with no agreement with Syria, the road to a formal resolution of the Arab-Israeli conflict was closed. Still, Rabin was not in a hurry. Much had been accomplished in only a few years, and the difficult job of completing the final-status negotiations with the Palestinians and the arduous negotiation with Syria would have to be carried out during a second term.

Peres, as we have seen, approached the peace process in an entirely different way. He was mindful of all the difficult political and territorial disputes between Israel and its Arab neighbors, but to him these were not the crucial matter. They would be addressed in the first, transitional phase, during which trust and confidence should build, but "in the second, decisive phase of the peace process the specific nature of peace is the dominant issue."[14] And its nature would be determined by the interplay between Arab-Israeli relations and the larger regional developments of which they were a part. In short, a durable solution to the Arab-Israeli problem could be achieved only when the Middle East had established a regional system, and the formation of such a system depended on the resolution of the Arab-Israeli conflict. Put differently, Israel could not enjoy a stable peace so long as the Middle East was beset by severe social and economic problems, and Israel's neighbors could not overcome their problems so long as they failed to settle their conflict with Israel. The foreign minister's vision was stated boldly:

> Peace between Israel and its Arab neighbors will create the environment for a basic reorganization of Middle Eastern institutions. Reconciliation and Arab acceptance of Israel as a nation with equal rights and responsibilities will sire a new sort of cooperation—not only between Israel and its neighbors but also among Arab nations. It will change the face of the region and its ideological climate. . . .
>
> The problems of this region of the world cannot be solved by individual nations. . . . Regional organization is the key to peace and security. . . . Our ultimate goal is the creation of a regional community of nations . . . modeled on the European community.[15]

As Rabin's foreign minister and partner, Peres was given considerable scope to try to implement some of his ideas. He helped initiate the "donors' conference" in Washington, two weeks after the signing ceremony on the White House lawn; this was intended to orchestrate a large-scale international boost to the Palestinian economy and to raise living standards in the Gaza Strip and the

West Bank. Indeed, the point was to recast the economic relationship between Israel and the West Bank and the Gaza Strip (the legal framework having been defined in the Paris Agreement in July 1994). This campaign was motivated by more than the obvious and familiar idea that Arab peacemakers should be rewarded economically. As American and Israeli policy-makers saw it, Hamas and the other fundamentalist groups who opposed Arafat fed on poverty; by creating new sources of employment, by providing housing projects and better schools, the Palestinian Authority could better build a constituency that supported peace with Israel. A different way of saying much the same thing was to say that over time it would be hard if not impossible to maintain peace between a society enjoying a per capita income of $18,000 a year and a society with a per capita income of less than $1,000 a year. That is difficult enough between neighboring states separated by clearly defined boundaries, and even more so in the case of two societies whose lives are closely intertwined.

Israel's effort to get financial and economic aid to the Palestinian Authority was a controversial aspect of the Rabin-Peres policy—controversial in Israel and among Jewish communities abroad. After years of mobilizing *against* Arafat and the PLO, it was difficult to accept the reconciliation, the recognition, the symbolism of a handshake, and even harder to imagine Israeli leaders and diplomats lobbying to obtain financial resources for yesterday's enemies. Yet this went to the core of the new reality that Israeli policy-makers were seeking to shape. Israelis have yet to decide whether they want a clear-cut separation from the Palestinians or some form of association or integration. But whatever shape the final settlement takes, the very existence of the Oslo Accords means that it has ceased to be a zero-sum game. Mental adjustment to this revolutionary truth has lagged far behind, for understandable reasons. The Rabin government, and Foreign Minister Peres in particular, were way ahead of the public in adjusting to this new reality and molding it to fit into a new policy about Israel and its Arab environment.

Under Peres's direction, then, experts affiliated with the Foreign Ministry prepared an impressive dossier of joint economic projects. Of particular significance were the industrial parks proposed for several sites along the lines separating Israel from the West Bank and the Gaza Strip, to be financed by international agencies and private investors, and intended to provide employment for Palestinian workers while facilitating Israeli-Palestinian economic cooperation and minimizing friction or the appearance of Israeli economic domination. (The similarity to some of the ideas raised nearly twenty years earlier by Muhammad Sid Ahmed is quite striking.) In short order, a similar approach was likely for Israel's relationship with Jordan. King Hussein made clear that he expected "peace dividends"—debt relief and military aid from the United States and massive investments in Jordan's economy that would make up for the loss of remittances from Jordanian workers in the Gulf. He also indicated that he was willing to develop a "warm peace" with Israel, in stark contrast to Egypt's proverbial "cold" policy. The Foreign Ministry responded with a thick volume of projects focused on the Jordan rift valley. It included spectacular infrastructure projects (for example, a canal leading from the Dead Sea to a single Red Sea port just above the Gulf of Eilat, and a joint international airport for Eilat and Aqaba) as well as more conventional industrial parks in border areas.

It was during Peres's secret visit with King Hussein in November 1993 that an international business conference was first proposed. (Peres wanted to hold it in Amman.) The Israeli effort to take advantage of the Oslo Accords so as finally to make peace with Jordan had just begun, and Peres was seeking to expand the agenda. In the winter of 1993–94, the king was not quite ready for such a bold move, but the Clinton administration was persuaded to endorse the idea and helped to recruit Morocco's King Hassan: the first conference took place in Casablanca a year later, the second one in Amman in October 1995. Both conferences were impressive and successful gatherings of many Israeli, Arab, and international businessmen, though it is difficult to point out many joint Arab-Israeli business ventures that grew out of them; still, as a demonstration of the potentials inherent in the peace process, they were most effective. So Peres pushed on and tried to put together a regional bank for the Middle East, modeled after regional banks in other parts of the world. He came quite close to seeing this project through, but neither the Clinton administration nor most Arab states had been fully supportive of this concept, and with the waning of the peace process it was shelved *sine die*.

The differences between Rabin's and Peres's approaches to peacemaking were underlined by the changes Peres introduced when he assumed power in November 1995, after Rabin's assassination, in the conduct of Israel's negotiation with Syria. Rabin had assumed that Israel could not expect to obtain more than a "cold" peace with Syria, tailored by Assad to offer less than Sadat had given.

A warmer, closer relationship could develop only over time. But a contractual peace and satisfactory security regime would remove the danger of conventional war, push Iran back to the margins of the Middle East, resolve Israel's problem in Lebanon, and consolidate the agreements with Jordan and the Palestinians. These achievements would justify the concessions Israel would have to offer Damascus.

Peres was not interested in yet another version of Egypt's "cold peace" and thought it would be difficult to persuade the Israeli public to withdraw from the Golan Heights in return. But if Syria's economy could be tied more closely to the global economy, if investments were brought to it, if joint Israeli-Syrian ventures could be launched (even, if necessary, with American sponsorship or partnership), a web of interests would develop that would reduce the danger of renewed conflict. And if some of these joint ventures were established in the Golan Heights, this cordon would be hardly less valuable as security protection than yet another line of fortifications. And Syria would have to think twice before embarking on a course that would jeopardize its investments and interests in the Golan. Joint ventures in the Golan would also make Israeli concessions easier, blunting the sense of loss and departure. In the terminology of conflict-resolution theory—whereas Rabin was seeking a "settlement" with Syria, Peres was aiming at a "resolution."

Further, Peres wanted to make a prospective agreement with Syria a stepping-stone to a comprehensive Arab-Israeli settlement. In his discussions with the Clinton administration he explored the idea of a regional-security system in the Middle East, though the Americans regarded it as premature. Meanwhile, discussions between Israel and Turkey matured to produce a formal agreement on strategic cooperation. In theory, this Turkish-Israeli relationship could fit into a regional system inclusive of the major Arab states, but in practice Israel's Arab interlocutors, first and foremost Syria, viewed it as an anti-Arab measure, a revival of David Ben-Gurion's "alliance of the periphery" in the late 1950s.

Nor was Assad enamored of the economic aspects of Peres's peace policy, which he had already denounced as an Israeli scheme directed against Arab nationalism. He found the notion of joint businesses an offensive intrusion: any Israeli involvement in projects in the Golan Heights would be interpreted as perpetuating its presence there and denying him the chance for a full liberation of Syrian territories lost in 1967. As Assad's biographer, Patrick Seale, put it: "Most Syrians would have seen such a settlement as exposing their society, nascent industries, cultural traditions and national security to hostile Israeli penetration. For Asad it would have made a mockery of his entire career."[16]

It is telling that negotiations between Israel and Syria collapsed in March 1996 for reasons that had little to do with this dim view of economic relations with Israel in the event of peace and more to do with Assad's response to the initiative of an Israeli prime minister who was eager to come to an agreement with him. Assad had negotiated with Israel resentfully and grudgingly because it was something he had been forced to do, and now his policy options had diminished. As a grudging peacemaker, he would agree only to what he could not avoid, and he would demonstrate his dissatisfaction with the way things

were going. Assad at one and the same time criticized everyone who deviated from the course he had tried to pre-
scribe—who, in his view, gave Israel too much and undermined him—and was criticized by Syrians and others
adamantly opposed to peace with Israel, who expected or
wanted him to uphold the ideas and principles they had
once been identified with. For those who thought and
said that terms like "revolution," "Arab unity," and "Arab
socialism" had long ago lost their meaning, that the
Ba'ath had become a hollow term, but who were hoping
against hope that Assad would hold the line, his willingness to sign a contractual peace with Israel was a bitter
disappointment.

The lines separating Assad's position from that of his
critics and from that of the objects of his own criticism
are landmarks, and when we try to map out—and understand—Arab attitudes to peacemaking with Israel, we
must understand where they are. Each end of the spectrum is clear and distinct: the wholehearted opposition of
Islamic and other ideological opponents to any peace or
reconciliation, and open and unambiguous advocacy of
full peace with Israel. In the middle of the spectrum, subtle differences separate halfhearted endorsement of reconciliation from a grudging reluctance to agree to peace
and from criticism of all agreements with Israel.

As we saw above, in the twilight of Hafez al-Assad's
reign it was his foreign minister, Faruq al-Shara, who presented in an apologetic fashion the regime's version regarding its willingness to sign the peace treaty with Israel.
In essence, this version stated that signing the peace treaty
with Israel meant transition from "a struggle with an existential enemy" to competition with an adversary.

"Orphaned peace" is the term Fouad Ajami uses to describe a diplomacy that Arab opinion has accepted with many reservations.[17] Popular opinion in any country is difficult to measure, and especially in Arab countries, but there seems to be no discrepancy in this case between popular opinion and the positions articulated by public intellectuals and the intelligentsia. They are all informed with a sense of defeat. These were not good years in the Arab world. Old ideologies died or became stale and have not been replaced; the great hopes of the "oil decade" were long ago dashed. Saddam Hussein was defeated in the Gulf War, and though his immediate neighbors were relieved, there were those who had hoped for a revival of revolutionary zeal, spirit, and ideals, and they have been badly disappointed. The end of the Cold War and the disintegration of the Soviet Union left the United States with undue influence in the Middle East. Political Islam, a source of both threat and regeneration, seemed to have peaked. And even if the Arab regimes are remarkably resilient, durability does not go hand in hand with openness and innovation. Against that backdrop, peace with Israel achieved on terms closer to the Israeli than to the Arab position was received as yet another humiliation.

The expatriate Syrian poet Nizar Qabbani, one of the most eloquent and bitter critics of the "Arab order," wrote a particularly powerful and poignant poem, published in October 1995, expressing his disgust with the Oslo Accords and with the "Arab condition" exposed by them. "The last walls of embarrassment have fallen," he wrote; "we were delighted and we danced and we blessed ourselves for signing the peace of the cowards."[18] This was a humiliating surrender, with Arabs scrambling to kiss the shoes of "the killer. . . . In our hands they left a sardine can called Gaza and a dry bone called Jericho. . . . After the secret romance in Oslo, we came out barren. They gave us a homeland smaller than a single grain of wheat." And it was a deal made in the United States—"the dowry was in dollars . . . the cake was a gift from America." But Qabbani's real rage was directed at the Arabs' own political establishment, whom he held responsible for the misery and humiliation in the terms of the peace with Israel and for the larger decline of which the Oslo Accords were both a consequence and a symptom:

> Who would ask the rulers
> about the peace of cowards
> about the peace of selling in installments
> and renting in installments
> about the peace of the merchants
> and the exploiters?
> Who could ask them
> about the peace of the dead?
> They have silenced the street
> and murdered all the questions
> and those who question.

What Qabbani said in verse, others said in prose. The most prominent Palestinian intellectual, Edward Said, who had been one of Arafat's supporters several years earlier, denounced the Oslo Accords as a "sell-out." In *The Politics of Dispossession*, he wrote:

> With some of the euphoria dissipated after the great celebration surrounding the breakthrough, it now becomes possible to reexamine the Israeli-PLO agreements with the required common sense. What emerges from such scrutiny is a deal

that is more flawed and weighted unfavorably for the Palestinian people than many had first supposed. The show biz front of the White House ceremony on September 13, the degrading spectacle of Yasir Arafat thanking everyone for the suspension of most of his people's rights and the solemnity of Bill Clinton's performance . . . all these only temporarily obscure the truly astonishing proportions of the quite sudden Palestinian capitulation, which smacks of the PLO leadership's exhaustion and of Israel's shrewdness. . . .

In sum, we need to move up from a state of supine abjectness with which, in reality, the Oslo DoP was negotiated . . . into the prosecution of parallel agreements with Israel and the Arabs that concern Palestinian national, as opposed to municipal aspirations. But this does not exclude resistance against the Israeli occupation, which continues indefinitely.[19]

Qabbani's poem was entitled "Al-Muharwilun" (The hurried ones)—a castigating term for the Arabs who rushed to normalize relations with Israel. This term, used by an angry poet to denounce the Arab governments for endorsing hated agreements, diplomacy, and policies— the Egyptian and Syrian governments, notably—was the very term Arab governments themselves used to criticize those whom they accused of eagerness to "normalize" relations with Israel too rapidly. This underlines two important aspects of the Arab attitude to peacemaking with Israel: the centrality of the notion of "normalization," and the complex relationship between the ruling political classes and their societies on this particular issue. As Ajami has correctly pointed out, reservations with regard to peacemaking with Israel were one issue on which autocratic governments and their "civil societies" could agree, and in which they could have agreed on a division of labor, as it were. If it suited Sadat and Mubarak to keep the peace with Israel "cold," they might as well also let Egyptian professional associations boycott their Israeli counterparts, or let the Egyptian press vent their anger and frustration in anti-Israeli diatribes. By the same token, for a Syrian regime that was negotiating a peace with Israel and trying to achieve its extremely narrow concept of peace, statements made by Syrian writers or journalists condemning "normalization with Israel" would be useful. Nor could Arafat complain of Edward Said, Hisham Sharabi, or other prominent Palestinian intellectuals for criticizing the Oslo process when he himself publicly indicated that "the struggle continues."

During the mid-1990s, the term "normalization" came to replace "cold peace" as the key term in discussing the nature of Arab-Israeli peace. Curiously and significantly, this focused the debate on a notion that had been so cardinal to the original purpose of Zionism, which sought to normalize the condition of the Jews by establishing a state in which the Jewish people could develop a normal society and a normal economy. As we saw, this failed to happen in 1949. A Jewish state was founded and survived the 1948 war, but it could not obtain the Arab states' acceptance of its very existence. The most effective weapons in the Arabs' conflict with the Jewish state were refusal, rejection, and boycott. So the new state was rejected by its immediate neighbors, by the Muslim world, later by the Soviet bloc and much of the Third World. Israel did very well nonetheless, but its regional and international positions were not normal. Peace with the Arabs was the key to normalizing both. The end of the Cold War and the inauguration of the Madrid process improved Israel's

international position, but normalizing "the Israeli condition" could not be achieved without resolution of the
Arab-Israeli conflict.

As new agreements were being negotiated, signed, and
implemented in the years 1992–95, "normalization" acquired two different meanings: the establishment of bilateral "normal peaceful relations" between Israel and each
of its principal Arab counterparts; and the further normalization of Israel's position in the Middle East through
its participation in regional and international forums
along with Arab and other partners. The Arabs' response
to Israel's quest for normalization varied greatly. Syria's
original position in the bilateral negotiations of 1992–93
was that "normalization" fell outside the scope of the
"peace" legitimized by the Arab consensus for regaining
the territories Syria had lost in 1967. The Syrians grudgingly accepted the notion of a contractual peace, but continued to argue that the Israeli definition of normality—
in cultural, commercial, and economic relations, for in-
stance—concerned issues that "the society" and not the
government should agree to, and that conditions allowing
for such relations could develop only over time. In August
1993, when Rabin made his "hypothetical gambit" and
included "normalization" in Israel's peace proposal, Assad
responded by telling Warren Christopher that he "disliked" and "had difficulties" with that term; it took Syria
another year of trilateral negotiations with Israel and the
United States to agree to a limited, well-defined "normalization" as part of its prospective peaceful relationship
with Israel. This Syrian attitude clearly reflected the
Assad regime's negotiating style. All issues and details
were a matter of hard bargaining: the more eager Israel

was for normalization, the higher the price it would have
to pay for it.

Also, Syria was understandably trying to follow the
Egyptian precedent of "cold peace." Egypt had signed a
full-fledged peace treaty, with numerous annexes concerning normalization across the board, and it had subsequently found a way to turn these agreements into a dead
letter while keeping the essence and formality of a non-
belligerent relationship. Perhaps Syria could accomplish
the same result by avoiding the "normalization" issue altogether. Moreover, Assad felt he must do better than
merely replicate Egypt's agreement with Israel (if his
agreement with Israel looked like a copy of the Camp
David Accords, he would be hard put to explain why he
had not made it fifteen years earlier) and tried to achieve
something that at least in one major aspect would seem
better than the peace made by Sadat. In time, Assad discovered that he could not cite the precedent Egypt had
set in obtaining full withdrawal of Israeli troops from its
territory without offering an equivalent full contractual
"peace with normalization," at least on paper.

Beyond these considerations lay genuine fears of Israel's ambitions and schemes in the event of peace. Assad
was not about to open Syria up to Israeli business and
technology, or to contemplate the creation of a "new
Middle East" on the ruins of what was after all a predominantly Arab world. The thesis has been advanced that
Assad is so deeply concerned with the destabilizing effects
of peace with Israel that he does not actually want to consummate the deal and conducts negotiations in an "idle"
mode.[20] But this is an overstatement. Assad believes that
his regime can cope with the effects of peace and limited

normalization with Israel, but his aim is to contain Israel, not to integrate it into the Middle East. In October 1995, he lashed out against the very idea:

> I wonder about this notion in the far Arab future and what its values and role at present and in the future will be. . . .
>
>     This is the objective they are seeking. . . . Why is the Middle East being established? The Middle East already exists. The strange thing is that the Middle East is being presented as an alternative to Arabism. . . .[21]

As I have tried to make clear, Assad in 1995 was locked in an awkward position vis-à-vis the Israeli architect of an envisioned "new Middle East" who was willing to move much further than Rabin had been, but who insisted on "quality" and "depth" in the new peaceful relationship, and who saw normalization and economic cooperation as key to it. Assad's difficulties with this very approach were an important element in the subsequent failure to achieve a breakthrough.

As for Egypt, though there is a domestic dimension to its negativism about normalization with Israel,[22] the accent is clearly on the regional dimension. Egypt shared Syria's anxieties about a "new Middle East," but whereas Damascus voiced opposition and criticism from the sidelines, Cairo was forced, by virtue of being both a pillar of the peace process and a critic of its excesses, to adopt a much more complex policy. Its dilemmas were simplified by Netanyahu's victory and by the subsequent decline of peace diplomacy, for Israel's regional role diminished and Cairo could shift from subtle, indirect criticism of overly eager, hurried, and premature Arab willingness to normalize relations with Israel to outright criticism of nor-

malization as such. "Normalization is an Israeli inven-
tion," stated Osama al-Baz, a particularly thoughtful
Egyptian policy-maker, "which means the establishment
of a special relationship. Such a relationship must be
predicated on a common concept of and common interests in the future, and these are absent of true progress
and of a national, normal Israeli conduct, which meets
legal criteria; normal relations cannot be maintained lest
the balance be upset."[23]

Jordan formulated its peace policy in yet a third way.
It was willing to offer Israel a distinctly "warm" peace in
return for rewards it expected to gain from other dimensions of its relationship with its neighbor. The Hashemite
regime had no qualms about the effect of normalized relations with Israel in its own domestic sphere or about Israel's playing a regional role at the expense of some of Jordan's rivals. But the course of events in recent years has
made this policy untenable. Rabin's assassination, public
resistance at home, the failure of the anticipated "peace
dividends" to materialize, and the general decline of peace
diplomacy forced King Hussein to turn down the volume
on peace and normalization. And now Israel's relationship
with Jordan does not appear very different from its relationship with Egypt.

At the same time, the Palestinian approach is remarkably uninhibited. This may sound surprising, given the
ferocity of the Israeli-Palestinian conflict, but it is quite
understandable when the realities of two societies intertwined with one another are taken into account. In any
event, the Palestinians' leverage in the peace process derives primarily from their centrality in determining the
legitimacy and finality of a settlement. This crucial issue

goes to the core of Israel's relationship with the Arab world. Israel appears to Arabs as a powerful, aggressive, and threatening entity, but in fact it is a country haunted by a sense of vulnerability and persecution. Arabs believe as a rule that time is on their side, and many Israelis agree. But they have different views of a final settlement as a result. As Israelis see it, they are offering, irreversibly, to give up tangible assets, and they would like to be reassured that the consequent settlement is definitive and final, not open-ended. This is matched by a tendency on the Arabs' side to deny Israel that very asset—a reassuring sense of finality.

Since the Cairo conference in June 1996, there has been an official Arab definition of the terms under which a comprehensive Arab-Israeli peace might be established (and, implicitly, the Arab-Israeli conflict might end):

> Adhering to their national responsibility, the Arab leaders assert that the establishment of a comprehensive and just peace in the Middle East requires Israel's complete withdrawal from all occupied Palestinian territories, including Arab Jerusalem, and enabling the Palestinian people to exercise their right to self-determination and to establish an independent state with Arab Jerusalem as its capital. This is because the Palestinian issue is the crux of the Arab-Israeli conflict. The Arab leaders also call for Israel's complete withdrawal from the Syrian Golan Heights to the June 4, 1967, line and for Israel's full and unconditional withdrawal from southern Lebanon and the western al-Biqa to the internationally recognized borders, in implementation of Security Council Resolutions 242, 338, and 425 and the principle of land for peace. On these bases, they call for the resumption of talks on all tracks.

The Arab countries' commitment to continue the peace process to achieve a just and comprehensive peace under the aegis of international legitimacy is a goal and a strategic option. This commitment requires similar serious and unequivocal commitment on the part of Israel, which must work to complete the peace process in a way that will restore the rights and occupied territories and ensure balanced and equal security for all the states of the region, in accordance with the principles agreed upon at the Madrid Conference, especially the land-for-peace principles, and the assurances given to the parties.

The Arab leaders stress their adherence to the UN resolutions, which do not accept or recognize any situation resulting from Israeli settlement activity in the occupied Arab territories. They consider this settlement activity illegal, unlawful, and nonbinding. They consider the building of settlements and bringing settlers to them a violation of the Geneva Convention and the Madrid framework and an obstruction of the peace process. They call for a halt to all settlement activity in the occupied Syrian Golan Heights and the occupied Palestinian territories, particularly Jerusalem, and for the dismantling of these settlements. They also reject any change to the character and legal status of Arab Jerusalem. They emphasize that a comprehensive and just peace in the Middle East cannot be achieved unless a solution is found for the issue of Jerusalem and for the problem of *Palestinian refugees*, who *have the right to return* in accordance with international legitimacy and the UN resolutions.[24] (Italics mine)

By citing the Palestinian "right of return" as yet another condition, the Arabs introduced an element likely to perpetuate indefinitely the debate on a settlement. It is hard enough to formulate a definition of terms for a final settlement that will be acceptable to a large and diverse group, and within that group particularly important parts are played by the Palestinians and by Egypt. The "right of return" is an important issue of principle particularly for Palestinians living in the diaspora, but it is significant first and foremost as an issue likely to keep the peace process open-ended.

Egypt has been quite open and systematic in formulating a policy designed to achieve the same end. That policy was expounded in detail by President Mubarak in May 1998 at a forum of the French Institute for International Relations in Paris. "You may agree with me," he said (according to the unpublished minutes), "that the implementation of peace in the Middle East, as in other regions, requires elements that I will call indispensable elements, around which a national consensus can form particularly among the active sectors of the society." He then enumerated nine, beginning with "a popular perception that the proposed peace formula is a just formula that accomplished the required balance between the rights and commitments of the two parties. In the absence of such justice peace rests on a fragile base and will be blown by the first gust of wind. . . ." A stable peace, he went on, had to be based on international legitimacy, free will of and acceptance by the parties, comprehensiveness, and balanced security. As could be expected, he also said that Israel should give up its "military nuclear program" and sign the Nuclear Non-Proliferation Treaty.

Yet Egyptian policy on Israel has always had many strands. While formulating an open-ended definition of peace and pursuing a policy of cold peace, of opposition to "normalization," and of open enmity to Netanyahu's government, Mubarak's regime has also given a significant number of Egyptian intellectuals the green light to join a regional peace movement together with Israelis, Jordanians, and Palestinians. The group met for the first time in Copenhagen in February 1997 and has met several times since. Egyptian opponents of the peace process vehemently criticized the Egyptian participants, but Israelis were rightly impressed more by their willingness to articulate a public defense of peace with Israel than by these familiar denunciations.

In this context, Israeli and other observers anxiously monitored the arrest in the summer of 2000 of Professor Sa'd al-din Ibrahim, one of the prominent members of that Egyptian group. Ibrahim was arrested primarily because of his campaign for democracy and human rights in Egypt, but as part of the regime's campaign to blacken his name, his relationship with Israel was played up in a hostile fashion. Ibrahim was sentenced to prison and was subsequently released owing to American pressure, but the shadow of this affair was not removed by his release.

In this present phase of Arab-Israeli relations, there is no Arab consensus or dominant view with regard to peace with Israel. But in the gamut of Arab views, those of Egypt and of the Palestinians are notable. Egypt is, after all, the senior Arab state, and the Palestinians are the "core of the problem." Yet Arafat, the PLO, and the Palestinian Authority are not the sole spokesmen for the Palestinian cause. By signing the Oslo Accords and by administering an actual government with authority over land and people, Arafat and his organization became part of the established order. Political opponents and public intellectuals can articulate a Palestinian position free from the moderating effects of power and responsibility. It is interesting that two different Palestinian intellectuals operating in entirely different contexts have recently argued for a "bi-national state" as the preferred solution to the Israeli-Palestinian conflict.

Edward Said, whose break with Arafat and criticism of the Oslo Accords I have already mentioned, wrote a brief essay published on January 10, 1999, in the *New York Times Magazine* in which he argued that neither Israel's policy of separation nor the Palestinians' quest for independent statehood could work: "For all this, the problem is that Palestinian self-determination in a separate state is unworkable, just as unworkable as the principle of separation between a demographically mixed, irreversibly connected Arab population without sovereignty and a Jewish population with it. The question, I believe, is not how to devise means for persisting in trying to separate them but to see whether it is possible for them to live together as fairly and peacefully as possible."

Dr. Azmi Bishara, a member of the Knesset and an eloquent spokesman, in excellent Hebrew, for Israel's Arab citizens, in 1998 gave a lengthy interview to an Israeli magazine in which, among other things, he stated:

> I do not rule out a temporary solution of two states for two peoples, but this cannot be more than a temporary solution . . . ultimately the framework must be bi-national. . . .
>
> A distinction must be made between a historic compromise and a settlement. A settlement can be made without a historic compromise, but it would be limited in its time range and would lack the moral and historic dimensions. . . . [The Zionist left] speaks about the '67 problem as if the '48 problem did not exist. . . . If you ask me whether a Zionist peace is possible I would say that a settlement, maybe even a com-

paratively just settlement, is possible but not final, comprehensive peace, the end of the conflict. In such an event the struggle against Zionism will continue in other forms. It could possibly turn from a national to a civic struggle. In that case our role as Arab citizens of Israel could become the most important. . . .

If we speak of the national conflict the solution is the decolonization of the occupied territories in the West Bank and Gaza. But if we speak of the civic problem the solution is Israel's dezionization.

These various notions of peace among Israel's Arab partners do not mesh well with Israel's own biases and preferences. Israelis are preoccupied in this context with two principal issues: (1) the quality, or depth, of peace, and (2) the finality of the political settlement. As we have seen, there is widespread opposition in the Arab world to the very idea of normalization as such, but Israelis regard Arab willingness to offer it or refusal to do so as an important criterion for measuring the value, stability, and durability of an agreement. As we saw, Saudi Arabia took in 2002 a significant initiative in this context when Crown Prince Abdullah came forth with a plan to end the Arab-Israel conflict by offering Israel "full peace" and "normalization" in return for an Israeli withdrawal to the lines of June 4, 1967. The "Saudi initiative" was adopted on March 28, 2002, by the Arab summit in Beirut.

But the Beirut summit added to the original Saudi formula a reference to "the right of return." The Arab consensus thus endorsed the notion of normalization ten years after it had accepted the idea of peace with Israel but diluted the significance of its decision by linking it to an issue known to compound the quest for finality in Arab-Israeli relations.

Israelis attribute an even greater significance to the Arabs' attachment to open-ended formulations, and to other expressions of their reluctance to accept a definitive resolution of the conflict, all of which inflame the Israelis' underlying sense of insecurity. Whether it is the Egyptian practice of changing the definition of "satisfactory settlement" or the vows taken by radical Palestinian intellectuals and political activists never to accept the legitimacy of Zionism, the impact on the public and political debate in Israel is negative. Clearly better to have cold peace rather than hot war with Egypt, but the kind of peace Egypt offers reduces the Israeli motivation to leave the Golan Heights in return for a peace agreement with Syria when that agreement is likely to fall short of the familiar Egyptian-Israeli model.

These issues were brought into stark relief by Ehud Barak's failed quest for a comprehensive settlement with the Palestinians. As we saw, Barak was willing to go well beyond his original "red lines" in return for Arafat's formal acceptance of "the end of conflict," renunciation of additional claims from Israel, and agreement to settle the Palestinian demand for "the right of return" on the modest terms offered by Israel. According to the "orthodox" version, Arafat rejected Barak's offers and Clinton's bridging proposals precisely because he refused to offer Israel the finality it wanted and to give up the demand for "the right of return." Whether Arafat refused because he did not want to (or could not) end the conflict or because of tactical considerations (a sense that time was on his side and that additional concessions could be extracted from

Israel), he ended up seriously undermining the assumption that a historical compromise could be reached between Israel and the Palestinian national movement.

The impact of these developments was exacerbated by three years of Palestinian-Israeli fighting and the escalating spiral of blow and counterblow. They served to undo much of what had been accomplished in the mid-1990s and to radicalize both Israeli and Palestinian positions.

The launching of the "road map" in the spring of 2003 briefly revived the credibility of the prospect of a Palestinian-Israeli agreement. But its collapse in September 2003 and the sense that the Bush administration was beginning to distance itself from this issue underscored concerns that the parties were treading in a vicious cycle and that the prospect of a two-state solution was becoming dimmer.

# 8

# CONCLUSION

In September 2003, the British-Israeli scholar Ephraim Karsh published a brief monograph entitled "The Oslo War—Anatomy of Self-Delusion" under the auspices of the BESA Center at Bar-Ilan University.

As the title implies, the author draws a direct connection between the signing of the Oslo Accords in 1993 and the violence of the years 2000–2003. According to Karsh, Arafat had been seeking to establish a territorial base on the West Bank and in Gaza since 1968, from which he would be able to wage a campaign for Israel's destruction. The architects of the Oslo Accords therefore played into his hands, providing him with the territorial base he needed to launch the September 2000 offensive.

In the monograph's conclusion, Karsh asserts that "the Oslo Process was the single gravest strategic error committed by an Israeli government since the establishment of the state. Precisely twenty years after the failure to identify Anwar Sadat's willingness to take the path of

peace led to the October War, Israel's government erred
once more in reading the political map and co-opted an
Arab leader committed to Israel's destruction as a partner
for peace. This failure was much graver than its predecessor because the October War, serious and painful as it
was, had limited objectives. . . . The Oslo War, on the
other hand, is a total war, seeking to destroy the state of
Israel through ceaseless terror that would lead to massive
emigration and [through] Israel's acceptance of the 'right
of return' that would lead to its gradual collapse through
demographic undermining."

Karsh presents strident arguments that have also been
made by other participants in the academic and public-
political discourses. These arguments are not supported
by the narrative and analysis offered in this volume.
The Oslo process clearly failed. The underlying concept
of a five-year interim agreement between Israel and a Palestinian Authority—during which a measure of mutual
trust would be built between the parties and a reconciliation process would begin, enabling the parties to reach
a final-status agreement—did not materialize. The final-
status negotiations failed, and in that failure's aftermath
a violent confrontation erupted, exacting high tolls from
both sides.

There is no contesting the fact that the challenges Israel faced in fighting the current war of attrition were
significantly exacerbated by the need to contend with an
autonomous authority possessed of a militia-like police
force and intelligence and security services, and with terrorist organizations operating from autonomous territories. It is true that there were serious flaws in the construc-

tion of the Oslo process; however, it is equally true that the Oslo Accords were not implemented properly.

Led by Yasser Arafat, the Palestinian side projected a message of ongoing struggle rather than reconciliation. Arafat also failed to confront and take on the terrorist organizations. The Israeli side did not suspend the settlement project and failed to devote adequate effort to improving quality of life for the Palestinian population. Rabin's assassination removed a leader who could have navigated the Oslo process to a successful conclusion in the mid-1990s. The Palestinian terror wave in the winter of 1996 undermined the position of Shimon Peres and brought to power a prime minister critical of, if not hostile to, the Oslo process. It is therefore impossible to draw a direct line from September 1993 to September 2000. The debate on this matter will remain open and will continue to agitate both the academic community and the public arena.

Furthermore, the depth of the conflict in 2000–2003 does not, in fact, derive from the formation of the Palestinian Authority, but rather from the intensity of the conflict between two communities almost equal in size inhabiting the land west of the Jordan. In military terms, Israel is far more powerful than its Palestinian adversary, but it cannot translate its military superiority into a total, definitive victory. Seen in this context, the point of departure is not 1968 (as it was according to Karsh) but 1967— the year of Israel's victory in the Six-Day War and the establishment of its control over the West Bank and the Gaza Strip.

Since June 1967, the Israeli political system has unsuccessfully contended with both the challenges and the opportunities created by this new reality. Israel established and consolidated its presence in and control of the West Bank and Gaza, at the same time experimenting with a series of formulas to settle or resolve the issue: "The Alon Plan," Moshe Dayan's "living together," Menachem Begin's "autonomy plan," "the village leagues" during Sharon's tenure as defense minister, Rabin's autonomy plan as minister of defense and during his first months as prime minister, and then the "Oslo Accords." The outbreak of the "first *intifada*" in December 1987 was particularly significant in this course of affairs. As a genuine popular outburst, it marked the end of the twenty-year period in which Israel was able to control the West Bank and the Gaza Strip at a cost acceptable to Israeli society, allowing Israel to avoid painful and fundamental choices.

Yitzhak Shamir's willingness to go to the Madrid Conference and Yitzhak Rabin's willingness to accept the Oslo formula can be understood only against this backdrop. The Oslo formula failed, but the failure should be seen not only in the context of the years 1993–2000 but from a perspective dating back to 1967.

This is also the perspective in which one should view the four main options currently debated in Israel. The quest for a final-status agreement (despite the failure of 2000 and three years of violence) remains the first option. The principal manifestations of this quest are the "Ami Ayalon–Sari Nusseibah initiative" and the "Geneva Initiative." Ami Ayalon is the former commander of the Israeli navy and the former head of the GSS, Israel's security service. Sari Nusseibah is a prominent Palestinian academic and a member of a distinguished Jerusalem family. Together they drafted a statement of principles offering a framework for a final-status agreement, and obtained more than fifty thousand signatures from Israelis and Palestinians endorsing these principles.

In November 2003 in Geneva, a group of Israelis led by Yossi Beilin and a Palestinian group led by Yasser Abd Rabu (a former member of Arafat's cabinet) endorsed the text of a would-be Israeli-Palestinian final-status agreement. The Geneva Initiative has been more ambitious and more controversial than the Ayalon-Nusseibah initiative, insofar as it purported to act in a quasi-governmental capacity and was implemented on the international stage. However, its real significance was not the mutually agreed-on text itself but the demonstration that a group of Israelis and Palestinians could agree on such a text. In other words, it was an act not of diplomacy but of public diplomacy.

The second option is the effort—presently suspended—to reach an interim agreement either through the "road map" or through another route.

Then there is the option of adopting a unilateral Israeli decision implementing the equivalent of an interim or final-status agreement without a Palestinian partner. The obvious advantage of this option—in both its modest and its more ambitions versions—derives from the possibility of circumventing the current Palestinian leadership. But this attractiveness is counterbalanced by two principal difficulties. In the absence of a Palestinian partner, there would not be immediate political dividends to compensate for unilateral concessions (such as withdrawal, or dismantling of settlements). Also, Israel would be taking the calculated risk of coming under criticism by acting alone and confronting the Palestinians and the world with a fait accompli.

The final option is an effort to perpetuate the status quo through inertia, either through unhappiness with the three first options or through the strength of ideology and belief in Israel's eventual victory over Palestinian nationalism.

Ariel Sharon and his government have been shifting among the last three options. Sharon formally endorsed the notions of Palestinian statehood and interim settlement, and reinforced his policy by adopting a rhetoric that went so far as to condemn "the occupation." But Sharon continued to support the expansion of settlement activity—and his lukewarm attitude contributed to Abu Mazen's failure. In December 2003, the pendulum swung yet again in the other direction as Sharon's deputy and confidant, Ehud Olmert, spoke publicly about the need to implement a far-reaching unilateral settlement including territorial concessions, the dismantling of settlements, and concessions in Jerusalem. And more significantly, Olmert predicated his position on the "demographic argument"—namely, that if Israel did not disengage from the bulk of the West Bank and Gaza, it would lose its "Jewish character." Olmert was thus embracing the left's chief argument in the post-1967 debate.

The issue of the "separation fence," and the manner in which it has unfolded throughout the last two years, demonstrates the degree to which the lines separating the four options have become blurred. As its name implies, the notion of the fence was adopted at the height of the terrorist wave of 2001–2, by the advocates of unilateral separation. They insisted that the fence be constructed

close to the "green line" (the pre–June 1967 armistice
line) to normalize life in Israel by stopping suicide bomb-
ers and achieving maximum separation between the two
populations. Sharon and the bulk of the right were opposed to the idea. They suspected that by placing the
fence more or less along the "green line," Israel would in
fact be drawing the future boundary with the Palestinian
state. They were also opposed to the idea of leaving a
large number of settlers and settlements "beyond the
fence." As the casualties mounted and public pressure
built up, Sharon's government was forced to endorse the
fence and to start building it. But the task was undertaken
without enthusiasm and the fence was pushed eastward,
into the West Bank. The construction of the fence became more controversial as it was built inside the West
Bank and after a major wave of suicide bombings had
already subsided. The Palestinians adroitly called it
a "wall"—rather than a fence—and complained about
"ghettoization," while most Israelis were hard put to understand where exactly the fence was being constructed.

The options mentioned above all deal primarily with
the Palestinian issue. Indeed, the quest for a comprehensive Israeli-Arab settlement has been abandoned. Arab-
Israeli diplomacy is predicated now on the assumption
that the larger Arab-Israeli relationship would be improved by the calming or stabilizing of Israeli-Palestinian
relations. A final settlement could not be achieved without an Israeli-Syrian settlement, which neither Jerusalem
nor Washington presently wishes to pursue. However, in
late 2003, an intriguing discrepancy arose. While the
Bush administration and the Sharon government were
manifestly not interested in a resumption of the Israeli-

Syrian negotiation, Bashar al-Assad launched a "charm offensive" designed to advertise Syria's interest in such resumption.

These issues are unfolding in a changing Middle Eastern arena. In Iraq, the end of the war inaugurated the struggle over the nature of the Iraqi state. The prewar expectations of the war's architects—that a swift, impressive military victory would produce a democratic regime in Iraq and provide an impetus to democratic forces in the region—failed to materialize. Instead, the absence of a genuine Iraqi political community has been exposed, as the main ethnic and religious groups, including Sunnis, Shi'ites and Kurds, fight over the future of the Iraqi state and their respective positions within it. The cause and outcome of this conflict will have important repercussions for Israel's relationship with the Arab world.

Planners of the war also expected that Saddam's fall would encourage the opposition to the ayatollahs' regime in Iran, and would reinforce its efforts to topple the regime. Such a change has yet to happen, but Iran is approaching a moment of truth over the issue of nuclear weapons in its relations with the United States and the international community. Iran's attempts to conceal its efforts at developing nuclear weapons failed, and a decision to proceed with them could pit Iran against the United States and part of the international community. Such a course of events would have a direct and far-reaching impact on Israel and its strategic environment. The Iran of the ayatollah has defined itself as a bitter enemy of Israel. Should Iran come into possession of nuclear weapons and delivery systems, it would change the deterrence equation and the rules of the game currently upheld in the region. Iran is now engaged—through Hizballah and such radical Palestinian groups as Islamic Jihad—in an effort to exacerbate the Israeli-Arab and Israeli-Palestinian conflicts and to disrupt all attempts to resolve them. The direction of Iranian politics in the coming years will have a direct bearing on these issues.

Iran is not the only Middle Eastern state likely to undergo political change. Personal—let alone more profound—changes during the present decade in countries like Egypt, Saudi Arabia, and Syria could affect Arab-Israeli relations. Beyond the political chronology in particular Arab states, larger trends cast a shadow on the region. The Middle East and the Arab world have not fared well in the last few decades. The region's population grew dramatically without a commensurate development of economic resources and political structures. Without such a development in the coming years, the Middle East is likely to be buffeted by endemic instability—an instability that is bound to deny Arab-Israeli reconciliation and peace the environment indispensable for their success.

# NOTES

## 1. THE BACKGROUND

1. For two overviews of the Arab-Israeli conflict, see Elie Kedourie, "The Arab-Israeli Conflict," in *Arabic Political Memoirs* (London, 1974), pp. 218–31; Shimon Shamir, "The Arab-Israeli Conflict," in *The Middle East: Oil, Conflict and Hope*, ed. A. L. Udovitch (Lexington, Mass., 1976), pp. 195–231. For more detailed accounts, see Nadav Safran, *Israel—The Embattled Ally* (Cambridge, Mass., 1981); Don Peretz, *Palestinian Refugees and the Middle East* (Washington, D.C., 1993); Fred Khourie, *The Arab-Israeli Dilemma* (New York, 1968).

2. On the Madrid process, see James A. Baker, *The Politics of Diplomacy* (New York, 1995), pp. 417–20, 425–28, 447–49, 454–57, 459–63, 468–69, 487–89, 500–507; Eithan Ben Tzur, *Haderekh Lashalom Overet be Madrid* (The road to peace goes through Madrid) (Tel Aviv, 1997).

3. For an original, classic account of the Cold War in the Middle East, see John Campbell, *Defense of the Middle East* (New York, 1960). For a subsequent complete study of U.S. policy in the Middle East and relations with Israel, see Steven Spiegel, *The Other Arab-Israeli Conflict* (Chicago, 1985).

4. See William Quandt, *A Decade of Decisions* (Berkeley, Calif., 1997).

5. See Benny Morris, *1948 and After* (Oxford, 1994) and *Righteous Victims: A History of the Zionist-Arab Conflict* (New York, 1999); Avi Shlaim, *The Politics of Partition: King Abdallah, The Zionists and Palestine 1951–1971* (Oxford, 1990) and *The Iron Wall: Israel and the Arab World since 1948* (New York, 1999); Ilan Pappe, *The Making of the Arab-Israeli Conflict 1947–1951* (New York, 1988); Efraim Karsh, *Fabricating History: The New Historians* (London, 1997); Shabtai Teveth, "Charging Israel with Original Sin," *Commentary*

88 (September 3, 1989): 24–33; Zeev Sternhell, *The Founding Myths of Israel: Nationalism, Socialism and the Making of the Jewish State* (Princeton, N.J., 1998); Rami Tal, "No Subject Is Taboo for the Historian" (an interview with Anita Shapira), in *Zionism—The Sequel*, ed. Carol Diament (New York, 1998).

6. See Itamar Rabinovich, *The Road Not Taken* (New York, 1991); Neil Caplan, *Futile Diplomacy*, vol. 3 (London, 1997); Neil Caplan and Laura Zittrain Eisenberg, *Negotiating Arab-Israeli Peace* (Indiana, 1998).

7. For a cogent presentation of an Arab point of view, see Boutros Boutros-Ghali, "The Arab Response to the Challenge of Israel," in Udovitch, *The Middle East: Oil, Conflict and Hope*, pp. 231–50.

8. See Yehoshafat Harkabi, *Arab Attitudes to Israel* (Jerusalem, 1976); Yehoshafat Harkabi, *Arab Strategies and Israel's Response* (New York, 1977).

9. See Shimon Shamir, "The Middle East Crisis: On the Brink of War (14 May–4 June)," in *Middle East Record 1967*, ed. D. Dishon (Tel Aviv, 1971), pp. 183–204.

10. For a penetrating assessment of the major currents of opinions and the national mood in Israel, see Amos Oz, *In the Land of Israel* (London and New York, 1983).

11. See Fouad Ajami, *The Arab Predicament* (Cambridge, 1982).

12. See Helena Cobban, *The Palestine Liberation Organization* (Cambridge, 1984); Avraham Sela and Moshe Maoz, eds., *The PLO and Israel* (New York, 1997).

13. See Shlomo Avineri, *Israel and the Palestinians* (New York, 1971).

14. For the Israeli and American perspectives on the September 1970 crisis in Jordan, see Yitzhak Rabin, *The Rabin Memoirs* (Boston, 1979), pp. 186–89; Henry Kissinger, *The White House Years* (Boston, 1979), pp. 597–617. For a contemporary exposition of Likud's view that "Jordan is Palestine," see Benjamin Netanyahu, *A Place among the Nations* (New York, 1993), pp. 343–45.

15. For a critical view of Israeli policy at the time, see Ezer Weizman, *On Eagles' Wings* (London, 1976), pp. 279–95.

16. See Zeev Laqueur, *Confrontation* (London, 1974).

17. See William B. Quandt, *The Peace Process* (Washington, D.C., and Berkeley, Calif., 1993); Malcolm Kerr, ed., *Rich and Poor States in the Middle East* (Boulder, Colo., 1982); Moshe Dayan, *Breakthrough* (New York, 1981).

18. See Kissinger, *Years of Upheaval* (New York, 1982), pp. 747–98.

19. See Rabin, *Memoirs*, pp. 253–300; Itamar Rabinovich, "The Challenge of Diversity: American Policy and the System of Inter-Arab Relations 1973–1977," in *The Middle East and the United States*, ed. I. Rabinovich and H. Shaked (New Brunswick, N.J., 1980), pp. 181–96.

20. See Kissinger, *Years of Upheaval*; Rabin, *Memoirs*, pp. 799–853.

21. See Jimmy Carter, *Keeping the Faith* (Toronto, 1982), pp. 269–429, and *The Blood of Abraham* (Boston, 1985); Cyrus Vance, *Hard Choices* (New York, 1983), pp. 16–256.

22. See Quandt, *Peace Process*.

23. See Ze'ev Schiff and Ehud Ya'ari, *Israel's Lebanon War* (New York, 1984); Itamar Rabinovich, *The War for Lebanon, 1970–1983* (Ithaca, N.Y., and London, 1984).

24. See Fouad Ajami, *The Dream Palace of the Arabs* (New York, 1998).

25. See Shimon Peres, *Battling for Peace* (London, 1995), pp. 258–70.

26. See Baker, *Politics of Diplomacy*; Uri Savir, *The Process* (New York, 1998); and Itamar Rabinovich, *The Brink of Peace* (Princeton, N.J., 1998).

## 2. MADRID AND OSLO: YEARS OF HOPE

1. Studies and memoirs regarding this period include Itamar Rabinovich, *The Brink of Peace* (Princeton, N.J., 1998); Uri Savir, *The Process* (New York, 1998); David Makovsky, *Making Peace with the PLO* (Boulder, Colo., 1996); Warren Christopher, *In the Stream of History* (Stanford, Calif., 1998); Hanan Ashrawi, *This Side of Peace* (New York, 1995); Abbas Mahmud, *Through Secret Channels* (Reading, UK, 1995).

2. See Joseph Alpher, "What Went Wrong?" (The American Jewish Committee, New York, 1998).

3. See Robert Slater, *Rabin of Israel* (London, 1996). See also the memoir by Rabin's widow, Leah Rabin, *Our Life—His Legacy* (New York, 1997).

4. For Baker's surprisingly brief version of this, see James A. Baker, *The Politics of Diplomacy* (New York, 1995), pp. 555–57.

5. See FBIS, July 27, 1992, pp. 5–6, "Final Statement Issued."

6. On Hamas and Islamic Jihad, see Ziad Abu-Amr, *Islamic Fundamentalism in the West Bank and Gaza* (Bloomington, Ind., 1994); Hisham H. Ahmad, *From Religious Salvation to Political Transformation: The Rise of Hamas in Palestinian Society* (Jerusalem, 1994).

7. See Martin Indyk, "Dual Containment," lecture at the Washington Institute, May 18, 1993.
8. See Yossi Beilin, *Laga'at BaShalom* (To touch peace) (Tel Aviv, 1997).
9. See Shimon Peres, *Battling for Peace* (London, 1995).
10. For a detailed version of this episode, see Rabinovich, *Brink of Peace*, pp. 108–15. My version of the event is contested by the Syrian view that Rabin actually "committed Israel to a withdrawal from the Golan." For the Syrian version, see Ambassador Walid Muallem's interview in *Journal of Palestine Studies* 26, no. 2 (Winter 1997): 401–12.
11. The only detailed account of the Israeli-Jordanian negotiations is in Moshe Zak, *Hossein Oseh Shalom* (Hussein makes peace) (Ramat Gan, 1996).
12. See Uri Savir, *The Process* [in Hebrew] (Tel Aviv, 1998), pp. 346–50.
13. See Shimon Peres, *The New Middle East* (New York, 1993).
14. See FBIS, October 12, 1995, pp. 50–61, "Radio on Al-Assad's *Al-Ahram* Interview."
15. See Shai Feldman, *Nuclear Weapons and Arms Control in the Middle East* (Cambridge, Mass., 1997), pp. 7–15, 153–58.

### 3. YEARS OF STAGNATION

1. See the official text: "The Wye River Memorandum Signed at the White House, Washington, D.C.," United States Information Center.
2. So far, two biographies of Benjamin Netanyahu have been published in Hebrew. I give their titles in English here: Ben Kaspit, *Netanyahu: The Road to Power* (Tel Aviv, 1997); and Ronit Vardi, *Bibi–Who Are You, Mr. Prime Minister?* (Jerusalem, 1997).
3. See the interview with him in *Ha'aretz*, September 18, 1998.
4. See Benjamin Netanyahu, *A Place among the Nations: Israel and the World* (New York, 1993), pp. 256–328.
5. See ibid., pp. 350 ff.
6. See ibid., pp. 351–53.
7. For an illuminating study of the 1996 elections and their social context, see Daniel Ben Simon, *Another Country* [in Hebrew] (Tel

Aviv, 1997); also Daniel J. Elazar and Shmuel Sandler, *Israel at the Polls: 1996* (London, 1998).

8. See Netanyahu's interviews with David Makovsky, *Jerusalem Post*, May 10, 1996, and with Shimon Schiffer, *Yediot Ahronot*, May 23, 1996.

9. See ibid.

10. See FBIS, May 23, 1996, "Likud Issues Platform," p. 4.

11. See interview with Makovsky, *Jerusalem Post*.

12. See FBIS, June 18, 1996, "Netanyahu Government Presents Basic Guidelines," pp. 32–36.

13. See FBIS, June 24, 1996, "Final Communiqué Issued by Arab Summit," pp. 13–16.

14. See Itamar Rabinovich, *The Brink of Peace* (Princeton, N.J., 1998), pp. 256–64.

15. See the chapters on Israel in Bruce Maddy Weizman, ed., *Middle East Contemporary Survey, 1996* and *1997* (Boulder, Colo.).

16. For an excellent synoptic survey of the events that led to the signing of the Wye Agreement, see David Makovsky's article in *Ha'aretz*, December 4, 1998.

17. For a critical biography of Ariel Sharon, see Uzi Benziman, *He Does Not Stop at the Red Light* [in Hebrew] (Tel Aviv, 1985).

18. The document was first published in *Ha'aretz*, November 16, 1998.

## 4. EHUD BARAK AND THE COLLAPSE
## OF THE PEACE PROCESS

1. The first book written on the Barak period was by the journalist Raviv Druker, *Hara-kiri* [in Hebrew] (Tel Aviv, 2002). It is a critical book, relying mainly on interviews with disappointed assistants and partners and internal material from the Prime Ministry Office that was handed to the author. Later on another book was published, Ran Eddelist, *Ehud Barak: His War against the Demons* [in Hebrew] (Tel Aviv, 2002). This book attempts to form a reaction to Druker's book, and it is based, although this is not explicitly stated, on long hours of conversations with Barak himself as well as with other participants in the events of the period.

2. Ibid. and Aluf Benn in *Ha'aretz*, July 19, 1999.

3. Ibid.

4. For an overview of the Israeli-Syrian negotiations during Barak's period, see Eyal Zisser, "The Israel-Syria Negotiations, What Went Wrong?" *Orient* 42 (June 2, 2001): 225–51.

5. See Uri Savir, *The Process* (New York, 1998), pp. 298–326, and Itamar Rabinovich, *The Brink of Peace* (Princeton, N.J., 1998), pp. 248–93, 305–19.

6. For the public diplomacy in the Israeli-Syrian negotiations, see Itamar Rabinovich, "Public Diplomacy and Apologetics—the Israeli-Syrian Negotiations during the End of Asad's Reign," in *Religion and State in the Middle East*, ed. David Menashri (in press).

7. Ibid.

8. See Druker, *Hara-kiri*, pp. 70–110; American ambassador in Israel Martin Indyk in *Yediot Ahronot*, March 16, 2001. Ehud Barak's version was published in an interview for *Ha'aretz*, May 19, 2000; Uri Sagie (during a conversation with the author, May 2003). Another American version is that of Robert Malley, a member of the National Security Council during the Clinton administration; see Robert Malley, "Middle East Endgame III: Israel, Syria and Lebanon—How Comprehensive Peace Settlements Would Look," *International Crisis Group Middle East Report* 4 (July 16, 2002): 4.

9. See Robert Malley and Hussein Agha, "Camp David: The Tragedy of Errors," *New York Review of Books*, August 9, 2001.

10. Zisser, "The Israel-Syria Negotiations," p. 237.

11. Aluf Benn in *Ha'aretz*, January 4, 2000.

12. Rabinovich, "Public Diplomacy and Apologetics."

13. Ibid.

14. See Zisser, "The Israel-Syria Negotiations"; Malley, "Middle East Endgame III." Additional details of the negotiations can be found in Madeleine Albright, *Madam Secretary* (New York, 2003), pp. 476–82.

15. For an analysis of the new power equation created in South Lebanon, see another monograph by Malley: Robert Malley, "Old Games in Search of New Rules," *International Crisis Group Middle East Report* 7 (October 29, 2002).

16. Druker, *Hara-kiri*, pp. 189–208.

17. Ibid, pp. 167–78.

18. Shlomo Ben-Ami, interviewed by Ari Shavit, *Ha'aretz*, September 14, 2001; Gilead Sher, *Within Reach, the Peace Negotiation 1999–2001: A Testimony* (Tel Aviv, 2001), pp. 80–96.

19. Ben-Ami interview.

20. Ibid. and Sher, *Within Reach*, pp. 153–235. A Palestinian version of the course of affairs can be traced in the notes of Akram Hanieh, which were published originally in *Al-Ayyam* (between July 29 and August 10, 2000). A shorter version was published in English: Akram Hanieh, "The Camp David Papers," *Journal of Palestine Studies* 30, no. 2 (Winter 2001): 75–97.

21. Sher, *Within Reach*, pp. 360–74.

22. Ibid., pp. 397–415; Yossi Beilin, *A Guide for a Wounded Dove* [in Hebrew] (Tel Aviv, 2001), pp. 198–222.

23. *Ha'aretz*, January 28, 2001.

24. For the dispute regarding Taba, see Ari Shavit, "Taba's Principle of Return," *Ha'aretz*, July 11, 2002, and Yossi Beilin, "What Really Happened in Taba," *Ha'aretz*, July 15, 2002.

25. Michael Hirsh, "Clinton to Arafat: It's All Your Fault," *Newsweek*, June 27, 2001.

26. *Ha'aretz*, October 8, 13, 2000; *Newsweek*, July 23, 2001.

27. "Dennis Ross's Exit Interview," *New York Times Magazine*, March 25, 2001.

28. Daniel Mandel, "Dennis Ross: The Man in the Middle," *The Review* 26, no. 6 (June 2001).

29. Dennis Ross, "Camp David: An Exchange," *New York Review of Books*, September 20, 2001.

30. Malley and Agha, "Camp David: The Tragedy of Errors."

31. Beilin, *Wounded Dove*.

32. Ron Pundak, "From Oslo to Taba: What Went Wrong?," *Survival* 43, no. 3 (2001): 31–46.

33. Uri Savir interviewed by Ben Kaspit, *Ma'ariv*, March 9, 2001.

34. Amos Gilead during a lecture at the Jaffa Center for Strategic Studies, Tel Aviv University, May 23, 2002.

35. Henry Kissinger, *Does America Need a Foreign Policy?* (New York, 2001), pp. 164–88.

36. Menachem Klein, *The Jerusalem Problem: The Struggle for Permanent Status* (Gainesville, Fla., 2003).

## 5. SHARON, BUSH, AND ARAFAT

1. See chap. 3, pp. 113–16. Also see Sharon's autobiography, Ariel Sharon and David Chanoff, *Warrior* (New York, 1989).

2. Uzi Benziman, *He Does Not Stop at the Red Light* [in Hebrew] (Tel Aviv, 1985).

3. See Bob Woodward, *Bush at War* (New York, 2002).
4. Ibid., pp. 60–61.
5. Mahmud Abbas's "Call for a Halt to the Militarization for the Intifada," *Journal of Palestine Studies* 32, no. 126 (2003): 74–78.
6. Khalil Shikaki, "How to Reform Palestinian Politics," *New York Times*, July 9, 2002. See also Dr. Mahdi Abdul Hadi, "Reforms in Palestine," *Passia* (Palestinian Academic Society for the Study of International Affairs, Jerusalem), July 2002. I am indebted to Brigadier General (reserve) Shlomo Brom, a senior researcher at the Jaffe Center for Strategic Studies, Tel Aviv University, for most useful conversations about these issues.
7. *Ha'aretz*, December 24, 2001.
8. Woodward, *Bush at War*, pp. 17–18.
9. For an in-depth analysis of this issue, see Fouad Ajami, "Iraq and the Arab's Future," *Foreign Affairs*, January–February 2003.
10. *Yediot Ahronot*, April 16, 2003.
11. *Ha'aretz*, May 27, 2003.

## 6. THE WEB OF RELATIONSHIPS

1. See Elie Kedourie, "The Arab-Israeli Conflict," in *Arabic Political Memoirs* (London, 1974), pp. 218–31; Shimon Shamir, "The Arab-Israeli Conflict," in *The Middle East: Oil, Conflict and Hope*, ed. A. L. Udovitch (Lexington, Mass., 1976), pp. 195–231.
2. See Shimon Shamir, ed., *Egypt from Monarchy to Republic* (Oxford, 1995); Israel Gershoni, *The Emergence of Pan-Arabism in Egypt* (Tel Aviv, 1981); and *Rethinking the Egyptian Nation: 1930–1945* (Cambridge, 1995).
3. See Abraham Sela, "The Question of Palestine in the Inter-Arab System, from the Foundation of the Arab League until the Invasion of Palestine by the Arab Armies, 1945–1948" [in Hebrew], Jerusalem, 1986.
4. See P. J. Vatikiotis, *Nasser and His Generation* (London, 1978), *Conflict in the Middle East* (London, 1971), and *The History of Modern Egypt* (London, 1991).
5. See William B. Quandt, *The Peace Process* (Washington, D.C., and Berkeley, Calif., 1993).
6. See Fouad Ajami, *The Dream Palace of the Arabs* (New York, 1998).
7. On the nuclear dimension of Israeli-Egyptian relations, see Shai Feldman, *Nuclear Weapons and Arms Control in the Middle East* (Cambridge, 1997), pp. 206–24.

8. For the history of Israel and the Zionist movement's contacts with various groups in Lebanon, see Laura Zittrain Aisenberg, *My Enemy's Enemy* (Detroit, 1994); Benny Morris, "Israel and the Lebanese Phalange: The Birth of a Relationship 1948–1951," *Studies in Zionism* 5, no. 1 (1984): 125–44.

9. See Ehud Ya'ari and Ze'ev Schiff, *Israel's Lebanon War* (New York, 1994); Itamar Rabinovich, *The War for Lebanon, 1970–1983* (Ithaca, N.Y., and London, 1984).

10. See Avi Shlaim, *Collusion across the Jordan* (Oxford, 1988); Dan Shiftan, *Optzia Yardenit* (Jordanian option) (Efal, 1986; Moshe Zak, *Hossein Oseh Shalom* (Hussein makes peace)] (Ramat Gan, 1996), and "Israel and Jordan: Strategically Bound," *Israel Affairs* 3, no. 1 (Autumn 1996): 39–60. See also Uriel Dann, *Studies in the History of Transjordan, 1920–1949* (Boulder, Colo., 1984).

11. See my *The Road Not Taken* (New York, 1991), pp. 111–67.

12. For a Jordanian version of the 1967 crisis and war, see Samir Mutawi, *Jordan in the 1967 War* (Cambridge, 1987).

13. See Asher Susser, *On Both Banks of the Jordan* (London, 1994).

14. See chap. 1, n. 14.

15. It is significant that, though King Hussein publicly announced his country's disengagement, the formal annexation act was never abrogated, nor has Jordan's constitution been amended. It still stipulates that the "territory [of the kingdom] is indivisible and no portion of it may be ceded." The Constitution of the Hashemite Kingdom of Jordan, chap. 1, art. 1, as found in Muhammad Khalil, ed., *The Arab States and the Arab League* (Beirut, 1962).

16. See Harold Saunders, *The Other Walls* (Princeton, N.J., 1991).

17. For several classic statements of Israel's outlook on the Palestinians, see Shlomo Avineri, *Israel and the Palestinians* (New York, 1971).

18. For a sympathetic history of the Palestinian national movement, see Helena Cobban, *The Palestinian Liberation Organization* (Cambridge, 1984).

19. For two basic and very different views on the subject, see Jacob Landau, *The Arabs in Israel: A Political Study* (London, 1969), and Ian Lustick, *Arabs in the Jewish State: Israel's Control of a National Minority* (Austin, Tex., 1980).

20. See Majid Al Haj and Henry Resenfeld, *Arab Local Government in Israel* (Tel Aviv, 1988); Jacob Landau, *The Arab Minority in Israel, 1967–1991: Political Aspects* (London, 1994); C. Klein, *Israel as a Nation State and the Problem of the Arab Minority in Search of a Status*

(Tel Aviv, 1987); David Kretzmer, *The Legal Status of the Arabs in Israel* (Tel Aviv, 1987); Sammy Smooha, *Arabs and Jews in Israel*, 2 vols. (Boulder, Colo., 1989–92); Elie Rekhess, "Resurgent Islam in Israel," *Asian and African Studies* 27, nos. 1–2 (March–July 1993), and Rekhess, ed., "Arab Politics in Israel at a Crossroad," *Occasional Papers 119* (Tel Aviv, 1991); Nadim Ruhana, "The Political Transformation of the Palestinians in Israel from Acquiescence to Challenge," *Journal of Palestine Studies* 18 (1989).

21. A particularly radical version of this position was offered by Dr. Azmi Bishara, currently a member of the Knesset, in a lengthy interview he gave to *Ha'aretz*, May 29, 1998.

22. After the 1948 war, the Iraqi government conducted a study of the Arab debacle in Palestine that offers important early insights into the Arab, and specifically Iraqi, view of the conflict. See Shmuel Segev, *In the Eyes of an Enemy* [in Hebrew] (Tel Aviv, 1954).

23. Shmuel Segev, *The Iranian Triangle* (New York, 1988).

24. On the Iran-Iraq war, see Anthony H. Cordesman and Abraham R. Wagner, *The Iran-Iraq War* (Boulder, Colo., 1990). On Saddam's Iraq, see Efraim Karsh, *Saddam Hussein: A Political Biography* (London, 1991); Ofra Bengio, *Saddam Speaks on the Gulf Crisis* (Tel Aviv, 1992); Amatzia Baram, *Culture, History and Ideology in the Formation of Ba'thist Iraq, 1968–1989* (Hampshire, UK, 1991); and Samir Al Khalil, *Republic of Fear: The Politics of Modern Iraq* (New York, 1990).

25. See Avner Yaniv, "Israel Faces Iraq: The Politics of Confrontation," in *Iraq's Road to War*, ed. Amatzia Baram and Barry Rubin (New York, 1996).

26. See *Al Thawra*, April 3, 1990. See also "President Warns Israel, Criticizes U.S., April 1, 1990," in Bengio, *Saddam Speaks on the Gulf Crisis*.

27. See Judith Miller and Laurie Mylroie, *Saddam Hussein and the Crisis in the Gulf* (New York, 1990).

## 7. PEACE AND NORMALIZATION

1. See Muhammad Sayyid [Sid] Ahmed, *After the Guns Fall Silent* (London, 1976).

2. See ibid., p. 67.

3. See ibid., p. 111.

4. See ibid., pp. 111–13, passim.